WITHDRAWN

Understanding the
Little Rock Crisis

Understanding the Little Rock Crisis

AN EXERCISE IN REMEMBRANCE AND RECONCILIATION

EDITED BY

Elizabeth Jacoway
and C. Fred Williams

THE UNIVERSITY OF ARKANSAS PRESS, FAYETTEVILLE 1999

03 02 01 00 99   5 4 3 2 1

Designed by Ellen Beeler

⊜The paper used in this publication meets the minimum requirements of the American National Standard for Permanence of Paper for Printed Library Materials Z39.48-1984.

Library of Congress Cataloging-in-Publication Data

Understanding the Little Rock crisis : an exercise in remembrance and reconciliation /
    edited by Elizabeth Jacoway and C. Fred Williams
        p.   cm.
    Includes bibliographical references and index.
    ISBN 1-55728-529-2 (cloth: alk. paper). —ISBN 1-55728-530-6 (paper: alk. paper)
        1. School integration—Arkansas—Little Rock—History—20th century. 2. Central
High School (Little Rock, Ark.)—History. 3. Afro-Americans—Education—Arkansas—
Little Rock—History—20th century.   I. Jacoway, Elizabeth, 1944–   . II. Williams, C.
Fred.
    LC214.23.L56U53   1999
    379.2'63'0976773--dc21   99-38024
                                                                                                CIP

ACKNOWLEDGMENTS

In any long-term project such as this, many people contribute to the completion and success of the endeavor and deserve recognition and thanks. It is my pleasure and privilege to be able to thank the people who gave so generously of themselves to make this project a reality.

First and foremost, I want to thank Olivia Guggenheim for suggesting that I plan a conference of outstanding scholars in Little Rock. Without her clear-sighted suggestion, I would undoubtedly still be stewing about the shortcomings of the group effort known as the Little Rock Central High Museum Planning Committee.

I am deeply grateful to three members of that planning committee, Ethel Ambrose, Bill Asti, and Wieke Benjamin, who early in the conceptualization process saved this conference and volume from oblivion when my child developed a medical emergency. These three friends took me by the hand and led me through a series of fund-raising efforts, ultimately promising to assume responsibility for raising the money, if need be, because they thought my ideas had merit. I shall always be grateful to these friends for helping me stay the course through some perilous waters.

My good friend Fred Williams of the history department at the University of Arkansas at Little Rock stepped forward when I needed him and agreed to co-chair this conference and help me secure the funding for it, ultimately persuading his chancellor to sponsor both the conference and the resulting volume. While I flew off for a summer at the Mayo Clinic, Fred undertook the tedious details of planning a conference. I shall be eternally grateful to this old friend; when I count my blessings, I count him twice.

Chancellor Charles Hathaway of the University of Arkansas at Little Rock took the bold step of underwriting this conference and volume, even though I had no institutional affiliation to shore up my credibility and had been described to him as "controversial" (surely a feat for this stay-at-home mom), probably because I have argued in several venues that any complete understanding of the Little Rock crisis will have to include a thorough examination of the segregationist mentality. For this chemist-chancellor to transcend the constraints of "political correctness" and place the imprimatur of the university on this endeavor took intellectual and intestinal fortitude, and I want to offer here, once again, my heartfelt thanks.

I also want to thank all of the conference participants, especially those whose papers are not included here, who took time out of a busy fall semester and came to Arkansas to help make my ideas a reality. I shall be forever indebted to Numan Bartley, Margaret Bolsterli, Dan Carter, David Chappel, Charles Eagles, Jimmie L. Franklin, Willard Gatewood, John Graves, Adam Green, Paul Greenberg, Alton Hornsby, Winthrop Jordan, Janetta Kearney, Linda Reed, Rita Roberts, Beth Roy, Patricia Sullivan, Everett Tucker III, Lee Williams, and Odessa Woolfolk. They give meaning to the term *collegiality.*

Two friends at the University of Arkansas Press, Kevin Brock and Beth Motherwell, encouraged me at every stage of the process. They liked my ideas from the outset and encouraged me to proceed; they attended the conference and offered valuable insights; they kept up their spirits and mine when the press found its livelihood threatened; and they even offered to help me find another publisher if that were to become necessary. From my perspective they are the shining stars of the University of Arkansas Press and two of the strongest arguments in favor of its continued existence. I am grateful both for their friendship and their support.

My wonderful neighbor and computer expert, Elisabeth Curtner, shepherded me through the murky corridors leading from legal pads to word processors; she literally came through dark of night to save me from a thousand errors and the imminent destruction of my word processor. If I had any hope of getting rich from this book I would send her on a family ski vacation in the Colorado Rockies; alas, my gratitude will have to suffice. All proceeds from the sale of this book will go to UALR.

I must also thank my husband's secretary, Lesley Howard, who contributed countless hours and much patience—and many times her word processor—toward making me computer literate. Without her calm and reassurance, the completion of this manuscript would have caused considerably more brain damage.

My good friend Ralph Brodie, who was president of the student body at Little Rock Central High School in 1957–58 deepened the channel and corrected the course in my introductory chapter. His patient and cogent reading of every draft saved me from many errors. I shall be forever grateful to this lifelong friend for his gentle encouragement and unfailing support.

As in all things, my dear friend Elizabeth Payne has enriched this endeavor. She listened patiently to my frustrations about the Little Rock Central High Museum Planning Committee, encouraged my idea to plan a conference, sat by my bedside in Minnesota when I gave my son a kidney, attended and critiqued the conference at UALR, read and contributed to every draft of this manuscript, and helped me always to believe not only that this was a worthwhile endeavor but that I could do it. I am in awe of her strengths and gifts, and most of all that she has chosen me to be her friend.

My deepest thanks go to the three men in my life who give meaning to everything I do. Tim, Timothy, and Todd Watson have lived in a state of chronic messiness while the woman who was supposed to be attending to their needs closeted herself in her upstairs office or flew off to Little Rock to do mysterious things. They fed and entertained themselves while she served on the aforementioned planning committee, planned a symposium, sweated through a fortieth anniversary commemoration and conference, slaved over a steaming word processor, talked to contributors at length, slaved over a steaming word processor, lived through a looming threat to the University of Arkansas Press, and slaved over a steaming word processor. My family does not have a clue what I do, but their presence in my life gives me the energy and the sense of purpose to do it, and I offer them, as always, my unbounded thanks.

Writers always wonder if their words, and the pursuant expenditure of energy, will hit their mark. It is my fondest hope that this volume may deepen and enrich the understanding of its readers, and that it may in some way contribute to the healing and the reconciliation so urgently needed in Little Rock and all across America. For the possibility that I may contribute to this process, I am most deeply grateful.

Elizabeth Jacoway
Newport, Arkansas

CONTENTS

Understanding the Past: The Challenge of Little Rock

ELIZABETH JACOWAY

In the fall of 1957, during an episode remembered as the Little Rock crisis, the new medium of television brought the realities of American racial inequity into the national consciousness. Racism and discrimination were not, of course, products of Little Rock; they were an American legacy of three centuries of slavery and segregation. But the Little Rock crisis put faces on these evils and brought them with shocking force into living rooms around the world. No longer could white Americans maintain the fiction that their society ensured "liberty and justice for all"; and in time this dawning realization provided the foundation for many of the gains of the ensuing civil rights movement. The city of Little Rock, however, did not experience such a satisfying conclusion to the dilemmas its desegregation struggles created. The prolonged crisis left an aftermath of racial and class-based mistrust within the city, and the perceptions of Little Rock and of Arkansas beyond the region have continued for forty years to be tied to the images of hatred and strife that emanated from the streets outside Central High.

As the fortieth anniversary of the 1957 crisis approached, various groups in Little Rock recognized the wisdom of marking the occasion. Many saw this as an opportunity to demonstrate to the world, and to each other, that the people of Little Rock openly acknowledge the errors of the past; this was to be a cleansing, an opening of a festering wound that has plagued the city for forty years, in order to administer a healing dose of self-examination, confession, and repentance. As the chairman of the city's Fortieth Anniversary Commission remarked two days after the return of "the Little Rock Nine" to Central High: "We have bared our souls to the nation, and in many respects we have finally shown ourselves and the nation that we can face what happened here in 1957. By acknowledging it and facing it, we can see where we are and decide where we want to go on a more positive basis. Who knows what it will hold for us?" [1]

Among the many who expressed an interest in commemorating the fortieth anniversary of the 1957 crisis was a group that had been working for two years to create a Central High museum. The story of the Little Rock Central High Museum Planning Committee's attempts to agree on even fundamental approaches to the 1957 experience provides an instructive commentary on the difficulties of the historical reconstruction process, especially when the key questions at issue, in this case racial inequities, remain unresolved. As the country begins its rounds of fortieth and fiftieth anniversaries of civil rights battles and milestones, it could be beneficial to learn, once again, from the experience of Little Rock.

As a Little Rock native and a historian of the modern South, I received an invitation to participate in the planning of this museum; I was a busy mom living well over an hour away from Little Rock, but my long-standing professional interest in the Little Rock crisis compelled me to accept. My service on the Little Rock Central High Museum Planning Committee was to be one of the most fascinating, frustrating experiences of my professional career.

For over two years I made monthly trips to Little Rock, meeting in extended sessions with an interesting collection of neighborhood activists, businessmen, personnel from various existing museums, and representatives of both the black and white local press. I was the lone southern historian in the group, and it was a humbling experience for me to realize that everyone on the committee had their own interpretation of the Little Rock crisis—replete with their own set of information and experiences—and that my perspectives on the past carried no more weight than anyone else's.

In our mission statement, crafted early on, we described our aim: "To empower, inform, enlighten and challenge people by interpreting, documenting, discovering and preserving the history of the 1957 Central High crisis and its context. To create opportunities for people to gain a more complete understanding of and to be transformed by the environment and circumstances surrounding the 1957 Central High crisis."[2] Crafting the mission statement proved to be an easier task than carrying out our mission. Encouraged at every meeting to "think big" and to plan a museum that could be a model of its type, most of us began to bond around a growing sense of the importance of what we were about. There was significant give and take within the group and a growing respect for other points of view. This was my first experience with creating history by committee, and I could see from the outset that what we were about was not the kind of historical reconstruction I had learned about in graduate school. We were, instead, engaged in constructing a product that could accommodate competing agendas and perform a vast array of functions. It was a learning experience for all of us.[3]

Through all of the planning committee's deliberations I found myself saying time and again: "You have to consider the background and the context!" Increasingly it became clear to me that few of my colleagues had a real grasp of the very complex legal, political, and social issues that had converged to create the crisis in Little Rock. Even worse, from my perspective, many of them believed that getting at the "truth" of 1957—just telling the story—would be the easy part of our task, and the hard part would involve finding solutions to the myriad problems of Little Rock's ongoing racial conflicts; sympathetic as I was to my colleagues' desire to improve race relations in our state, it did not seem to me that finding those solutions was our charge. I yearned for other voices to speak to the difficulties and complexities of historical reconstruction—and especially of the healing power inherent in understanding the past. At length a sympathetic listener suggested another path: that I might plan a conference of nationally recognized scholars to provide Little Rock with a crash course in southern history and race relations. This volume is the result of that suggestion.

Drawing on all that I had learned from this experience about the misperceptions, justifications, distortions, and oversimplifications concerning the desegregation crisis that were prevalent in Little Rock, I began to dream of a symposium that would also address the needs for healing that my work with the planning committee had led me to recognize. Not only was there widespread community embarrassment about the long-standing and continuing perception among outsiders of Little Rock as a degenerate and racist backwater, and not only were there the customary divisions and mistrust between black and white elements of the community—much of which stemmed from a distorted or incomplete understanding of 1957— there were also troubling divisions within the white community over the motivations and legitimacy of various white activities and attitudes during the period of the crisis, as well as divisions within the black community over the ultimate wisdom of desegregation and the lionization of the Little Rock Nine. All of these things cried out for the healing balm of reconciliation, an acceptance of the past that could come only through clear-sighted understanding and a spirit of forgiveness. But without an attempt to present a reasonably accurate historical understanding of what happened in Little Rock in 1957–59, I believed that the planning committee could not fulfill its stated mission, and that other efforts to enhance the public understanding of those crucial years in Little Rock's past—and to promote the healing process—would fall wide of the mark.

It has been my good fortune to know and work with some of the finest historians in the field of modern southern history. For years I have attended scholarly conferences, worked within professional historians' organizations, and read and reviewed the literature being produced in southern history. Through all of these activities I have been a keen observer and consumer of the work being done in my field. Now I began to ask some of the people whose work had impressed me as being most fair-minded and balanced if they would come to Little Rock for a laymen's conference on the 1957 crisis. I had no money and no institutional backing, but they responded with a resounding, gratifying "Yes!"

At this point my good friend C. Fred Williams of the University of Arkansas at Little Rock invited his chancellor to sponsor this conference. A member of the LRCH Museum Board of Directors, Chancellor Charles Hathaway had already articulated his desire to have the university commemorate the fortieth anniversary in some meaningful and significant way, and a scholarly conference was what he had in mind. My impressive list of participants closed the sale, and Dr. Williams undertook the task of making all the arrangements for a conference on his campus.

In planning a conference on any topic, one is constrained by the work that scholars are currently doing—or have done in the past—in the field. I had the good fortune of having a deep pool of reputable scholars from which to draw, and the ones I invited performed admirably in fashioning papers that would fit my conceptual scheme. What I envisioned was a conference, and a volume, that would paint in broad strokes the outlines of southern race relations beginning with an overview of the history and the lived experience of segregation and then narrowing by stages to focus on the racial climate in Arkansas, the political and economic climate in Little Rock, and the legal and constitutional dimensions of the crisis.

In my instructions to the conference presenters, I noted that in observing the preparations for the fortieth anniversary, it seemed to me that "almost everyone has an agenda that is shaped more by present needs than by past realities." Some in Little Rock were clearly self-interested, whether in jockeying for advantage in helping showcase the Arkansas-born president of the United States as he welcomed the Little Rock Nine back to Central High, in working to ensure that their own role in the crisis was portrayed sympathetically, or in placing their contributions or institutions in the limelight. Others were good-hearted but ill-informed, wanting to use the anniversary to draw attention to present dislocations in the body politic or to assign blame for current problems to a mythologized past. My charge to the conference presenters was to provide the intelligent lay person with the information and the tools to begin to build a more meaningful dialogue about race-related problems in Little Rock, past and present. It was a tall order, but I was not to be disappointed.

>> <<

To get a clear perspective on what we are calling the Little Rock crisis requires a brief overview of the three years preceding 1957 and the two years immediately following. On May 17, 1954, the U.S. Supreme Court handed down the decision entitled *Oliver Brown et al. v. the Board of Education of Topeka, Kansas*, which put an end to the sixty-year-old policy of "separate but equal" in public school education. Under the leadership of Superintendent of Schools Virgil T. Blossom the Little Rock School District announced almost immediately that it would comply with the *Brown* decision, and within a year it announced its Blossom Plan for gradual school desegregation in Little Rock, to begin in the fall of 1957.[4]

The NAACP filed a lawsuit against the Little Rock School District in February 1956 (*Aaron v. Cooper*), arguing that the district was not moving fast enough in its desegregation efforts. The Capitol Citizens' Council (the Little Rock chapter of a southwide organization of respectable, middle-class opponents of desegregation), then mounted a campaign in the school board elections in March 1956; although they lost at the polls, they began to attract a growing following from the blue-collar neighborhoods around Central High School. On March 12 all of the members of the Arkansas congressional delegation (along with the majority of their peers in every other southern state) signed the Southern Manifesto, which articulated their vigorous opposition to the *Brown* decision and their belief that *Brown* was not a legitimate exercise of federal judicial power. In August 1956 the Federal District Court ruled in favor of the Little Rock School District in *Aaron v. Cooper*, but Federal Judge John Miller of Fort Smith retained jurisdiction in the case, thus removing the voluntary aspect of the Blossom Plan.[5]

In the November 1956 general election, the people of Arkansas approved by wide margins several measures designed to preserve segregation; furthermore, in February 1957 the Arkansas General Assembly passed four laws to maintain racial segregation in the public schools. In Little Rock, however, two segregationist, blue-collar candidates for the school board met defeat in March 1957, losing to candidates of the businessmen's lobby who ran on a platform of compliance with federal mandates. Little Rock's traditional leaders, the civic elite of downtown business and professional men, worked that spring to promote what they billed as a "good government campaign"; winning approval for a city manager–council form of government, they thereby left a lame-duck, discredited mayor until the November 1957 elections.[6]

A key element of the Blossom Plan would enable the community's leaders to send their children to unintegrated Hall High School, slated to open in the fall of 1957. The movement west into newer, more affluent neighborhoods had escalated since World War II, and the result was a new class division in the city along residential lines. As a "man of the people" of humble origins, and with few social pretensions, Governor Faubus felt a natural kinship with the working-class families whose children would attend Central High; and as the pressures for him to intervene in local affairs mounted, he remained true to his populist heritage.[7]

In public statements, Faubus claimed repeatedly that he had no intention of taking a stand either for or against integration in Little Rock. He had always maintained that, in all matters, he would support the will of the people in any particular locality (and he had done so by refusing to intervene in the desegregation controversy in Hoxie, Arkansas, in 1956). He believed that his involvement in the desegregation process would be politically costly, no matter what position he took, and his primary interest was in improving the economic and social conditions of the average Arkansan. Midway through the summer of 1957, however, the governor began to receive reports of impending violence at Central High, many of these reports coming directly from Superintendent Blossom himself. He may also have made promises to key political operatives in eastern Arkansas that he would oppose integration in return for their support of his legislative agenda. Whatever the motivation, it is clear that by early August, Faubus had concluded that he could not avoid playing a role in the upcoming drama in Little Rock.[8]

Governor Faubus appealed first to the Justice Department, calling Assistant Attorney General William Rogers to ask what assistance the federal government might be able to provide in the event of an emergency in Little Rock. Rogers sent a member of his staff, Arkansas native Arthur B. Caldwell, to Little Rock to meet with Faubus, but the governor was able to draw little comfort from Caldwell's position that the government could not intervene in the absence of a dead body.[9]

Faubus and Blossom both realized that Little Rock's lame-duck mayor, Woodrow W. Mann, would not be able to command the loyalty of the city's police and fire personnel. Gradually Faubus moved toward the conclusion that only state authority could provide a force strong enough to control or contain an emergency in the capital city; Faubus considered briefly using the state police, but apparently about this time he settled instead on the Arkansas National Guard. Repeatedly, Superintendent Blossom and others appealed to Faubus to make a public statement, much as North Carolina's Gov. Luther Hodges had done, to the effect that he would not tolerate violence at Central High. Faubus declined.[10]

Through August 1957 Little Rock witnessed a flurry of legal activity as various lawsuits sprang up in chancery court in an effort to block desegregation. At one point, in response to a suit filed by the newly formed Mother's League of Central High School (an auxiliary of the Citizens' Council) Chancellor Murray Reed issued an injunction against the Blossom Plan. Within a matter of days, however, newly appointed Federal Judge Ronald Davies of Fargo, North Dakota, overruled the chancery court decision and suspended the injunction, demanding that desegregation proceed as scheduled.[11]

Into this charged atmosphere stepped Gov. Marvin Griffin of Georgia. The invited guest of the Capitol Citizens' Council, he spoke to a large and enthusiastic audience at the civic auditorium about his handling of desegregation in Georgia. Assuring the crowd that Georgia's schools would remain segregated under his tenure, he left his audience with the question: "Why do you have to have integration here?" Why, indeed? That was the question on everyone's lips as the day for school opening drew near.[12]

A part of the conventional wisdom about the Little Rock crisis holds that Orval Faubus manufactured a crisis at Central High to win election to an unprecedented third term as governor of Arkansas. Faubus said at the time, and maintained ever after, that he acted to prevent violence and bloodshed in Little Rock. Many have questioned the governor's reasoning and intentions over the years, but whatever his motivation, Gov. Orval

Eugene Faubus placed the Arkansas National Guard around Little Rock Central High School on September 2, 1957, thereby precipitating a major constitutional crisis over the extent of state versus federal authority.[13]

Three weeks of inconclusive maneuvering ensued in the local courts, at the White House, and behind the scenes from Little Rock to Washington. After two weeks Arkansas Congressman Brooks Hays proposed that Governor Faubus and President Dwight Eisenhower meet face to face in an effort to resolve the crisis. Arranging the meeting through his friend Sherman Adams, administrative assistant to the president, on September 14 Hays flew with the governor to Newport, Rhode Island, to meet with the president at a favorite golfing retreat. Faubus and Eisenhower both believed that during their private meeting they arrived at a workable solution; since, however, Faubus had short-sightedly failed to take along a lawyer, he had to yield to U.S. Atty. Gen. Herbert Brownell's insistence that the proposed agreement was unacceptable. The governor returned to Arkansas empty-handed to face a court date with Judge Davies, who enjoined him on September 20 from interfering further with the desegregation of Central High. Faubus then removed the Arkansas National Guard soldiers from their posts around the school and flew off to the Southern Governors' Conference at Sea Island, Georgia.[14] The mayor replaced the guard with Little Rock city police, who put up barricades in the middle of the streets outside the school.

On Monday, September 23, the nine black children slipped into a side entrance of Central High School, precipitating rioting among the angry crowd gathered in the streets out front. The Little Rock police were no match for the emotional protesters outside the school, and by noon Assistant Police Chief Gene Smith removed the nine from the school "for their own safety." At the urging of a group of concerned citizens including former governor Sid McMath, his law partner Henry Woods, Congressman Brooks Hays, *Arkansas Gazette* editor Harry Ashmore, and Virgil Blossom, Mayor Mann called President Eisenhower and requested that he send troops to restore order in Little Rock. Wednesday morning, September 25, Little Rock awakened to the eerie spectacle of U.S. Army paratroopers in full battle gear stationed around Central High. The famed Screaming Eagles of the 101st Airborne Division stood just an arm's length apart in the middle of the streets surrounding Central High, with bayonets affixed to their weapons, while military helicopters flew overhead and landed on the practice field. The Little Rock Nine entered the school this day through the front door,

with full military escort, and desegregation in Little Rock was under-
way.[15]

Confusion reigned among the traditional leadership of the city, the
downtown businessmen. These were the same men who had worked for a
decade to reverse the fortunes of the pre–World War II economy in
Arkansas. They had lobbied successfully for industrial development and an
improved image for their city and state, and they had just launched a
movement to clean up city government and make it more amenable to the
needs of the business community. These men now feared that all they had
worked for was jeopardized. As one of them lamented: "we *knew* that we
were more progressive in the beginnings of racial integration than most of
the South, and most *all* of the North, so our feelings were: Why us?"[16]

The twenty-four former presidents of the chamber of commerce began
meeting daily in an effort to ascertain what steps could be taken to resolve
the crisis. All came to naught, however, as opinion was too divided within
the group to arrive at any commonly shared understanding. Some among
the businessmen resented the fact that Eisenhower had sent troops into
their city; others were relieved that he had. Many were enraged that the
military was being used to force an end to segregation in their city but
nowhere else in America. In this situation of high emotion, embarrassment, and outrage, a vacuum in local leadership became readily apparent.
In this climate the few voices raised in favor of compliance became suspect
as agents of the "enemy" forces, as advocates of integration, and increasingly Governor Faubus moved center stage.[17]

The October 5 launching of the Soviet spaceship *Sputnik* took Little
Rock off the front pages of the world's newspapers, but as the weeks wore
on with little abatement of the tension in Arkansas's capital city, Virgil
Blossom and his school board found themselves under mounting local
criticism for continuing to work to implement the Blossom Plan. In the
face of proliferating Citizens' Council activity and visibility, the chamber of commerce group eventually decided that the most feasible means
of easing the tension would be to persuade the school board to appeal to
the federal court for relief. Surely in this situation of high emotion and
with the continuing threat of violence, they reasoned, the court would
allow a cooling-off period to permit the school board to devise a more
workable plan. A former football coach and a large man in will and size,
Virgil Blossom refused to consider retreat. His decision to hold out
against both the downtown leadership and the governor predictably
pushed him and his board into an isolated and lonely position. Harassing

phone calls and even threats, which had become routine for Virgil Blossom and his family, now became a distressing reality for members of the school board, who were serving voluntarily out of a sense of public spirit and goodwill.[18]

Harassment extended as well to the nine black children. At the out-set of the school year, some white students had made overtures of welcome and friendliness toward the nine, but as the city's adult segregationist forces became more organized and more emboldened by the governor's supportive position, a small cadre of white tormentors began to poison the environment inside Central High, and the black children found them-selves increasingly isolated within the fortresslike walls of the school. Of course it did not foster the prospects for positive social interactions that each of the nine had a military escort and that they left their classes sev-eral minutes before the end of each period, or even that the vast majority of Central High students went about their business with no thought of harassing or condoning harassment of the black children. But from the perspective of the nine black students, they had made their way inside the fortress; now they were under siege from within.[19]

A pall descended upon Little Rock. High hopes had been dashed on all sides: the black community now saw the limited extent of their city's commitment to desegregation; the business community despaired over the damage to their city's image; the school board realized belatedly that their carefully crafted plan was woefully inadequate; some few in the white community began to recognize and contemplate their own racism. Two generations of legally enforced segregation had blinded the races to seeing each other whole, but few understood the impairment or thought in terms of remedy. Anger and resentment prevailed.[20]

At length the chamber committee persuaded the school board to seek relief through the federal courts. Support for the school board position had evaporated, leaving the individual members under siege and the com-munity viewing desegregation as the school board's problem. Only the *Arkansas Gazette* spoke out publicly in favor of supporting the board; Harry Ashmore's editorials were to win him a Pulitzer Prize but would cost his paper millions of dollars in lost subscribers and advertising.[21]

In February 1958 the school board's attorneys petitioned the federal district court for an immediate postponement of desegregation in Little Rock. The petition described the school board as "standing alone, the vic-tim of extraordinary opposition on the part of the state government and apathy on the part of the federal government." In this context the board asked for a delay until the courts clarified the concept of "all deliberate speed," the nebulous terminology employed in the *Brown* decision.[22] On May 27, 1958, Central High's first black graduate, Ernest Green, graduated with 602 other seniors in a historic but uneventful ceremony.

In June 1958, Federal Judge Harry J. Lemley of Hope, Arkansas, found in favor of the school board and granted the requested two-and-a-half-year delay of integration. The NAACP appealed this decision immediately to the Eighth Circuit Court of Appeals in St. Louis, which overturned the Lemley decision in August. While the school board appealed its case to the Supreme Court, Governor Faubus called a special session of the Arkansas General Assembly, which passed quickly a series of stridently anti-integration bills. One of these empowered the governor in the event of forced integration to close the schools and then hold an election within thirty days to determine whether voters wanted to keep them closed or to reopen them on a desegregated basis.[23]

On September 15, 1958, the U.S. Supreme Court, meeting in an unusual, called summer session, handed down the decision entitled *Cooper v. Aaron*, which instructed the Little Rock School Board to proceed immediately with the Blossom Plan. Governor Faubus responded by closing the city's four high schools.[24]

Not far from the governor's mansion that afternoon one of Little Rock's most revered senior citizens picked up her telephone and started organizing a movement of women that would, within a matter of months, resolve the crisis in their city. The Women's Emergency Committee to Open Our Schools (WEC) came into being in the living room of Adolphine Fletcher Terry's antebellum mansion, beneath the portrait of her father in his Confederate uniform.[25]

The WEC's first effort was a campaign to educate the public and get out the vote in the hastily scheduled September 27 election. The Faubus forces had worded the ballot to read "*For* racial integration of all schools within the School District" (that dreaded word—*integration*—now carried overtones of federal coercion, race mixing, and community embarrassment) or "*Against* racial integration of all schools within the School District," with "for integration" being the choice to mark for open schools. Although the movement for open schools went down to defeat by an almost three-to-one margin, the WEC leadership felt encouraged that 7,561 citizens were willing to mark "for integration" on their ballots, and the women set about the business of developing a highly structured campaigning and information-distributing apparatus.[26]

With the schools now closed and the Blossom Plan thoroughly repu-
diated, the school board members concluded that they had reached the
end of their effectiveness. Despite opposition from their superintendent,
the board now bought out Virgil Blossom's contract and, with the exception of one outspoken segregationist member, Dr. Dale Alford, they resigned
en masse. The Women's Emergency Committee went to work to recruit
new members for the school board, as did the Capital Citizen's Council
and other segregationist groups. In the November 1958 elections, Dale
Alford ran a last-minute, write-in campaign against long-time Congressman
Brooks Hays and won.[27]

In the meantime, all of Little Rock's public high school students
found themselves without schools. Some went to other towns to live with
friends or relatives, some went on to college, most stayed at home. Many,
unfortunately, never would go back to school. The segregationist forces
created a private school corporation and considered ways to transfer all the
public school assets and buildings to it. The teachers in the city's four public high schools sat in empty classrooms, occasionally teaching their
courses to each other.[28]

In the December school board election the WEC demonstrated the
effectiveness of its carefully crafted precinct-by-precinct organization.
Forging an alliance between the affluent voters in west Little Rock and
the largely black precincts downtown and to the east, the women succeeded in electing three "moderate" school board candidates who had the
endorsement of the businessmen's lobby. The segregationist forces also
elected three members, so conflict within the newly constituted school
board was undoubtedly inevitable.[29]

In January 1959 the in-coming president of the Little Rock Chamber
of Commerce shocked the crowd gathered at the civic auditorium to cel-
ebrate his inauguration when he suggested that the time had come to put
an end to the crisis. Breaking through the wall of silence that had stifled
the traditional leadership of the community for over a year, E. Grainger
Williams called for "the re-establishment of all areas of communication,
so that we may be able to discuss our principles...our feelings...our differences...our problems...without anger or hatred...without fear of
reprisal...but with understanding, tolerance, intelligence and respect for
each other." In early March 1959 his chamber of commerce conducted an
internal poll and found that more than 800 members favored reopening
the schools "with a plan of controlled minimum desegregation," while only
250 opposed reopening. The realities of living without schools had forced

Little Rock's businessmen to reexamine their priorities and discover that continued economic growth was more important to them than continued separation of the races.[30]

Rumors of a purge of the "integrationist" teachers circulated in Little Rock throughout the spring of 1959, and in an early May board meeting the segregationist faction initiated such an undertaking. The moderate faction walked out of the meeting, thinking that without a quorum their segregationist colleagues could not continue. The remaining three declared that a quorum had been established at the beginning of the meeting, and they proceeded to fire forty-four Little Rock School District employees, among them some of the most respected, beloved teachers in the school system.[31]

At last Little Rock's traditional male leadership found its voice, rallying now around the issue of fairness for the teachers. Having found a way to sidestep the issue of integration, the men formed a new organization called Stop This Outrageous Purge (STOP); engaging the WEC's organizational structure and workforce, the STOP leadership initiated a recall of the offending segregationist board members. The segregationists countered by forming an organization entitled Committee to Retain Our Segregated Schools (CROSS), and they, too, rallied for a recall election.[32]

In the ensuing election on May 25, the now-familiar alliance of affluent-white and black precincts carried the day, if just barely. The three segregationist board members lost their seats, soon to be replaced by three "moderates" who had the stamp of approval of the WEC and STOP forces and who campaigned on a platform of reopening the schools integrated. With public opinion in Little Rock now demonstrated to be in favor of open schools, and with unanimity of purpose now reestablished within the school board, the crisis phase of Little Rock's school desegregation troubles was over. Not so easily resolved would be the underlying problems of racial and class-based divisions and the challenges of integrating disparate cultural norms and expectations into a unified educational system.[33]

>> <<

In the sweltering heat of a mid-September Arkansas morning in 1997, hundreds of Little Rock's citizens gathered to hear an eclectic group including politicians (from the mayor to the senator), former students, neighborhood activists, and museum board and planning committee members dedicate the Little Rock Central High Museum Visitors Center.

Speaker after speaker called for a celebration of the distance we have trav-eled since 1957, though longtime black leader Annie Abrams hit the high note when she prayed in her invocation that all who visited the center could go out as "ambassadors for justice," and that the Lord would "give us the courage and strength to go forward from here to complete the wisdom of the [planning committee's] Mission Statement." She prayed as well that the visitors center could become "the flagship that will steer us through the turbulent waters that we will encounter as we travel the long journey toward understanding our history in all its complexity."[34]

Several days later President Bill Clinton came home to Arkansas to lead the Little Rock Nine up the steps of Central High, and Arkansas Gov. Mike Huckabee captured the dominant feeling of the commemoration when he called for an end to the evils of racism that have kept Americans apart. Everywhere the theme of reconciliation was the order of the day, but historical inaccuracies and misperceptions abounded, seemingly pro-viding a perfect prelude for the conference entitled "Remembrance and Reconciliation: Understanding the Little Rock Crisis of 1957" that fol-lowed within a matter of hours at the University of Arkansas at Little Rock.

Keynote speaker Sheldon Hackney, former chairman of the National Endowment for the Humanities, set the tone for the conference when he described the Little Rock crisis as a form of "political theater" that both dramatized the evil of excluding blacks from full participation in the American Dream and rendered that exclusion intolerable in popular thinking throughout the country. Despite the gains of the civil rights movement, however, and the very real changes in American hearts and minds, Hackney argued that "the full realization of racial equality...has not been achieved yet." Equally distressing, white Americans in recent years have come to believe that racial discrimination is no longer a serious problem, while "significant majorities of African Americans perceive racial discrimination to be a constant and oppressive fact of their daily lives." Hackney concluded that Americans must close the gap between the principle and the practice of equality of opportunity if there is to be a rec-onciliation between the two groups, and he suggested that this is "the challenge of the current era."

David Goldfield, author of a widely acclaimed study of southern race relations entitled *Black, White and Southern*, addressed the conference with a meaty yet fast-paced overview and analysis of the era of segregation. Noting that southern race relations remained fluid through the 1880s,

Goldfield argued that the imposition of segregation functioned as a means to solidify racial and gender hierarchies in the New South, and that the intent of segregation by law was "not merely to separate the races but to denigrate one and elevate the other." Segregation therefore made whites feel good about themselves and solved the political problems of white leaders by creating a common bond among all whites; it fit well with the New South booster rhetoric because it promised to promote the peaceful conditions necessary to attract northern industry; and it was affirmed in southern churches as well as in the national Congress and the federal courts. In short, according to Goldfield, "southern whites went about their lives oblivious to the misery in their midst," and as a result, the adverse impact of segregation on blacks, whites, and the South is now incalculable. With the *Brown* decision and the civil rights movement whites saw "how they had strayed from the basic principles of Christianity"; but just as whites experienced this revelation, blacks began to back away from their commitment to integration, eventually emphasizing the importance of group identity and entitlements. Goldfield concluded with a ringing charge for a renewed commitment to an integrated society; acknowledging that reconciliation requires goodwill, he seconded Congressman John Lewis's call for a society that transcends race, "where you can lay down the burden of race—I'm talking about just *lay it down*—and treat people as human beings, regardless of the color of their skin."

Two papers included in this volume by George Wright and Joel Williamson contrast the experience of a young black and a young white growing up in the segregated South. George Wright, author of a pathbreaking study of black life in Louisville, Kentucky, acknowledges that his life and experiences are not "typical" of all southern blacks, primarily because he grew up in the relatively benign racial climate of Kentucky; nonetheless, he notes that the patterns of racial segregation and discrimination in Kentucky mirrored the experiences of blacks farther South. As a child in the 1950s, Wright rarely saw white people, and this isolation, as well as the protection provided by his family and the black community, shielded him from the worst aspects of racial discrimination and allowed him to have a normal, if not idyllic, childhood. He notes that during the summer of the 1963 March on Washington he, like teenage boys everywhere, was more interested in making the all-star baseball team than in the civil rights movement. In reflecting back, however, he realizes that the conditions for his parents in that era were far from equal to what whites in post–World War II America were experiencing, especially in terms of employment opportunities. He also learned in his integrated high school the withering effects of white racism, and he believes that the effects of racism and segregation are still present in the lives of many black Americans, especially in terms of what he calls "poverty of the spirit." He concludes with the hope that reconciliation can come through a greater white understanding of what his parents and contemporaries have had to face through years of segregation and discrimination.

Joel Williamson, author of the landmark study of southern race relations entitled *The Crucible of Race*, describes a very different experience as a white boy growing up in small-town South Carolina in the 1930s and 1940s. Surrounded by blacks in his town, and even in his home, he did not realize until adulthood that he really knew very little about the people with whom he lived in such close proximity. Even in the navy and in graduate school he missed any awareness of black people, except where they deviated from South Carolina norms of behavior, which was a part of his legacy of segregation. Williamson argues that "We have created two cultures in America based on fictions of color, and we seem unable to let these constructs go." What is needed, he suggests, is an approach that will get us beyond the physical fact of the integration of bodies to the psychological and emotional awareness of the feelings in race relations. "That," Williamson concludes, "is the test of America's commitment to democracy."

Anthony Badger is the Paul Mellon Professor of American History at Cambridge University. He has been working for several years on a study of "the Southern Manifesto" of March 1956, the document signed by a majority of southern congressmen that vowed defiance of the 1954 *Brown* decision. In his essay, Badger traces the white reaction to *Brown* in Arkansas; noting that Arkansas had boasted a liberal tradition in the years before 1954, he asks "what went wrong?" in Little Rock in 1957. Arguing that "the political dynamics of the race issue, which inhibited an effective policy of compliance with desegregation, were already in place by March 1956," he then dissects the inner workings of those political dynamics, demonstrating that the movement to secure the signatures of Arkansas's congressional delegation revealed the depth of white commitment to resist desegregation, despite a parallel commitment to remain law abiding. He also argues that the Southern Manifesto demonstrated in Arkansas that "if you disavowed compliance with the Supreme Court, you were in no position to control the segregationist pressure groups that resolutely opposed any compromise with desegregation"; therefore, he argues, a moderate like

Gov. Orval Faubus would find it impossible to defuse the extremist threat. "It was difficult," Badger concludes, "to try and convince people that there was no alternative but to obey the law of the land, that they should accept the inevitable, when leading politicians in the state were proclaiming that there was an alternative, that desegregation could be avoided."

Building on the work of his mentor at Cambridge, John Kirk traces the reactions to the *Brown* decision in Arkansas, arguing that a "profound regional difference [within the state] in attitudes and approaches to school desegregation brought a deadlock over the issue at a state level." Furthermore, the "finely balanced position of the state between a willingness to accept the 1954 *Brown* decision as the law of the land and attempts to circumvent the Supreme Court ruling served to heighten the importance of the Little Rock School Board's stance on desegregation." With the handing down of *Brown* II in 1955, which equivocated by telling local school boards ambiguously that they must desegregate "with all deliberate speed," Little Rock Superintendent of Schools Virgil Blossom modified his original Blossom Plan to reduce substantially the amount of integration that would occur in the Little Rock School District, indicating "a subtle yet significant shift from a stance of begrudging compliance to active reluctance to implement the law." According to Kirk, "This more than served to "encourage the development of a massive resistance movement in the state amongst militant die-hard segregationists." Kirk concludes that right up to the time of the school crisis "there were chances for constructive dialogue and orderly school desegregation" in Arkansas, and that "the failure of school desegregation at Little Rock was a result not of the strength of the segregationists, but a failure of moderates in having the conviction to uphold the law."

Roy Reed is the author of a sensitive and compelling new biography of Gov. Orval Faubus entitled *Faubus: An American Prodigal*. In his conference paper included here he tests the theory that the Arkansas governor precipitated the Little Rock crisis in order to guarantee himself a third term in office. Tracing Faubus's Socialist upbringing, his racial moderation (before 1957), and his liberal friends, Reed argues that it was Faubus's fate to be governor "when several opposing forces of history collided in the capital of the state," and he found himself caught uncomfortably in the middle with no palatable options. Reed demonstrates that "Faubus continued to maneuver for the political center even as it crumbled under his feet." Navigating between the segregationist extremism of his political opponent Jim Johnson and the pleas from Superintendent Virgil Blossom that he use the power of the state to preserve order, Faubus eventually "betrayed the better instincts of his state and his own nature, and he began his descent into the dark side of history."

James Cobb has written numerous books and articles about the South's business and industrial development. In this paper he challenges the popular notion that economic modernization goes hand in hand with social and political democratization, arguing instead that segregation had been one of the "invented" traditions that had accompanied the New South's industrialization and urbanization processes." "Far from a capitulation to the past," he writes, "segregation was the wave of the future in the New South of the late nineteenth and early twentieth centuries," primarily because it provided the stable racial climate that was essential for a stable investment climate. Cobb argues that the New South strategy prevailed over the next three-quarters of a century, but in the wake of the *Brown* decision "Faubus and other economic development-oriented, southern politicians found it increasingly difficult to sidestep the question of whether they would actually defy any federal attempt to force integration of the public schools." When Faubus finally chose to block integration, Little Rock's business and industrial development leaders quickly found that "they could stir up little or no interest among industrialists in moving to Little Rock." Cobb argues that business leaders in other southern cities quickly grasped "The Lesson of Little Rock," and that consequently cities such as Raleigh, Atlanta, Charlotte, and Dallas managed effectively to avoid civil rights disturbances. Ominously, however, one Arkansas business leader seemed to speak with authority when he suggested that "the industrial prospect doesn't give a hoot whether your schools are integrated or not, but he wants no part of disorder or violence." In conclusion, Cobb argues that "The Lesson of Little Rock might well be expanded to suggest that while racial conflict may be incompatible with economic progress, economic progress cannot guarantee racial progress unless those who seek a developed economy are equally committed to a developed society as well."

Kermit Hall is a noted constitutional and legal scholar who writes here that "the constitutional lessons of the Little Rock crisis remind...us how much our constitutional world stays the same even as it changes." Arguing that one of the important contributions of the Little Rock crisis was "to the incremental growth of federal judicial authority," he notes the irony of our now witnessing the California Civil Rights Initiative's challenge to this assertion of federal judicial supremacy. Hall argues that "at the outbreak of the Little Rock crisis there was considerable uncertainty about the breadth of judicial power and corresponding questions about the willingness of the executive branch and Congress to implement desegregation," and as a consequence, "segregationists drew the predictable conclusion that they had everything to gain by resisting rather than cooperating." Governor Faubus in particular believed that the federal government wanted "a constitutional scheme in which it could dictate to the states but shirk responsibility for implementing its decisions and ignore the wishes of the majority of its citizens," and so he resisted. Hall argues that Faubus and his fellow southern governors and legislators demonstrated that the doctrine of state sovereignty did not die with the Civil War as is generally believed, and that "Faubus's position was real and legitimate, so much so that the Supreme Court [in Cooper v. Aaron] felt compelled to reject it vigorously, a sure indication of its vitality." Hall demonstrates that the Cooper decision gave rise to a much more aggressive effort to achieve equality than the Brown decision had envisioned, and he concludes that the Cooper decision was "an important weigh station on the road to what some have called the imperial judiciary, but it is perhaps even better understood as a singular moment in affirming the power of law to transform social evil. What the Court defended in Cooper was a process ...by which the supremacy of federal law would permit local minorities to address through the federal judicial system social concerns beyond their reach."

Tony Freyer is the author of The Little Rock Crisis: A Constitutional Interpretation. In this paper he draws heavily on that study to argue that "any remedy for the [Little Rock School District's] current problems could benefit from understanding the extent to which a moderate constitutional vision of public school desegregation prevailed in the Little Rock crisis of 1957–59." Freyer argues that in the forty years after 1957, "because successful defense of constitutional rights became synonymous with coercion, progress was limited and ambiguous, vulnerable to the social and economic forces identified with white flight." Viewed from the perspective of 1957, Freyer argues that the Blossom Plan adopted by the Little Rock school board steered a moderate course between the more extreme demands of the segregationists for outright resistance to the Brown decision and the NAACP for a more aggressive course toward the implementation of integration. According to Freyer, Governor Faubus understood the wisdom of this moderate course and supported it until such support was no long tenable politically; and after Faubus's capitulation to federal power a consciousness developed in Little Rock "that justified desegregation primarily in terms of deference to the constitutional supremacy of federal power." Freyer concludes with the hope that Little Rock can transcend this minimalist approach to race relations and develop instead "a heightened consciousness grounded on trust." Only then, he suggests, can "Little Rock's future...at last [be] freed from its past."

The scholars who came to Little Rock in September of 1997 detailed over and over the connections between remembrance and reconciliation, the need to understand the past in order to move beyond it. As southern writer William Faulkner suggested many years ago: "the past is never over; it isn't even past." Community activist Annie Abrams expressed it this way: "Our lack of knowledge and sharing is a part of our problem; we are on a journey of continuing to learn, and the more we know about our past, the more we'll be prepared to contribute to the process of reconciling our differences."

>> <<

In a special kind of poetry, the fortieth anniversary of the Little Rock crisis produced a powerful image of reconciliation. Two days before the president spoke at Central High the *Arkansas Democrat-Gazette* carried on its front page the picture of two middle-aged women who might seem unremarkable to the casual observer. Forty years ago, when they were fifteen, photographer Will Counts captured their images in a picture that has become an icon of the civil rights movement. There was young Elizabeth Eckford, composed and stoic, walking along the line of National Guard soldiers at Little Rock Central High School, while she was being heckled and tormented by an unnamed white girl whose face was twisted in anger and hate. That young white girl was Hazel Bryan, now Hazel Massery; forty years after that episode Hazel Bryan Massery went to Elizabeth Eckford's home and apologized for the venomous outburst that had scarred both of their lives. Since that day, as improbable as it might seem, the two adult women have begun to build a friendship.[35]

I interviewed Hazel Massery early in 1996 and discovered that she is a compassionate, interesting, reflective woman. She told me that after the birth of her first child when she was nineteen, she had had a blinding realization of the pain she had inflicted on another woman's child outside of Central High; holding her new baby had been a transformative experience for her, as it is for many women, and she called both Elizabeth

Eckford and her grandmother at that time and apologized to them. She told me that she has been haunted for years by the enormity of the error she made when she was fifteen, and she has worked in a variety of causes to, in effect, do penance for that early mistake.

That interview with Hazel Massery haunted me. It was such a far cry from what I had expected to hear, and it planted a seed of hope in my mind that perhaps racial reconciliation in this country is, after all, within our grasp. Young Hazel Bryan had acted out of a set of assumptions about black people that her parents' and grandparents' lives under a system of segregation had led all of them to adopt. She had never examined her racial assumptions nor had cause to do so; but when she did find a compelling reason to rummage through her mental inheritance she discovered that some of it needed to be left behind. Perhaps it was the Christian teachings in her upbringing that caused her to find her racism unpalatable after careful examination; perhaps it was the grounding in democratic values as a part of her public schooling. Whatever the explanation, while the world continued to think of Hazel Bryan and the legions she represented as being trapped in the snapshot of one moment in this country's racial awakening, Hazel Bryan Massery actually moved light years beyond the thought patterns captured in that image.

Not long after my interview with Hazel Massery, I suggested to the Little Rock Central High Museum Planning Committee that in our visitors center we could communicate volumes about Little Rock's growth and health if we juxtaposed two pictures at the entrance to our exhibit—one of Hazel Bryan and Elizabeth Eckford as Will Counts had captured them in 1957 and one of the two women as adults, if they would consent to come together in such a reunion. I felt that Hazel would welcome an invitation to begin the process of reconciliation, but I had always been told that Elizabeth had been so traumatized by the events of 1957 that she made very few public appearances. The planning committee was skeptical about my suggestion, and the opportunity passed.

On the day of the visitors center dedication in September 1997, I spotted photographer Will Counts in the crowd, made my way across the blistering parking lot and introduced myself to him. Begging his indulgence if he thought me presumptuous, I offered him the suggestion that I had made to the planning committee, that he should capture an image of the two adults whose picture forty years ago had brought him worldwide recognition at the outset of his career. Counts looked at me with a kind of startled recognition and confessed that he had had the same idea, that within the last hour he had proposed it to Elizabeth Eckford and she had agreed, but that no one seemed to think the white girl would consent. I gave Counts Hazel's number and encouraged him to call her.

Will Counts arranged the meeting of the two Little Rock women he had photographed as girls, and he went on to capture another image outside Central High, this one of the two adults who have begun the process of coming to terms with their own past. Finally they are through reacting in anger, they are through making excuses, they are trying to understand, and they are beginning to heal. In the past two years they have made numerous public appearances together, they have spent considerable private time together, and they are now writing a book together. As girls, these two gave the nation and the world a classic image of white persecution and black suffering; as women, they have begun the process of reconciling their differences, understanding each other, and moving into a better future.

Some suggest that we should forget the past, rise above it, let it go. But just as in personal relationships unresolved differences fester and thwart unity of purpose, so in societal relations a failure to understand and be sensitive to our past masks our ability to see each other whole. As a part of the fortieth anniversary commemoration activities in Little Rock, Arkansas Gov. Mike Huckabee explained before a national television audience at Central High that even though some had questioned the wisdom of reopening the wounds of 1957, he believed it was important to "confront the pain of the past" in order to move beyond it. Likening America to the tribes of Israel, Huckabee suggested that in many ways his state and the rest of the nation have "wandered for forty years in the wilderness as it relates to race relations."[36]

Americans have been wandering for forty years in a wilderness of misunderstanding, recrimination, and blame; lacking a Moses to lead us, or perhaps not knowing how to follow, we have remained lost in a wilderness that will continue to claim us as long as we fail to understand each other. Surely forty years of wandering is enough; surely we shall rise to the challenge of our time. Finding our way is within our grasp, but only if we commit ourselves to a fearless exploration of the past, unencumbered by the baggage of preconceived notions, hidden agendas, and facile moral judgment. With reconciliation and forgiveness as beacons to guide us, may we find our way through, at last, to that American Promised Land of "liberty and justice for all."

Little Rock and the Promise of America

SHELDON HACKNEY

Early in the twentieth century, in 1903, W. E. B. DuBois predicted in his classic book, *The Souls of Black Folk*, that in the United States the problem of the twentieth century would be the problem of the color line. In 1944, in another classic study, *An American Dilemma*, Gunnar Myrdal noted that "America is continuously struggling for its soul," a struggle occasioned by the harsh gap between the reality of racial discrimination and the uplifting ideals of the "American Creed." Near the end of the century, in 1992, while block upon block in South Central Los Angeles smoldered both literally and figuratively, Rodney King spoke plaintively to the people of his city and beyond, "Hey people! Can't we all get along?"

Using these three data points alone, one is tempted to conclude simply that racism persists and that all the blood and ink spilled in the cause of racial justice and reconciliation has been spilled in vain. That conclusion not only would be wrong and would denigrate some remarkable achievements, but it would also mask a fundamental shift in the nature of the problem. Over the course of the twentieth century glorious new chapters have been written in the story of America's advance toward the ideal of human equality that our founding documents envisioned. Nevertheless, racism persists, and it has not only become more complex as our population has become more diverse in recent years, it has also changed in a fundamental way since the Little Rock crisis of 1957.

The Little Rock crisis was one of those critical moments in our national life when nine brave teenagers, through the commonplace act of going back to school in September, forced the country to recognize that we were falling inexcusably short of the ideals set forth in our nation's Constitution and

Declaration of Independence. Those nine heroes and heroines paid a high price for their acts of courage, and we have all benefited.

We have gathered here forty years later to try to understand that event, to assess the degree to which it constituted a step forward in the struggle for human equality, to wring some meaning from it that might bring us together as an increasingly diverse and progressively atomized society. Having just discussed this episode with my freshman seminar at Penn, I approach our task with a spirit chastened by the relentless power of history to change the meaning of the past and by the sobering accumulations of the intervening years. My students, you see, were born in 1979 and 1980. Their *parents* were too young to have been aware of the Little Rock crisis of 1957!

Moreover, after they had watched Henry Hampton's marvelous documentary "Eyes on the Prize," my students were virtually speechless. They simply did not recognize the America in which the drama of 1957 Little Rock played out. They are not innocent of racism, nor of the subtleties of current discrimination, but they simply could not comprehend a society that practiced legal segregation, a society in which the raw ugliness of violent hatred was so near the surface, and one in which the federal government was so timid in the pursuit of justice. For them, mostly white and completely nonsouthern, with ideological orientations ranging from polite liberalism to gracious conservatism, there is the unspoken assumption that African Americans are full participants in the same moral universe as all other Americans.

That is one measure of the impact of Little Rock. Recall that in 1942, 68 percent of white Americans supported racially segregated schools; by 1985 only 7 percent did. In 1944, 55 percent of whites nationally believed that whites should receive preference over blacks in job hiring; by 1972 only 3 percent supported that reasoning. At the level of principle, at least, African Americans are now full participants in the American mainstream. We owe that leap forward to Little Rock and to the civil rights movement it helped to ignite.

A great chasm separates us today from the society of the 1950s, largely because the turbulent sixties redirected the course of history and changed America in fundamental ways. The change is so complete that young people have trouble imagining a different America. In my thinking, the sixties began with the *Brown* decision, the Montgomery bus boycott, the Autherine Lucy case at the University of Alabama, and the integration of Little Rock Central High School.

No one doubts the primacy of the 1954 *Brown* decision in accelerating the pace of changes that had been moving toward racial equality since at least the New Deal. A case can also be made for the primary importance of the 1955–56 Montgomery bus boycott. Out of that experience emerged a new leader, Martin Luther King Jr.; a new civil rights organization, the Southern Christian Leadership Conference; and a philosophy of protest, nonviolent direct action—all of which were to play important roles in the civil rights movement over the next decade.

Nevertheless, the crisis at Central High provided something else, something especially compelling. In addition to a set of heroes, the Little Rock Nine and Daisy Bates, whose performance encouraged the mobilization of black communities throughout the country, Little Rock provided for all the world to see a morality play whose meaning was unmistakable. When the Arkansas National Guard turned back the nine black teenagers, literally blocking the door that led to educational opportunity and preventing model young Americans from treading the primary avenue of self-improvement that Americans had come to recognize as a fundamental right, the public saw a dramatization of the evil of exclusion. Because the drama in Little Rock was about the exclusion of blacks from education and thus from full participation in the American Dream, it communicated what was to become the theme of the era in a particularly powerful and clear way. By humanizing Gunnar Myrdal's social science research and translating his elegant words into a form of spectacle—of political theater —Little Rock provided the theme, the images, and the powerful narrative that sped America along the road to full inclusion. The successes of the civil rights movement grew from the movement's emphasis on inclusion. When put into a human drama, it was hard for Americans to imagine why young African Americans should be denied access to the means of self-improvement. The promise of American life has always involved equal opportunity; one of the duties of American life has always been the obligation for self-improvement. The visual drama of the confrontation in Little Rock drove home the moral lesson throughout the country that excluding any American from this central dynamic was intolerable. Forced to confront the contradictions in their beliefs, white Americans actually changed their hearts as well as their minds.

As fundamentally important as was the dismantling of the legal structure of segregation and the shift of white attitudes nationally, the full realization of racial equality was not achieved in 1957 and has not been achieved yet. There is still a disturbing gap between principle and practice. Indeed, one of the most discouraging developments of the past twenty years is that a steady diet of distorted media images and soundbites about welfare queens and Willie Hortons, frequently manipulated for political advantage, has convinced the public that the problem of equal opportunity has been solved. In the eyes of some, there is no more real discrimination, so no government action is needed (in fact, would be counterproductive), and the natural processes of democracy and the market, if left unhindered to work their magic, will integrate whites and blacks in a natural and unforced manner.

Unfortunately, we know from opinion surveys that substantial majorities of white Americans believe that racial discrimination today is not a serious problem. They are aware that discrimination exists, but they believe that the incidence is minor and that it can be overcome easily by individual effort. We also know that significant majorities of African Americans perceive racial discrimination to be a constant and oppressive fact of their daily lives. In itself, this is a dangerous disparity, as if whites and blacks were not living in the same society or were not talking with each other. Consider the immediate reactions to the verdict in the O. J. Simpson criminal trial: 70 percent of whites thought it was jury nullification, while 70 percent of blacks thought the verdict was proper. When perceptions of the same event can be so different, what chance does society have to develop the level of social trust to make collective decisions about common problems?

More important, we know from carefully done studies that significant racial discrimination does exist in housing, jobs, education, banking, the criminal justice system, and the ordinary encounters of daily life. Yet whites do not perceive these continuing injustices, perhaps because they continue to harbor negative stereotypes of black Americans. This is the challenge of the current era.

In our media-drenched environment, how do we break through the noise of distorted messages to communicate a clear and compelling portrait of the gap that still exists between the principle and the practice of equality of opportunity? Even though it sounds completely inadequate, given the magnitude of the task at hand, talk helps. Talk may not be all we need, but the more we talk to each other across all the lines of difference that separate us, the harder it is to sustain those negative stereotypes that inhibit full understanding. That is one of my conclusions from the three-year project of the National Endowment for the Humanities that has just been completed. It was called "A National Conversation on American Pluralism and

Identity". It brought Americans together in face-to-face groups, by radio and television, and on the Internet, to talk and to listen to each other about what holds us together as a society in the midst of our increasing diversity, what values we share and need to share, and what it means to be Americans as we prepare to enter the twenty-first century.

From my persistent eavesdropping on the national conversation, I can confirm the impression that is broadly held among journalists and social critics that Americans are worried about the fragmentation of society. They sense that we are drifting apart—into edge cities and homogeneous suburbs and gated communities, sitting isolated in front of our television sets and computer terminals, into multicultural identity groups. Robert Bellah and his colleagues refer to this as a "crisis of civic membership."[1] Robert Putnam has started a "great debate" nationally about the depopulation of "civil society," that common space that is neither governmental nor privately personal where Americans historically have come together to pursue common interests and to solve common problems.[2]

The good news is that there is an enormous amount of goodwill among Americans. They are eager to work with others from groups different from their own to find solutions to social problems and to overcome barriers of suspicion. This is an important clue to a strategy for the needed crusade for reconciliation. Multicultural task forces at the local level, brought together to study and to solve locally identified problems, are a wonderful way to improve the community while building civic commitment and breaking down the barriers that separate groups.

One of my other discoveries in the NEH's National Conversation is that Americans actually share a lot of attitudes and beliefs without being fully aware of it. Most important, they overwhelmingly revere the Constitution and the Declaration of Independence. They are firmly committed to the political values that underlie our founding documents, and especially to the simultaneous pursuit of human equality *and* individual liberty. Those two ideals sometimes pull in opposite directions, but Americans are committed to both.

Similarly, Americans are committed to a spacious sphere of life into which all come on a basis of complete equality, judged by the same standards, and expected to obey the same rules, a sphere of "just Americans" without any hyphenations or group modifiers. At the same time, they also want to be able to preserve the diversity of cultural heritages that serve to enrich our lives and connect us to our ancestral traditions. They respect diversity, but they also want this to be "one America, indivisible."

That determination to be a single nation was also the answer to the challenge put to the nation by the Little Rock Nine, Daisy Bates, and those who tried to accomplish that great step forward peacefully and in accordance with the law of the land. The sympathies of an aroused nation, and the intervention of the federal government, affirmed that we were to be a single society, a unified nation.

Perhaps somewhere in our examination of the Little Rock experience we will identify the next step that our society must take toward the full realization of America's promise. Our guiding principle must be the observation of Martin Luther King Jr., "This is not a war between the white man and the Negro, but a conflict between justice and injustice."

The events in Little Rock forty years ago helped us realize that our fates as Americans are intertwined despite all our differences. We are bound together across barriers of time and boundaries of race, playing roles in a common story, sharing the shame of our shortcomings as well as the glory of our triumphs. The crisis in Little Rock is part of that grand narrative of expanding opportunity and equality, the progressively perfected inclusiveness of America.

Segregation and Racism:
Taking Up the Dream Again

DAVID R. GOLDFIELD

In 1885 T. McCants Stewart, a black newspaperman from New York, traveled to his native South Carolina expecting a rough reception once his train headed south from Washington, D.C. To his surprise, the conductor allowed him to remain in his seat while whites sat on baggage or stood. He provoked little reaction among whites when he entered the dining car. Some of them struck up a conversation with him. Stewart, who admitted he had begun his journey with "a chip on my shoulder... [daring] any man to knock it off," now observed that "the whites of the South are really less afraid to [have] contact with colored people than the whites of the North." In Columbia, South Carolina, Stewart found that he could move about with no restrictions. "I can ride in first-class cars.... I can go into saloons and get refreshments even as in New York. I can stop in and drink a glass of soda and be more politely waited upon than in some parts of New England."[1]

Seven years later, three prominent black men, Tom Moss, Calvin McDowell, and William Stewart, opened a grocery on the south side of Memphis, an area with a large African American population. The People's Grocery prospered while a white-owned store across the street struggled. The proprietor of the white-owned store, W. H. Barrett was incensed. He secured an indictment against Moss, McDowell, and Stewart for maintaining a public nuisance. Black community leaders responded with a protest meeting at the grocery, during which two people made threats against Barrett. Barrett learned of the threats, notified the police, and warned the gathering at the People's Grocery that whites planned to attack and destroy the store. Nine sheriff's deputies, all white, approached the store to arrest the men who had threatened Barrett. Fearing an assault, blacks in the grocery fired on the deputies, unaware who they were, and wounded three. When the deputies identified themselves, thirty blacks surrendered, including Moss, McDowell, and Stewart, and were imprisoned. Four days later, deputies removed the three owners from jail, took them to a deserted area, and shot them dead.[2]

Although southern blacks experienced segregation, intimidation, and discrimination during and after Reconstruction, race relations in the South remained remarkably fluid through the 1880s. Southern blacks purchased small farms, entered business, moved to towns and cities, established churches and mutual aid societies, cast ballots, and mingled and fraternized with whites in general stores, public conveyances, and saloons.

By 1892, the year of the People's Grocery lynchings in Memphis, the racial climate had changed in the South. Movements to codify racial segregation and bar blacks from the ballot box sprang up throughout the region. Although segregation would never become complete or uniform, it is not an exaggeration to state that after the 1890s blacks were excluded from meaningful participation in southern life. Effectively barred from the ballot, restricted for the most part to menial occupations, and legally excluded or separated from whites in a wide range of activities and venues, southern blacks took their inferior place in the hierarchy of white supremacy, a place they would hold until well into the next century.

A new generation of African Americans came of age in the South during the late 1880s and early 1890s. This was the first generation of freedom. But freedom per se remained a hollow promise so long as southern blacks could not enjoy all of the rights of American citizenship. As the young black editor of Nashville's *Fisk Herald* proclaimed in 1889, "We are not the Negro from whom the chains of slavery fell a quarter of a century ago.... We are now qualified, and, being the equal of whites, should be treated as such." Charles Price, an African American educator from North Carolina admonished colleagues in 1890, "If we do not possess the manhood and patriotism to stand up in the defense of ... constitutional rights and protest long, loud and unitedly against their continual infringements, we are unworthy of heritage as American citizens and deserve to have fastened on us the wrongs of which many are disposed to complain." The new generation of blacks, unwilling to accept the verdict of Reconstruction and anxious to expand their civil and social rights, pressed and protested.[3]

For many in the generation of southern whites who came of age in the same period, this assertiveness rankled. The prevailing white view of blacks during the slavery era was of a docile, childlike race. But the perceived experiences of Reconstruction and after changed whites' perceptions about blacks. Southern blacks competed for jobs with whites, they moved about at will, crowded together with whites in towns and cities, attired themselves in the latest fashions, and generally acted as if they were the social equals of whites. While the vast majority of southern blacks labored in the fields, growing numbers of freedmen found their niche in the cities, where their visibility and successes underscored the fluidity of southern race relations.

A successful black contradicted basic white assumptions about race and race relations; it upset white views of an orderly society; and it challenged religious beliefs that confirmed African American inferiority. Blacks who achieved not only threw the white worldview into question, but it seemed sacrilegious to the bargain. The popular press fanned the resentment by reporting alleged incidents of insolence and, more serious, assaults by black men on white women. Now that the controlling bonds of slavery had fallen away, whites believed, the true primitive nature of the black character was emerging and only a reassertion of white dominance would stay a racial rampage.

Young whites, constantly reminded of the heroism and sacrifice of the preceding generation in the Civil War and how their fathers had redeemed the South from Republican rule and Negro ruin during Reconstruction, felt honor-bound to uphold and preserve the legacy of their predecessors and undertake a second redemption, this time not to save the South from the Yankee, but whites from blacks.

The crisis in race relations seemed especially serious to whites during the early 1890s. The ruling Democratic party, whose leaders had supposedly redeemed the South from ruin and despotic rule, was under siege by the Populists, a group of distressed white farmers who sought relief from staggering debts, high interest rates, and discriminatory railroad charges. A shaky economy, which plunged deeper into depression after 1893, compounded the political uncertainty.

To worsen matters for southern white men, gender relations seemed as fluid as the racial and political situations in the 1890s. Race and gender were closely connected in the post–Civil War South. A key component of the Lost Cause ideal held that Confederates had fought to protect their homes and families, most especially the white women of the South. The reality was that southern men had often failed in this mission. One out of four Confederate soldiers never came home, and many who did continued to suffer physical and psychological trauma. A decade after the war, the leading expenditure of the state of Mississippi was for prosthetic devices for veterans. The war not only took life, but property and prosperity as well. White southern women assumed the roles of breadwinners after the war, entering the teaching profession, working in the fields, and taking up factory jobs. Although work outside the home was much more an economic necessity than an assertion of independence, the fact stood as a rebuke to the role of white men as protectors of white southern women.[4]

But white southern women did more; they took up leadership roles derived from their church work. They led temperance crusades, joined suffrage movements, opened settlement houses, dabbled in city planning and beautification, and pushed against the boundaries their men had established. Many shared the attitude of Galveston clubwoman Cordia Sweeny, who wrote at the turn of the century, "I feel humiliated over the position of woman and the way she has been looked on in the past, as a slave or a plaything. I want to be neither, and want woman equal with men before my daughter grows up."[5] Such an attitude contradicted the southern white male construction of what white women should be, just as the reality of black achievement challenged prevailing notions about race. Having failed to protect their women during the war, postwar southern white men created a woman whose protection was both necessary and demanding. They elevated her to a pedestal and dedicated themselves to keeping her there, above politics, beyond sex, and ineffectual in affairs outside the home. Yet, the economic necessities of postwar life, coupled with the growing assertiveness of southern women in public affairs, contradicted the pedestal image and challenged the role of men as protector.

If white men could not sustain women on the pedestal themselves, they could enlist, figuratively, of course, the black man's assistance. The changing perception of blacks as insolent ingrates and sex fiends dovetailed nicely with attempts to secure the elevated, yet subservient place of white women, for who could save their virtue from black men better than white men? Here was a crusade women could not undertake for themselves—a crusade worthy of the white knights of Dixie, a golden opportunity to restore blacks to their place and white women to their pedestals. The eagerness with which southern legislatures embraced segregation by law and disfranchisement, and the readiness with which whites of diverse social classes resorted to lynching to reinforce the place of blacks ordained by law, indicated the broader objectives which these devices served. They were not ends in themselves, but means to solidifying racial and gender hierarchies in the New South.

The intent of segregation by law was not merely to separate the races but to denigrate one and elevate the other; to offer constant reminders of inferiority as if repetition would bring a self-realization among blacks that they were, in fact, an inferior race. Facilities were rarely equal regardless of judicial admonitions to the contrary. Black schools were makeshift affairs, sometimes located in churches, rude cabins, or plain buildings erected with northern philanthropy. Educational funding in southern states increased dramatically after 1900; but, not only did the gap between white and black per-pupil expenditures widen, but black schools received less money than they had prior to 1900. Black children often walked past new and spacious white schools with landscaped lawns, gymnasiums, playing fields, and a library. Their school year was invariably shorter, usually from late October to the middle of April, when children were not needed in the fields. Pupil-teacher ratios ran as high as eighty to one in one-room schoolhouses. It was less the segregated facilities black children and their parents minded than what that segregation implied in facilities, textbooks, and teachers. As black North Carolina writer Pauli Murray noted of her childhood in the 1940s, "It was never the hardship which hurt so much as the contrast between what we had and what the white children had . . . Our seedy run-down school told us that if we had any place at all in the scheme of things it was a separate place, marked off, proscribed and unwanted by the white people."[6]

Segregation reinforced that impression time and again. If blacks were fortunate enough to have any parks at all, towns rarely provided maintenance. A stranger coming into a town or city always knew the location of black neighborhoods because that was where the pavement ended, where city services stopped or appeared sporadically. Law enforcement authorities scarcely noticed the vice and crime in black communities so long as it remained confined there.

As new technologies appeared, new ways of segregating the races also emerged. In the new downtown office buildings of the early twentieth century, blacks rode the freight elevator, used filthy rest rooms, and were rarely served ahead of whites no matter their place in a line, assuming local regulations permitted them to enter the building in the first place. Perhaps most demeaning, an elaborate etiquette accompanied the codification of segregation requiring African Americans to play a subservient role in all contact with whites. Don't appear to be too smart in conversation, never talk eye to eye with a white person, never complain or appear unhappy, never gossip about other white folks to whites, and never ever address a white woman directly beyond the perfunctory "good morning, ma'am." The extent to which these precepts were enforced depended on whites, so blacks became experts in "reading" the other race to determine what words and body language they should assume. But when confronting white strangers, the difficulty was compounded. In black writer Ernest J. Gaines's novel, *A Lesson Before Dying* (1993), Grant Wiggins, a black teacher in a small Cajun community, is invited to the home of wealthy whites. Wiggins muses, "I tried to decide just how I should respond to them. Whether I should act like the teacher I was, or like the nigger that I was supposed to be. I decided to wait and see how the conversation went. To show too much intelligence would have been an insult to them. To show a lack of intelligence would have been a greater insult to me. I decided to wait and see how the conversation would go."[7]

Under segregation black southerners became less a people than a form of behavior, as Quentin Compson observed in William Faulkner's *The Sound and the Fury* (1929): "a nigger is not a person so much as a form of behavior; a sort of obverse reflection of the white people he lives among."[8] The black southerner that evolved during the segregation era was a creation of whites, of how southern whites wanted to perceive their black neighbors now that whites had reestablished control over their communities and homes: docile, deferential, and basically content with the way things were. The vast majority of southern whites were not bad people. As time went on, they just assumed everything was fine; northerners might express their incredulity when white southerners asserted that race relations were fine in Dixie, but most southerners truly believed that to be the case. Nothing they saw or heard in their daily contact with African Americans contradicted that view.

Segregation then, not only sealed the victory for white supremacy, but it made whites feel good about themselves. Early in a white boy's life, he learned that no matter how poor he was, he was not black. Second, the behavior of blacks confirmed the wisdom of segregation. The potential loss of work, the alienation of white protectors, and the threat and reality of verbal and physical harassment ensured general compliance with the rules of white supremacy. Challenges occurred all the time, of course, between the 1890s and the 1950s. Rosa Parks was hardly the first southern black to challenge segregation. The NAACP kept up a steady stream of lawsuits from the 1920s onward, but these efforts had little effect on the lives most blacks led on the farms and in the towns or cities.

Third, segregation and the white supremacist ideals that framed it solved the political problems of white leaders. White supremacy became the common bond between whites of all social classes; to disrupt the bond implied the end of white supremacy and the beginning of Negro rule. To lend credence to this view, southern textbooks, movies, and popular literature created a historical fiction, depicting Reconstruction as an era of Yankee thuggery and black terror.

Fourth, segregation fit well with New South booster rhetoric. Segregation and modernization were quite compatible. As new technologies appeared, such as elevators, electric trolleys, and soda fountains, segregation sorted out the races helpfully. Segregation smoothed the disorder that accompanied urban and economic development. Blacks knew their place and provided the menial labor to support the growing urban economy, and white supremacy kept the baser instincts of black men in check so that racial peace and harmony could attract outside investment.

Finally, white ministers confirmed the hierarchy of races and asserted that segregation was not only good for blacks but the pattern God had intended. Most white churches affirmed that southern whites were not only carrying out the divine plan but also ensuring the peace and tranquillity of their homes, families, and region.

So southern whites went about their lives oblivious to the misery in their midst; real blacks and real black lives were invisible to them because the etiquette of segregation and the fact of separation ensured that invisibility. Whites were oblivious as well to the great contradictions of segregation, that blacks and whites came into intimate contact with each other as nursemaids, cooks, and domestics, yet they were systematically separated in theaters and parks, and blacks were excluded completely from white restaurants and hotels. Most southern whites were also oblivious to the bizarre rhythms of life that accompanied segregation: that whites when they left their homes rarely would lock the front door, but always the back door because that was where blacks entered; that blacks had to plan trips downtown carefully to ensure they would not need rest rooms or places to eat; that blacks could buy shoes and clothes, but could never try them on; that black doctors and lawyers existed in southern towns, even though whites often insisted that blacks could master only elementary material.[9]

As peculiar as many of these racial customs were, without the complicity of the rest of the nation they could not have existed, much less flourished. When the curtain formally descended between blacks and whites in the 1890s the majority of white Americans, northern as well as southern, subscribed to the notion that blacks were inferior to whites and deserved to be treated as second-class citizens. Contemporary depictions of blacks show scarcely human stereotypes: black men with bulbous lips and bulging eyes, heavyset black women wearing turbans and smiling vacuously, and black children contentedly eating watermelon or romping with jungle animals. These images appeared on cereal boxes, in advertisements, in children's books, in newspaper cartoons, and as lawn ornaments. Popular theater of the day featured white men in blackface cavorting in ridiculous fashion and singing songs such as "All Coons Look Alike to Me" and "I Wish My Color Would Fade." Among the widely read books of the era was *The Clansman*, a glorification of the rise of the Ku Klux Klan by Thomas Dixon, a North Carolinian living in New York City and an ardent white supremacist. D. W. Griffith transformed *The Clansman* into an immensely popular motion picture epic under the title *Birth of a Nation.*

Intellectual and political opinion in the North bolstered southern policy. Scientific racism purported to establish white superiority and black inferiority on biological grounds. Northern-born professional historians reinterpreted the Civil War and Reconstruction in the white South's favor. Historian William A. Dunning, the generation's leading authority on Reconstruction, wrote in 1901 that the North's "views as to the political capacity of the blacks had been irrational." Respected journals openly supported disfranchisement and segregation. The progressive journal *Outlook* hailed disfranchisement because it made it "impossible in the future for ignorant, shiftless, and corrupt negroes to misrepresent their race in political action." Harvard's Charles Francis Adams Jr. chided colleagues who disregarded the "fundamental, scientific facts" he claimed demonstrated black inferiority. The *New York Times*, summarizing this national consensus in 1903, noted that "practically the whole country" supported the "southern solution" to the race issue, since "there was no other possible settlement."[10]

These views permeated Congress, which made no effort to block the institutionalization of white supremacy in the South, and the courts, which upheld discriminatory legislation. The migration of blacks to northern cities merely confirmed northern views on southern race relations. As a delegate at the Alabama disfranchisement convention of 1901 noted, "The race problem is no longer confined to the States of the South, [and] we have the sympathy instead of the hostility of the North."[11] The Republican party, which stood to lose votes in the South if states disfranchised African Americans, nonetheless made no effort to protect black rights after 1890. By the mid-1890s, Republicans were so entrenched in the North and West that they did not need southern votes to win presidential elections or to control Congress. Besides, business-oriented Republicans found common ground with conservative southern Democrats on fiscal policy and foreign affairs.

As the white consensus on race emerged, the status of African Americans slipped in the North as well as the South. Although no northern states threatened to deny blacks the right to vote, they did increase segregation. The booming industries of the North generally did not hire blacks. Antidiscrimination laws on the books since the Civil War went unenforced. In 1904, 1906, and 1908, race riots erupted in Springfield, Ohio; Greensburg, Indiana; and Springfield, Illinois; matching similar disturbances in Wilmington, North Carolina, and Atlanta, Georgia.

The damage all of this did to black southerners is incalculable and, in fact, historians have scarcely begun to assess the adverse impact of segregation on blacks, whites, and the South. But autobiographies written by blacks who grew up under segregation—Richard Wright, Maya Angelou, Mary Mebane, just to name some of the more prominent writers—indicate that black communities dealt with white supremacy by scaling back ambitions and protecting their children by limiting their horizons.[12] For especially creative and stubborn youngsters, these protective features of life in the black community were both confining and infuriating. When Wright published a short story in a black newspaper in Jackson, Mississippi, for example, his friends expressed disapproval: "they looked at me with new eyes, and a distance, a suspiciousness came between us." At another point in his autobiography, *Black Boy* (1945), Wright noted, "I began to marvel at how smoothly the black boys acted out the roles that the white race had mapped out for them. Most of them were not conscious of living a special separate, stunted way of life. Yet I knew that in some period of their growing up...there had been developed in them a delicate, sensitive controlling mechanism that shut off their minds and emotions from all that the white race had said was taboo."[13]

North Carolina writer Mary Mebane recalls her frustration about voicing ambitions in her community. "Black women like me have scrubbed a hundred billion miles of tiled corridors and washed an equal number of dishes. I wasn't going to do that. I am going to live my own life, I secretly said. No, you aren't, said an adult. I am going to see to it that you don't. You might as well get those foolish notions out of your head, girl. That adult was my mother."[14]

But segregation hurt whites, too. Segregation and the etiquette required by it cut whites off from their fellow southerners who had shared and contributed to the South's culture, whose blood coursed in untold veins of whites, and whose mutual dependence went unrecognized. At some point in the lives of any southern white who thought about it—and there were some—the tug between the feeling of common humanity and the requirements of following the dance steps of segregation became painful; of something as simple and as unthinking as wanting to shake someone's hand but refraining from doing so both because of the disapproval that might be voiced by fellow whites and the embarrassed and even fearful reaction of the black. The effort and expense to maintain separate facilities, no matter how disparate in quality, drained the South of energy and vitality. As writer Lillian Smith noted in 1948, "In trying to shut the Negro race away from us, we have shut ourselves away from so many good, creative, honest, deeply human things in life."[15]

Without an appreciation of how segregation by law evolved and the purpose to which whites applied it and blacks were subjected by it, it is not possible to appreciate how southern blacks reacted to the *Brown* decision in 1954 and the subsequent decade we call the civil rights movement. Although *Brown* hardly emerged out of legal thin air, it gave a clarion call to action for southern blacks. One Alabama black leader recalled, "For the first time, folks in Greene County watching TV and listening to the radio became aware of what was going on in the world around them."[16] As Pat Watters suggested, "All Southern time must be measured before and after *Brown* because it so changed history, the fabric of life and the very feel of the institutions of government."[17] A chance at the mainstream of southern life galvanized the black South, imparted an identity, an importance to lives. The civil rights movement and its religious and moral message opened the eyes, if not the hearts, of southern whites to the discontent among them, the basic contradictions of their lives, and how they had strayed from the basic principles of Christianity. The movement was a mutually revelatory exercise, an education for blacks that they could effect change and to whites that change was not only good but that it would not destroy southern civilization; to the contrary, it would save it and make it better. Whites would no longer construct their present on past failure, but on the hope of the future.

It is important to emphasize the "bad old days" of segregation because of late some in the black community have begun to look upon that era with nostalgia or at least a wistfulness that life was somehow simpler if not better then. Yes, teachers bootlegged black history into black schools to an extent not evident today; yes, black businesses flourished on "Sweet Auburn" in Atlanta and along numerous other black main streets in the urban South; and yes, drugs, single-parent households, and physical decay were not endemic in black neighborhoods.

In part the nostalgia among some blacks for the segregation era derives from a need to possess a valid cultural heritage. Henry Louis Gates's *Colored People: A Memoir* (1994) depicts his childhood village in West Virginia as a self-enclosed community where children grew up surrounded by supportive family, teachers, preachers, and friends. Gates's town is like a womb—secure, warm, and confining. A similar text of memory is Raymond Andrews's *The Last Radio Baby* (1990), about growing up "colored" in Georgia in the 1930s and 1940s, where Andrews evokes with nostalgia the respect for elders and kin, the cotton-picking contests and songfests, and the excitement of the weekly trips to town. These memoirs stress the togetherness, community, mutual respect, and, above all, the safe world of blackness that enveloped such enclaves.[18]

But these memoirs are more reflective of the present than they are of the reality of the past, not that African American communities did not exhibit these strengths. The filter of memory forgets that these districts were not totally self-contained and isolated from the white South. As black writer Gerald Barly has noted, "In such a reading of American social history, black communities before 1954 were, segregation notwithstanding, or perhaps owing to segregation, the American equivalent of an Edenic Africa before the coming of the white man.... If the black world before integration was so attractive, why was there a civil rights movement?"

Recently, German historian Saul Friedlander published *Nazi Germany and the Jews: The Years of Persecution, 1933–1939* (1997) about the fate of the Jews in Nazi Germany before the Second World War and before the implementation of the Final Solution. Jewish culture flourished under the Nazis, Friedlander notes, as the authorities drove them out of theaters, orchestras, schools, and editorial boards. "German Jews educated and entertained each other, producing fine works of art, drama, fiction and scholarship."[19] But Friedlander recounts these "golden" years more with a sense of tragic irony than with nostalgia. We know, of course, what awaited these Jews, but we also know their resourcefulness occurred out of necessity, out of their powerless and submissive relationship to Aryan Germany. The full life they had led before 1933 may have lacked the brilliant luster of the cultural outpouring which occurred after 1933, but it was a life lived whole with little compromise and with participation in the larger German society on their own terms. After 1933, the Jews became increasingly invisible to the average German, increasingly confined to their own neighborhoods and institutions. Out of sight, they drifted out of mind. What the years before the Holocaust underscored was not the virulent hatred and anti-Semitism of average Germans, but their profound indifference once German Jews disappeared from participation in the broader society.

The thrust of the *Brown* decision and the all-out assault on segregation which followed looked forward to the full participation of blacks in southern and American life, nothing less. Separateness meant inequality and invisibility. But the ink was scarcely dry on President Lyndon B. Johnson's signature on the 1965 Voting Rights Act when the Watts section of Los Angeles exploded in racial conflict touching off a four-year period of civil disturbances throughout the urban North. The white South congratulated itself on its seeming immunity from such unrest, and black southerners went about the business of voting, holding office, and going to schools previously barred to them. The South was now the Sun Belt, a happy region of economic prosperity and racial harmony. Gradually, the resolve for integration weakened in the South. Southern whites, it turned out, really didn't mind going to school with blacks, as long as there weren't too many of them. Black children invariably bore the brunt of busing. Middle-class southern blacks complained of "white-folks overload," working with white folks all day who understood very little about black culture and feelings. The rise of the Republican party in the South ensured that racial issues persisted, though rarely with the demagoguery associated with one-party rule. Republican strength fostered political segregation as the overwhelming majority of blacks voted Democratic and a majority of whites consistently voted Republican.[20]

Black women, who played major roles in the era before *Brown* in organizing communities for self-help and, later, for civil rights protests—women like Daisy Bates, who led the nine black children in Little Rock; Jo Ann Robinson, who initiated the Montgomery bus boycott; Ella Baker, who founded the Student Nonviolent Coordinating Committee; and Fannie Lou Hamer, who transformed Mississippi politics—receded in prominence as black men, long stymied by fear and repression, stepped to the fore, but not with any coherent program that sought to take black southerners and black Americans into the mainstream of American life.

To the contrary, voices erupted during the last decade promoting identity politics, emphasizing alleged genetic differences between blacks and whites, and manufacturing an African American history that not only distorted the past as much as whites had distorted the Civil War and Reconstruction, but that depicted whites as congenital antagonists and killers of culture. And then there was a flurry of nostalgia memoirs, arguing that desegregation contributed to the fall from the black Eden.

Whites tuned in and dropped out. Southern whites are not generally racists, nor are they as powerful as some black leaders imply. They are simply too busy to care; the polls always show a strong majority in favor of the concept of integration, but don't expect most whites to do much about it. And, in any case, blacks today send mixed messages as to whether or not they even want an integrated society. The emphasis among many black leaders is on group ideology, group entitlements, and group identity. To be sure, the movement that destroyed segregation by law focused on the civil rights of a group, but Martin Luther King and his followers always emphasized that it was about the dignity of individuals as much as the uplift of any group. As black sociologist Shelby Steele has noted, "being 'black' in no way spared the necessity of being myself." More to the point, Frederick Douglass explained, "the only excuse for pride in individuals... is in the fact of their own achievements. If the sun has created curled hair and tanned skin, let the sun be proud of its achievement."[21] The focus on group exclusivity and uniqueness hampers integration efforts if difference becomes the sole definition of identity.

The emphasis on difference is often the case among certain advocates of black education. The Ebonics movement, which is widespread in California, is touted in the name of cultural sensitivity; but, "in practice it is a means to allow black youngsters to pass through the school system without ever mastering the basics of grammar, spelling and punctuation."[22] It is hardly surprising that those schools employing the Ebonics approach have dropped in reading and language skills on standardized tests.

The self-isolation of blacks is evident also in politics. Until the early 1990s blacks, Jews, and Latinos were the most loyal Democrats in the nation. Recent mayoral elections in Los Angeles, New York, and Chicago have indicated that a majority of Jews and Latinos have voted for Republican or moderate Democratic candidates, while blacks have stayed with liberal Democrats. The dividing lines have been crime and fiscal conservatism. In Houston, where there were indications in the 1980s that blacks and Latinos might make common political cause, that appears to be the case no longer. As one analyst explained, "blacks and Latinos [in Houston] don't live the same sort of lives."[23] In terms of unemployment, family structure, crime, and attitudes toward the police, a vast gulf exists between blacks and Latinos in Houston and between blacks and everyone else every place else.

Can we begin to renew our commitment to an integrated society, and, if so, where do we begin? Conventional wisdom fifty years ago was that segregation, like the Third Reich, would last for a thousand years. In our own lifetimes we have seen both Hitler and Jim Crow vanquished, the Berlin Wall go up and down, the Soviet Empire collapse, and a man walk on the moon. The point is that the seemingly impossible can become the probable very quickly and unexpectedly. And it does not take a large army to effect such "miracles," just the goodwill of some dedicated men and women of both races who can put aside the posturing and the suspicions in order to chart a course of recovery and reconciliation.

The initiative lies with both blacks and whites, but especially with middle-class blacks; they were the ones who persevered during the Jim Crow era and fought its restrictions and then led and defined the civil rights movement. And, as it has been with every ethnic minority in this country, the conformity must be with the host society; black leaders must be candid in noting that conformity does not and should not imply a loss of cultural identity any more than being American denies an individual's Jewish, Italian, Irish, or southern identity. As black Atlanta Congressman John Lewis, a civil rights veteran noted, "You can have an integrated society without losing diversity. But you can also have a society that transcends race, where you can lay down the burden of race—I'm talking about just *lay it down*—and treat people as human beings, regardless of the color of their skin."[24]

I believe that this leadership will come from people like Lewis, southerners black and white, because we have seen the horror of segregation as the handmaiden of white supremacy, the teacher of inferiority, the enforcer of humiliation, the siren of the false sense of security, and the killer of dreams. Lewis admits that his vision is "old-fashioned," that, as he says, "it's out of date—that for a black person, it's Tommin', it's weak, it's passive. It is a radical idea. It's revolutionary to talk about the creation of the beloved community, the creation of a truly interracial democracy, a truly integrated society."[25]

But revolutions have occurred in our lifetime, here in the South and right here in Little Rock. Let us use this wonderful occasion and its history and legacy to rededicate ourselves to the principles those young children cherished as they walked the difficult steps to Central High School. Let us speak with the confidence and commitment of Frederick Douglass when he posed the question in June 1863, "can the white and colored people of this country be blended into a common nationality, and enjoy together... under the same flag, the inestimable blessing of life, liberty, and the pursuit of happiness, as neighborly citizens of a common country?" Douglass answered his own question unequivocally: "I believe they can."[26]

Growing Up Segregated

GEORGE C. WRIGHT

Growing up segregated is a subject that I have been thinking about for years. I believe that my life experiences, coupled with my scholarship, have given me a number of insights into race relations in the American South of the 1950s. I have conducted primary research on the subject and interviewed dozens of blacks from that period. I have lived my entire life in the South. As a student, faculty member, and administrator, I have been affiliated with four schools: the University of Kentucky, Duke University, the University of Texas at Austin, and the University of Texas at Arlington, all southern schools. For both good and bad reasons, I have been viewed by my colleagues—this includes whites and blacks alike—as a southerner. Mentioning a few aspects of my own life will explain my perspectives or biases on my view of growing up segregated.

I am aware of the risk involved when someone chooses to use his or her own life experiences when discussing a subject. For one thing, personal recollections often are viewed as a form of self-glorification. I hope none of you reach that conclusion from hearing my remarks. I do not want to give you the impression that my life and experiences are "typical" for all southern blacks, because a number of factors account for the many different experiences that black people had in the 1950s. Also, it is important for me to keep in mind that I lived in Kentucky, an area that differed from the Deep South in some respects. What might have seemed overly oppressive to Kentucky blacks might be viewed as "benign" to others.

My scholarship highlights patterns of racial segregation and discrimination in Kentucky that mirrored the experiences of blacks farther South. Until the 1960s, black Kentuckians were prohibited from using most tax-supported facilities and institutions such as parks, libraries, and government housing. In a manner consistent with the South, Kentucky discriminated against blacks in meting out "justice" in courts of law. Discrimination in employment was widespread, resulting in blacks working the least-secure and lowest-paying jobs. Blacks in Kentucky could vote, but most often for the lesser of two anti-black candidates. Prior to the 1950s, racial violence was common in the Bluegrass State. When considering that the number of Afro-Americans in Kentucky declined at a steady rate, and thus were never a threat to whites that blacks farther south could be perceived as being, the numbers of lynchings, murders, and episodes of running blacks off their lands were shockingly high; indeed, they were quite similar to those in the Deep South and in some instances higher than most southern states. Moreover, as the twentieth century progressed, the high number of murders by lynch mobs was replaced with legal executions of blacks by the state, though in reality they were a continuation of the mob violence that had existed in Kentucky since the end of the Civil War.

Yet in Louisville, the largest and most cosmopolitan city in the state, and in Lexington, my hometown, there existed a form of racial etiquette that I characterize as "polite racism," a form of oppression that extended a few concessions to Afro-Americans as long as they accepted their place and remained at the bottom of society. In both Louisville and Lexington, whites helped create black institutions. And, of course, a segregated black school is better than no school. But, the segregated black school was vastly inferior to white schools, and the gulf between them tended to widen over time. The polite racism of whites was so effective that it tended to lull both Afro-Americans and whites into believing that conditions in Louisville and Lexington were not as bad as elsewhere, especially when looking southward. (In his work, my colleague Joel Williamson calls this *conservative racism*).

I was born in Lexington on the Negro ward of St. Joseph's Hospital in February 1950. At that time, Lexington's housing projects were segregated by race, and my family lived in Charlotte Court. As a young child, rarely did I see white people: I attended an all-black school; played at Frederick Douglass Park, which was segregated; and, on a weekly basis, I went to the only black movie theater in town. Lexington had a very fine public library, but blacks were served once every two weeks by a bookmobile. While blacks could frequent and spend their dollars in the downtown shopping area, we were prohibited from eating in the department stores and one never knew how kindly he or she would be treated when attempting to buy clothes or try on shoes. All of my life I have had something of a weird sense of humor, and during my childhood days I used to ask, "What do whites do in public bathrooms that we don't do in toilets?" since we were denied the right to go into the ones reserved for whites.

Two forms of discrimination remain vivid in my mind forty years later. Each summer, we traveled from Lexington to Cincinnati to see a baseball game or go to the zoo, and I remember the "half-way houses" between these two cities where blacks were refused service. As a result, my mother prepared fried chicken and other delicious foods for us to snack on during the trip, and we carried a pot to relieve ourselves. Also, Lexington had its own amusement facility, which was called Joyland Park. Toward the end of summer each year I looked forward to "Negro Day," the only time when we were allowed in Joyland Park.

Racial segregation was such a part of my early life, and left such a mark on my life, that thirty-five years later I am still reminded of Jim Crow Lexington. To this very day, I simply cannot take for granted that I can go to any restaurants or movies I choose. I always ask my wife, when we are being served in a fancy place and are being treated in an appropriate manner, "What did they think we would do in here but eat?"

In reflecting back, I am struck that in the 1950s my family, as well as the majority of blacks in my community, seemed to accept these forms of racial exclusion as normal and allowed most forms of racial segregation to go unchallenged. This differs from what John Hope Franklin remembers about his father, an educated attorney.

Those of you who are black, who are my age or older, will understand when I say that despite the presence of racial segregation, black people found numerous ways to have rich and fulfilling lives. My own life was no exception. Indeed, when reflecting on my childhood and all of the activities I participated in, I am certain that I had a very normal life for a kid.

Earlier this year after my mother passed away, one of her best friends gave me a picture of my mother, my sister, and me as we were boarding a chartered bus for our summer excursion to the amusement park in Cincinnati. That one picture and others taken later that day at the park say a great deal to me. The clothes we have on are beautiful, and, given the smiles on our faces, we had a great time. The fact that we traveled out of town to the amusement park, wearing what looked to be new clothing and sunglasses, suggested that we had the financial resources to partake of recreational activities.

Practically every day during the summer I went to Frederick Douglass Park for baseball games, swimming, and other activities. At other times of the year, I took piano lessons, went to the bowling alley, and participated in scouting activities. It was back during the 1950s, before I turned ten years old, that I began what has become my lifelong love of going to the movies. There was a stipulation attached to my going to the movies: since I always went on Sunday afternoon, my mother allowed me to go only if I had been to church earlier that day. She reasoned that if I had been too ill to attend church, then there was no way I could have recovered by the afternoon to go to the movies.

Much of our lives centered around Frederick Douglass School, a place offering athletic contests and a wide range of activities that brought entertainment and cultural enrichment to our lives. For many Lexington blacks older than me, Douglass was the only school they attended since its grades went from the first through twelfth. Given what scholars now know about the contributions of Afro-American teachers, I suspect that the highly dedicated teachers that I encountered at Douglass were found throughout black America in the 1950s and 1960s. My teachers had very exacting standards and refused to allow any misbehavior by their students, even if this unruly behavior took place after school hours or during the summer months. My teachers had a sense of pride in race and believed that any inappropriate act by students reflected poorly on the entire race. The music teacher at Douglass was Mrs. Mamie Grimsley (note her name, "Grim"-sley, and believe me she was no fun at all). Mrs. Grimsley hit you with a stick for not paying attention or for singing off-key. To this day, I am unclear as to how I got roped into taking piano lessons from Mrs. Grimsley, an assignment that gave her even more opportunities to hit my hands. But can you believe this: because my two sisters were also taking piano lessons from Mrs. Grimsley, she did not charge for lessons for me, the third kid.

Perhaps symbolic of my childhood was the summer of 1963, when the March on Washington occurred. Like everyone else, I was aware of the civil rights movement. There had been demonstrations in downtown Lexington, culminating in a boycott of clothing stores during the Easter season. But during that crucial summer and while the march was taking place most of my attention was directed at making the all-star baseball team, something very normal for a male kid, white or black, at that time. It is important for me not to give the impression that life was idyllic in segregated Lexington and that the blacks of my community were not offended by the presence of racial discrimination. When I describe my life and activities in a segregated society as being "normal," I am speaking of my life and those years through the eyes of a child.

A few years ago, Bill Moyers, a well-known journalist who appears to be a very introspective and sensitive human being, was the commencement speaker at UT-Austin, his alma mater. He discussed at length the 1950s, the time when he obtained his B.A. degree and started his first professional job. In using his life as an example, Moyers made the point that new opportunities were available to young Americans in the decade after World War II. Moyers noted that his starting salary after graduation paid much more than his father was earning after thirty years of work. I listened to Moyers with great interest and waited for him to tell the graduating class and their families about the restrictions that race placed on some Americans, to say it as only he probably could that this American society of unbounded opportunities unfortunately did not exist for all Americans. For whatever reason—maybe because it was a graduation speech and he wanted to keep it positive and upbeat—Moyers failed to acknowledge the presence of racism in America in the 1950s, the time of the Little Rock school incident.

My parents were born a few years before Bill Moyers but are of the same generation. Furthermore my father, unlike Moyers, I suspect, served in the military during World War II. The freedoms that black men fought and died for during World War II, and the resulting bounty that Bill Moyers reaped in the 1950s and 1960s, were not extended to black people of my parents' generation: instead, my parents and their contemporaries were subjected to racial hostility, insults, and other indignities that a child like me in the 1950s could not possibly comprehend. Can you imagine what it must have been like for a military veteran, like my father, to be prohibited from using public facilities, from being denied the right to compete for the new jobs that were there for the taking for Bill Moyers and his white contemporaries? My father loved to read: can you imagine how he felt about being denied the right to enter the library? He loved and collected classical music. I wonder if he ever wanted to attend the special concerts held at Transylvania College, the University of Kentucky, or at the Lexington Opera House. If I as a child came to the understanding that police officers were not friendly toward us, can you imagine how my parents felt about the law and how they were required to act if they wanted to survive when interacting with the authorities in any fashion?

For my parents, the greatest impact of living segregated in the 1950s and 1960s was the limited employment opportunities. During the 1940s, my mother attended Kentucky State College for Negroes for three years but left without her degree. My father, while still in high school, had been drafted into the army. Upon returning home after the war, he went immediately to work instead of returning to high school to complete his degree, a decision not at all uncommon to most black and white men of his generation.

Unlike Bill Moyers, neither of my parents had college degrees; therefore, it is perhaps unfair to compare their work experiences with his. Lexington of the 1950s had available for white males well-paying blue-collar jobs, positions as clerks and salespersons, and white-collar jobs that were closed to Afro-Americans. Indeed, in my research and oral interviews I encountered only a few instances in which black men the age of my father worked as mail carriers; and in every instance these men were college graduates. My father and the man who would become my father-in-law eventually found positions at Lexington's elite hotels and country clubs. Jobs as waiters and cooks paid relatively good wages in part because of tips and opportunities to work overtime on special occasions.

New employment opportunities became available to Lexington blacks around 1960 with the opening of an IBM plant. Unfortunately, my father and future father-in-law failed to take advantage of these new employment opportunities. Their reasoning was understandable: while these new jobs provided stable employment and security in the form of retirement pensions, they also meant pay cuts. Also, whites with no more education or any more significant work experiences than my father were hired in supervisory positions. So, despite the presence of better paying jobs by the early 1960s, racial discrimination still held sway in employment in Lexington. I am not making a bold statement when saying that if my mother had been white she would have easily found employment as a cashier, a sales clerk, secretary, or better. When I joined the faculty of the University of Kentucky in 1977, I met secretaries who were my mother's age who had worked for the university for more than two decades. These women have since retired and enjoy pensions and medical benefits. In the 1950s, my mother often worked as a servant in the homes of whites. On several occasions her employer gave her hand-me-down clothes, which my mother brought home and promptly threw away! (It is my guess that women who gave these worn-out clothes to my mother were more motivated by a need to ease their guilt feelings about the low salaries of house servants than by any humanitarian sentiments.) At least for Lexington—and I suspect this is true for all of America of that day—every black young woman, if she needed to work, was compelled to do service or domestic jobs at some point. My mother eventually found employment that provided health insurance, paid vacation, and sick leave: she became a nurse's aid at Eastern State Mental Hospital. She was employed there for thirty years, working the graveyard shift of 11:00 P.M. to 7:00 A.M. for twenty of those years. The civil rights movement eventually resulted in my mother obtaining a better job and better working hours at Eastern State. But, all was far from well on her new job: she noted on numerous occasions that her fellow white workers resented the fact that she was their equal on a job in which they directed recreational activities for the patients.

Cracks in the wall of segregation had been occurring throughout the twentieth century, and these breakthroughs increased in a significant way in the 1950s and 1960s. In Kentucky, the statewide NAACP fought consistently for justice and equality with the focal point of their activities being school desegregation at both the college and public school level. By the time of the Little Rock school crisis, school desegregation was under way in Lexington, Louisville, and a few scattered parts of the state, but for the most part change was slow and often instigated by the NAACP. Even in Louisville, which received national accolades for "peaceful desegregation," the school integration that was occurring was modest at best, relying almost totally on the concept of "freedom of choice," a practice that kept all whites in their schools and only a handful of blacks moving to white schools. But the number of blacks opting to attend white schools in Lexington grew steadily over the years to the point that in the mid-1960s the decision was made to close the only remaining black high school in the city. I experienced school desegregation in September 1964.

The teachers at Frederick Douglass had prepared us for school desegregation: very few black students lagged behind whites academically. Additionally, our teachers had gone overboard in lecturing to us on the proper mode of dress and manners to be displayed in an integrated setting. It turned out that white kids were no more concerned about having their shirt tails tucked in than I had been, and they had little knowledge of the appropriate table manners in the cafeteria. It is possible that my high school experiences, which occurred from 1965 to 1968, might differ from that of many of my black contemporaries. By that time, Lexington had four high schools, and the housing patterns of blacks resulted in their living within the vicinity of three of these schools. When my sister started high school in 1963, school officials decided to bring more integration to Lafayette High School by sending her and her classmates there. I started high school two years later and was given the option of attending Lafayette or going to Bryan Station High School, still a predominantly white school but the one that was closest to my house. I chose Lafayette and was one of twelve blacks out of seven hundred students in the tenth grade class. By comparison, blacks composed around 25 percent of the student population at each of the other three high schools.

This meant that in high school I experienced segregation within a predominantly white environment. Black students were not overtly excluded, we just were not included in school activities such as plays, student government, organizations, and the like, though room was made for us on athletic teams. Where previously I had found numerous forms of enjoyment behind the wall of segregation to such a degree that I was unaware that I was segregated, this did not prove to be the case in high school. I realized there that I was an outsider.

Making my situation worse was the attitude of Lafayette's white teachers and administrators. Again, while not overtly racist, school officials at Lafayette were at least very insensitive to their black students. One example was the way they handled bus transportation to and from school, with black students being inconvenienced on both parts of the trip. The school system provided free lunches to needy students. Since my parents had divorced by that time and we had moved from a housing subdivision back to the housing project, I easily qualified for free lunch. But, when asking how this was handled my first day of school, I was informed that while the cafeteria had a dozen lines for students to go through to pay for their lunches, there was only one free lunch line. I simply could not go through that line.

Undoubtedly, the student and his or her parents have the major responsibility to ensure that the student receives an education. That said, however, a number of my teachers in high school failed to give me the encouragement that is an essential part of their jobs. I firmly believe that teachers should not destroy the dreams of their students but should try to make their students look beyond their own limited visions. Too often back then—at least at Lafayette if nowhere else—my teachers looked only at the color of my skin or compared my family background to that of white students and found me lacking. The worst incident that happened to me in high school was not that a white student, male or female, rejected my attempt to befriend them, or that I got into a fight, or that I was excluded from some party, or that I was called the infamous "N" word, because none of these things happened to me. I never allowed myself to be put in a place where whites could reject me. But, on one occasion I told my history teacher of my dream: I wanted to be a high school history teacher. He said that I lacked the smarts to do that. That incident, which may seem minor to some of you, was the worst thing that happened to me in high school.

Fortunately for me, having enjoyed the positive side of a segregated environment held me in good stead when I encountered rejection in a white setting. My pastor had always told me that I was very smart (but very bad as well). My teachers at Douglass had said that also. And, above all, my mother, who had attended college, had instilled in me that I had no choice but to go to college if I wanted to be something in life. Yet, I am convinced that the indifferent attitude that I received from white teach-ers in high school was encountered by other blacks and it destroyed their dreams and led to their dropping out of school. This would prove to be the crucial event in their lives.

Even though the days of growing up segregated have long ended, I believe that their impact is still present in the lives of many black Americans. All of my life I have encountered blacks who are extremely pessimistic regarding race relations and their own lives and suffer from what I call "poverty of the spirit." These Afro-Americans have accepted defeat and lack confidence to change the most fundamental conditions of their lives. While poverty of the spirit is not limited to any one area, I see this sense of impoverishment among blacks very clearly in my hometown of Lexington, Kentucky. I am dismayed by the number of people my age— those who were born in the 1950s and grew up segregated—who have no jobs or prospects for employment and still live at home. Many of them spend their days in Douglass Park, playing cards and watching basketball games, just like I did thirty years ago. Is it a coincidence, I have wondered, that the very same people are always in the park on the rare occasions when I return to Lexington, and that they are there all day long, rain or shine, hot or cold?

On one occasion, I spent an afternoon searching for a particular grave site in Greenwood Cemetery, the place where blacks were buried during the days of segregation and where most still choose to be buried today. Eventually, I went to the area where people have been buried over the past ten years and discovered the final resting places of at least twenty people I knew very well. They were the victims of substance abuse, vio-lence, and poor health in general. But clearly despair had been a major problem in the lives of these people. I know black people in Lexington who have a hard time believing that there are members of their race who have "made it" (have well-paying jobs and control over their lives). These doubting Thomases, to state it simply, believe that the best things in this life are reserved—in fact are given—to white people. Years ago, there was a skit by Eddie Murphy on *Saturday Night Live* that parodied something that many black people actually believe. Murphy, after lightening his skin, boarded a bus. Nothing unusual occurred until the last black person got off the bus. After checking to be certain that all of the Afro-Americans had left, the driver brought out refreshments, including soft drinks, wine, and cheese. The whites had a great time. The height of this farce occurred when Murphy entered a bank with the hopes of obtaining an installment loan. The lending officer, again after checking to make certain no blacks were within earshot, said to Murphy, "Here take it." Murphy was unclear as to what he meant, but the loan officer persisted. Instead of having to borrow money, Murphy was simply being given an unspecified amount, something that all whites supposedly received on a regular basis. I found this skit to be brilliant because it portrayed—in the form of a farce—something that many blacks in my hometown of Lexington believe: that whites have it made and receive certain special benefits denied Afro-Americans. I wonder if Murphy and the producers knew what they were depicting or if they had simply developed a skit that they thought was totally absurd. White racism is at the root of poverty of the spirit among blacks. Obviously, some of the racism goes all the way back to the days of slavery; but for many of my black contemporaries, the roots of their problems go back to the 1950s and 1960s, when they lived in a segregated society and were denied the many opportunities whites took for granted. Many white and black conservatives fail to acknowledge vestiges of historical racism and the legacies of slavery and segregation, and often they tend to blame the victims of that racism for the problems many blacks face.

Reflecting on growing up segregated I realize that, in spite of the opportunities available to me in the late 1960s that resulted in my obtaining three college degrees without any significant costs to me and my becoming a professor and administrator at several white universities, I harbor some resentment. I am not resentful because of anything that happened to me in Jim Crow Lexington, because, as I have already stated, as a child and teenager during those years, my family and community shielded me from the worst aspects of racial discrimination.

I resent that opportunities were denied my parents and blacks of their generation and that they were forced to conform to the racial status quo of that time. The jobs available to them were low paying and they were often supervised by whites, some of whom in a fair competitive world would have been working under the direction of my parents instead of supervising them. Furthermore, my parents, like all Afro-Americans of that day, were compelled to act in a certain manner if they wanted to keep their jobs. From her work experiences with whites, my mother told me repeatedly that she had to take it, to conceal her true feelings, to hold her tongue. (For example, Lexington whites loved Adolph Rupp and University of Kentucky basketball and wanted loyalty from blacks on that issue.)

Over the past few years, my wife and I while on vacation have met white couples who are the exact age of my parents. These working-class whites can afford vacations and seem to be financially secure because of the jobs they worked at for decades, the very jobs that were closed to my parents in the 1950s. My father-in-law, who is now in his seventies, is not retired. He still goes to work five days a week.

There were many, many positive aspects of Afro-American life in the 1950s, the time when racial segregation was still the norm. I do hope, however, that whites have a better understanding of the fact that it is not enough just to say that those times have ended. While my life is materially better for the changes that came about with the end of segregation, that is not the case for blacks of my parents' generation. People of my parents' generation have lived under the vestiges of segregation all of their lives.

Growing Up Integrated

JOEL WILLIAMSON

Segregation was not just a matter of separating bodies; it was also a matter of segregating hearts and minds, of creating cultures that were different in important ways even as they shared the same geography. Integration was not just a matter of mixing bodies—African American and white; it was also a matter of changing hearts and minds, of merging in some higher degree the two cultures. Integration was not just a physical matter; it was a psychological matter, a matter of thinking and emotions. What happens after the bodies are mixed poses the real issue.

I first began to realize that mixing the bodies was not enough in the early 1960s. I was coming to an end of writing my dissertation on the African American experience in South Carolina during Reconstruction from 1861 to 1877. About the same time that I was writing my conclusion, a number of African American students entered what I took to be Atlanta's equivalent of Little Rock's Central High. A day or so later, some of these—two or three—came out. After all that work by black people and white people to get these children in, they were voluntarily coming out, reeling out almost, of the schoolhouse door.

With a moment's reflection, I thought I knew why they came out. Never mind bodies, life for them in that school was an emotional hell. They were, in fact, Kurtz in Joseph Conrad's *Heart of Darkness*. They were pushing their sturdy but small boat up the river into a dark continent. Always the threat of attack, sometimes the overt attack with the spear penetrating your body. Sometimes meeting natives, armed natives, standing along the river bank or along the schoolhouse hallway and not knowing what they are thinking or what they intend to do. Then passing safely by. "Am I paranoid?" they might ask themselves. "These folks seem really friendly."

By about 1963, when I was writing about Reconstruction in South Carolina, the accepted interpretation was that Reconstruction ended in 1877 with African Americans only half free. True enough if rather simplex. But what about the other half? How would African Americans become wholly free? Pondering this in my conclusion, I raised the idea that possibly American democracy, after all, did not have the power to solve the race problem. We could handle physical integration all right, but psychological integration was a much more difficult matter and one we seemed ill-equipped to manage. In South Carolina black Americans came as close as ever in America to turning a black majority in a state's population into political power in an entire state, yet the political power of black South Carolinians was largely destroyed by violence, intimidation, and fraud, which essentially all white America either tolerated or endorsed.

My dissertation director at Berkeley was Kenneth Stampp. In 1956 he had published the pioneering and most deeply researched book yet to appear on American slavery. My idea about the weakness of American democracy in the face of white racism infuriated him. I needed to drop that paragraph or two from my dissertation, and, furthermore, he insisted, I had better rethink my thinking. I dropped that part from the dissertation, but I put the essential idea back into the book, which came out in 1965 and was called *After Slavery*. The runner-up for a title was *First Freedom*. The words *after slavery* suggested that the legacy of slavery was wide and deep and persistent, and the race problem more severe than we had thought thus far in the civil rights movement. It persists still, and I would add disfranchisement, segregation, and lynching to the sum of our inheritance.

About this time civil rights historian Howard Zinn created the allegory of the bus rider to explain how desegregation was going to work. He imagined a white man standing at a bus stop in a southern city. The bus came up loaded with black people. Would the white man walk the several blocks or more to his destination or would he get on the bus? That is, would he integrate? To ask, Professor Zinn seemed to think, was to answer yes. Looking at this man historically, however, he might or might not get on the bus. Materially, white southerners for years had been paying dearly for segregation, and they might continue to do so. Ironically, white southerners made their racism pay in slavery, and after slavery they paid for their racism, seemingly willing enough. Indeed, our man might walk.

Further, even if he did get on the bus, what will he be thinking, how will he *feel?* And how will African Americans feel about this white man in their midst? Given the facts that we in America have created two cultures and that I am white, I cannot speak for the reaction of the African American riders. I have an idea that the white rider is furious. He is say-ing, "I have to go along with this for now, but there will be a payday some day." If the white rider stays on the bus for ten years, twenty years, thirty or forty years, he might begin to say that these folks are essentially just like him. They are somewhat different, but he can give them space and have his space too. He might come to like a fellow rider, even "love" or make an emotional commitment to some individual fellow rider. But "getting over" in this way requires conscious effort and hard labor. It does not just happen.

If integration means putting black bodies next to white bodies or vice versa, I have been integrated all my life. I was born in Anderson County, South Carolina, on October 27, 1929. Two days later, the stock market crashed. My parents did claim me but denied that their extravagantly amorous behavior—and my arrival—had any relation to the latter disas-trous event. Soon after I was born, my folks moved from the country to the town. It happened that we moved into what had been one of the "best" parts of town in the 1920s. There were white Americans and African Americans living nearby all around, "the salt-and-pepper" pattern of hous-ing as it is sometimes called.

Three houses up the street lived "Captain" Marshall. The Marshalls had been planter slaveholders, and it still showed. Captain Marshall was the conductor on the only passenger train that came in and out of town on a short-line railroad, the Blue Ridge Railroad. The Marshalls owned a piece of the railroad. Ike Marshall lived in a small—almost tiny—one-room structure behind the Captain's house. Ike was black; he was the Captain's valet and chauffeur. It was a marvel for a little towheaded boy to watch: Ike getting the long, high car with shiny plateglass windows out of the garage, engine running, sitting at the wheel with his chauffeur's cap on, waiting, and presently the Captain coming out of the house and climb-ing into the rear seat of the car. Then the two of them driving up the street called Marshall Avenue. Ike Marshall and Captain Marshall driving up Marshall Avenue, stiff backed, looking straight ahead in a perfectly silent communion.

One-half block westward up Marshall was North Fant Street. One block north on Fant, across Calhoun, was my grammar school. A bit beyond midway in that block there was a one-story frame house painted dark yellow with a porch across the front. It was close to the sidewalk as some older houses in town were. It was on a huge lot, three times the size of others, though the house itself was comparable to the stoutly middle-class houses around it. There were gardens all around in the yard, including one in the narrow space between the porch and the sidewalk. There was a wire fence all around the property, but the part along the sidewalk had columns of wire capped by rounded arches, all interlaced.

I walked by that house at least twice a day during the school year and numerous other times. I was interested in the wire arches, blue metal gracefully shaped in an intriguing, repetitive interlocking pattern, intricate like lace. I would touch the arches lightly with my fingertips, trace out the form, feel the blue, marbled metal. I would sometimes see a woman in a bonnet in the yard doing something in the garden. She was tall for a woman, slight in build, and about forty years old. I knew she was "black" even though she was nearly as white as I. I also came to know—in time I just knew—that she lived there all alone and it was her house. Decades later, my father told me she was the daughter of one of the town's most prominent bankers, a white man, of course. Her father had provided for her in this way. It was a Charles Chesnutt *House behind the Cedars* thing.

In our house, there was always a black woman. Most memorable were Julia, Aunt Lulu, and Dempie—Aunt Lulu extraordinarily so. Aunt Lulu was born in or near Washington, Georgia, in 1881; she had—and sometimes showed—a silver dollar bearing that date that itself virtually said Lulu was born in this year. I would hold it sometimes, read the date, turn it over and look at the back. It was a marvelous coin—bigger, heavier, and somehow more solid than any other I had known. I would lower and raise my hand to feel its heft. When she got to be one hundred years old, the president of the United States sent Lulu his congratulations on a piece of thick paper, probably by way of the Social Security Administration. Lulu outlived all of her children, most of her grandchildren, and a lot of her great grandchildren. She died in the same nursing home my parents died in—that by way of racial integration and Medicaid. The last time I saw her, she sent me out to buy her a can of Red Man snuff. She was emphatic about the Red Man part. The right brand was important.

I am always skeptical when I hear white people talk fondly about the African American women who practically raised them, just like a mother and so on. Lulu didn't raise me, my parents definitely did that. But I had a deep and lasting relationship with Lulu. For one thing, it involved banana pudding. I loved banana pudding. Every so often, I would be walking home from grammar school. We got out about 1:00 P.M., no lunch, no cafeteria. Lulu might come on about 6 A.M., do breakfast and "dinner"—nobody said lunch, we were country people—clean up and go home about the time I left school. She would leave my lunch on the kitchen table. Passing the yellow house with the round-arch wire fence, I would be saying: "If I don't step on a crack all the way home, Lulu will have banana pudding for me." Somehow she always did that; it would be there on the table with a handy spoon when I got home.

Aunt Lulu's body was proximate to our bodies. Usually when we had dinner, sometimes joined by country cousins in town on some errand, Lulu would fix herself a dinner on a tray and sit with us in a corner of the dining room. She would join freely in the always smoothly flowing conversation, voicing opinions that carried weight. Lulu lived alone in a small wooden house among a dozen or so small houses in the middle of the block behind my schoolhouse. Large white houses ringed most of the block. Lulu walked about as far to our house every morning as I walked to school. Not far.

I left home in 1946 to go to the University of South Carolina and rarely came home afterward. Then into the navy in 1951, Berkeley in 1955, the University of North Carolina in 1960. Meanwhile, my older brother became Aunt Lulu's "white man." He was a very successful businessman, a closet Republican, and a conservative somewhere to the right of J. Strom Thurmond, for whom he always voted. Indeed, it was Strom who let him out of the closet when he became an overt Republican. He was also a thorough racist with an alarmingly disarming friendly and genteel manner. He and Lulu were close; he would go see her after she retired on her social security and just talk. Long after I left home I learned from him he always knew what was really going on locally—that Lulu had a secret life that I never guessed existed, an ignorance, I daresay, that my parents shared. Aunt Lulu was a *bootlegger*. She did quite well cashwise selling whiskey illegally. Sometimes her stock was legal whiskey, which she sold when the liquor store was closed and drinkers got desperate. Sometimes she sold moonshine. I think the police winked at Lulu's "technical" violations. Some of them were probably her customers. My brother certainly was.

I thought I knew Aunt Lulu very well—the Queen of Banana Pudding—and it turned out that I had no idea about a substantial part of her life. I was thrown off in part by the fact that Aunt Lulu was a good but not demonstrative Christian. In my folks' church they would find out about such a thing and kick you out of the church and all hopes of heaven too. They didn't drink alcohol, much less sell it.

So, the point is I didn't know much about the lives of African Americans even though I lived squarely among them. At the University of South Carolina in Columbia in the late 1940s there were about forty-seven hundred students, not one of whom was black. I was not around black people there. One day my roommate came home in a state of hilarity. He had been on a bus with a couple of black college students, both male. He listened to them talking in the back of the bus. One, he said, asked the other: "Is you done your Greek yet?" The incongruity, as he saw it, of getting Greek and missing English convulsed him. He had been a Machinist Second Class on a seagoing tug in the Pacific during World War II. He was on the GI Bill. His father worked in a textile mill. He went on to become an engineer working for Duke Power Company or Esso— now Exxon—or some company like that. All my roommates were World War II veterans, and they all took jobs like that and prospered in the 1950s.

I was ripped in full time from my South Carolina womb by the Korean War. I was ready, even eager, to come out. In July 1951, I headed for Newport, Rhode Island, and the U.S. Navy's officers' training school. In Washington I changed trains and proceeded north. I had never been north of North Carolina before. I was sitting in my seat when a shocking thing happened. This brown hand and arm rose above the seat in front of me. It was moving in a sort of lazy stretch. It was brown, not black, but it was definitely the arm of a "colored person." That had never happened to me before. Never had an African American sat in any conveyance, public or private, in front of me. (My father did not have a valet and chauffeur as did Captain Marshall.) Keeping cool, I asked myself: What is my duty in these circumstances? Then it hit me. With Washington, D.C., rapidly receding behind me, I was up North. This was their country, not mine, and they did things differently up here. "When in Rome, do as the Romans do," I quoted silently. This is Rome, I thought. Then I settled back and began to watch these curious people.

In Officer Candidate School I think I remember one young black man—already a sailor with one or two stripes on his arm, making him a petty officer—among some 240 whites from places like Princeton, Yale, Dartmouth, and the University of South Carolina. He didn't stand out because of his color; rather he was lost in spite of his color. At sea for two years, I think I saw only one African American naval officer. He was an ensign on a battleship, probably the *Missouri* or *Wisconsin*. I saw him through a spyglass as we steamed along together somewhere in the Atlantic. He was tall, handsome, and very light of skin. We all, my men and I, took turns looking at him through the glass because this was remarkable. A "colored" officer! African American sailors were all cooks, stewards, and boatswains. The cooks and stewards had their own guns at battle stations, two batteries on the forecastle. Segregated. They worked diligently at their marksmanship. There were often shooting matches between gun crews. The cooks and stewards were freely recognized as the best shots.

Harry Truman had desegregated the military in 1946. The generals and the admirals dragged their feet. Up around the Yalu River in Korea, the generals began to realize they had been underusing an asset when Chinese soldiers suddenly poured over them in human wave attacks. At sea, the admirals were not so quick. I saw a lot of covert and overt discrimination "on the line" in the navy, more stories than I can tell here.

My last year and some months in the navy was spent on an army base in Germany. In the fall of 1953, I went over on the USS *Randall*, the same ship that Elvis Presley went over on five years later, a fact that has brought us very close together. The army on that ship on that crossing was very much integrated. Black and white soldiers ate together, they slept together, and, when the sea rose a bit, they vomited together.

The army was integrated in Europe, the navy was not. In my unit of about forty people, one was an African American. Ours was a communications unit, highly skilled, intelligent people with IQs running up—well up—from 110. The navy had few blacks in our ratings—electronic technicians and radiomen, who in our unit were also cryptographers, usually a task reserved for officers only. Our single black sailor had been a boatswain's mate for which no IQ was required. But he had risen to become a first class boatswain's mate, equivalent of a middling sergeant in the army. This man was so smart that he passed the test for first class radioman after some integration in the navy began. He changed ratings without loss of rank. The difference was prestige not pay, and, perhaps, physically more comfortable duty.

But this only began this man's story. There was another integration shock here. This man lived off base with his white German lover. Interracial sex. Down South this was a lynching offense. Miscegenation. The greatest taboo in the Deep South whence I sprang. I watched this one too. Particularly, I watched the white southern men in our unit. They did not blink an eye. Had they heard the thing about being in Rome that I had heard? Must have. At that time, I never saw or sensed any discrimination against this man. Remarkable. And that might have come from our commander, an old navy man who went by the book. I think the admirals did not care what you *thought* about black people, but there would be no overt discriminatory *behavior* in the ranks.

After I began to study race relations, I thought a lot about that miscegenation situation in Bremerhaven, Germany. Lots of variables in play to produce a result. One was that many single sailors and some not single had their own *schatzes* (treasures), lovers, in the city to whom they gave precious coffee and cigarettes—items more valuable than gold in that still painful postwar economy. German men and boys were missing in massive numbers. Sex was open and easy, a shock in itself to these young, essentially puritanical Americans. It was a different world. Many single men married their *schatzes* and brought them to America.

Finally, decades later, I remembered a unit photograph we had made. We all got dressed up in our blues—our showcase uniform—and posed on the drill ground of the Marina Schule, where we lived. It was where the Germans had trained submarine officers during World War II. I remember our commander, who was very paternalistic, helped man the station while we all went out to pose. At least one other man would have to be scanning the frequencies with him. I looked for and found my copy of the photograph. The African American sailor was *not* in the group. But everybody in the photograph was so proud of this symbol of service to his country, this indelible document of manliness, sending home copies to their families, and so on. Somehow, this black man got left out—along with our kindly commander. Somehow, our single black sailor became an invisible man.

Berkeley in and after 1955 was another whole story—so many so-called races, so many cultures. If you treated each one differently you would be so busy changing gears you would never get anywhere. Some sort of toleration seemed necessary simply to go about your business and survive. But another interesting black-white thing happened to me. As a graduate assistant, I was loaned out to a political science professor named Thomas C. Blaisdale. Dr. Blaisdale had been a New Deal economist with an Asian specialty. He had risen to become an assistant secretary of commerce under Truman and, of course, lost his place to the Eisenhowers in 1953. Hired at Berkeley he started building his own empire in international studies. He created an office of several persons to receive and organize visitors to the campus from abroad. Many, many visitors and many bizarre stories come out of that. Probably, our most famous visitor was President Sukarno of Indonesia. We were all saddened by the intensity with which he attempted to seduce our beautiful boss, Miss Dora Seu, Hawaiian Chinese American. I suppose it was a joke, but I heard he offered her elephants.

Working with me in this office was a political science graduate student from Wisconsin. He was bright. He was informed. He was articulate. And he was black. He was black and he hated me. He just hated me. There was a sort of seething fury behind his hatred. It was startling and confusing to me. No amount of friendliness on my part seemed to lessen the intensity of his hatred. I was nonplussed. He didn't know me; how could he hate me so? Soon enough it came to me in a flash. He hated me simply because I was white and southern. Because my skin happened to be white, he hated me. It was all so unfair, I thought, and unnecessary. I was outraged. Then another thought came to me: black people must often feel this way with whites. I knew well what white people thought, both good and especially bad, about black people.

Deciding to write my dissertation and first book on black people in South Carolina was probably a lot more personal than I will ever know. Clearly, I was going home again to study not myself but the other. Still, the carefully chosen key figure on the dust jacket of the book that resulted is the yin-yang symbol—how two different things, black and white in this case, are yet one. I came to the concept first through my Chinese studies at Berkeley. Researching and writing my dissertation was a continuing education. My whiteness enfolded the seed of the other. Had I been black back then and down there, I decided, I would have thought and acted as they did. To write a book that held together, I had to make up my mind what I thought about race. I concluded that the idea of race is a snare and a delusion.

Race is a construct, a false construct. But ethnicity is real. There are different cultures. I thought I was writing black history. Later I understood that I was writing a history of relations between two cultures. I was a white man using mostly white sources to write about black people. I had deceived myself again, and so late in life. How could I presume to write black history? No more could I than Elvis could presume to sing black songs. I was ignorant of the deep history of blackness in the Marshall family. I had missed the meaning of the mulatto woman up the street. I had missed Aunt Lulu's other life. I had not noted the missing sailor. I was nonplussed by the black graduate student at Berkeley. I did not know a lot, after all, about African Americans.

We have created two cultures in America based on fictions of color, and we seem unable to let these constructs go. We have twenty-five-year-old citizens now, African Americans and white Americans, who have never known official, regular, relentless physical segregation. There are young whites who can look at a black competitor for promotion in a profession and say: "Why should you get any preference? You were right beside me at every step I took to get to this point." The rising young black sees the same equal preparation, and her or his question is why did they chose her or him and not me for promotion. Why am I left out of the group photograph that gives you so much pleasure, such a sense of being and belonging?

We see that we can handle fairly well the bodies in race relations in America. We can fix it so that practically every one will get on the bus and ride for a while. We need now to turn our attention to the emotions, the feelings in race relations. That is a gigantic and more difficult challenge. That is the test of America's commitment to democracy.

Arkansas governor Orval Eugene Faubus created a major constitutional crisis in September of 1957 when he attempted to use the power of the state government to block federally mandated desegregation at Little Rock Central High School. *Photo by Larry Obsitnik, courtesy of the* Arkansas Democrat-Gazette *and Special Collections Division, University of Arkansas Libraries, Fayetteville.*

VOTE **FOR** ☒ SEGREGATION

SUMMARIES OF SEGREGATION MEASURES ON GENERAL ELECTION BALLOT, NOV. 6, 1956

PROPOSED CONSTITUTIONAL AMENDMENT NO. 47

Requires General Assembly to oppose in every constitutional manner, including, interposition and nullification, all deliberate, palpable and dangerous invasions or encroachments upon the rights and powers belonging to the states and the people thereof by the government of the United States or any of the departments thereof; to provide by law for enforcement of this Act; to require General Assembly to exercise police powers of the state to regulate health, morals, education, marriage, good order and to insure the domestic tranquility, etc. (Sponsored by former Senator Jim Johnson)

VOTE **FOR** ☒

RESOLUTION OF INTERPOSITION

An Act calling for amendment to Constitution of the United States prohibiting federal government from exercising power over the operation of public schools in Arkansas; pledging the people to take all appropriate measures to resist illegal encroachment on the power of the state to control its domestic institutions calling on people of other states to assist in prohibiting further encroachment by the federal government. (Sponsored by Governor Faubus)

VOTE **FOR** ☒

INITIATED ACT NO. 2

Board of Directors of each school district authorized and required to provide for enrollment of children in public schools and for assignment of children to schools, with authority of such Board to be complete and final. Each applicant for admission to public school shall be assigned to such school as will have a tendency to decrease or eliminate any feeling of inferiority on the part of the pupil. Section 4 specifies factors on which School Board to base its decision, and Section 5 provides for appeals from decisions of local School Boards. (Sponsored by Governor Faubus.)

VOTE **FOR** ☒

COMMENTS

Proposed Constitutional Amendment 47 represents the strongest measure devised so far to provide for a continued segregation society in the State of Arkansas, and is designed to put into effect in Arkansas the strongest program yet conceived in the South to stop integration in the State and contemplates the adoption of such strong legislation as was enacted in Virginia recently to avoid any integration to any extent.

All these measures endorsed by

Association of Citizens' Councils of Arkansas

P. O. Box 597   PINE BLUFF, ARKANSAS

READ AND PASS ON

Segregationist handbill circulated by the White Citizens' Council of Little Rock. *Courtesy Arkansas Council on Human Relations, Broadside B4-647, Special Collections Division, University of Arkansas Libraries, Fayetteville.*

Gov. Marvin Griffin of
Georgia prepares to address a
White Citizens' Council rally
in Little Rock, August 22,
1957. *Photo by Larry Obsitnik,
courtesy of the* Arkansas
Democrat-Gazette *and Special
Collections Division, University
of Arkansas Libraries,
Fayetteville.*

Federal judge Ronald N. Davies
of Fargo, North Dakota served
temporarily in Arkansas during
the build-up to the crisis. *Photo
by Larry Obsitnik, courtesy of
the* Arkansas Democrat-
Gazette *and Special Collections
Division, University of Arkansas
Libraries, Fayetteville.*

The crowd outside Little Rock Central High School on September 5, 1957.
Photo by Larry Obsitnik, courtesy of the Arkansas Democrat-Gazette *and Special Collections Division, University of Arkansas Libraries, Fayetteville*

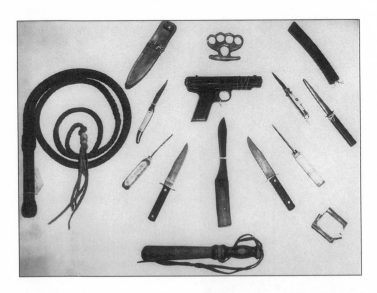

Weapons supposedly found on people around Central High by Arkansas State Police. *Courtesy of Orval E. Faubus Papers, Special Collections Division, University of Arkansas Libraries, Fayetteville.*

Little Rock police detectives examine partially burned cross outside the home of L. C. Bates and his wife, NAACP state president, Daisy Bates. *Courtesy of Daisy Bates Papers, Special Collections Division, University of Arkansas Libraries, Fayetteville.*

President Dwight Eisenhower, Congressman Brooks Hays and Gov. Orval Faubus after an inconclusive meeting at Ike's favorite golfing retreat at Newport, Rhode Island, September 14, 1957. *Courtesy of L. Brooks Hays Papers, Special Collections Division, University of Arkansas Libraries, Fayetteville.*

The Arkansas congressional delegation, all of whom had signed the Southern Manifesto opposing integration in March of 1956. *Left to right,* Jim Trimble of Fayetteville, Brooks Hays of Little Rock, E. C. "Took" Gathings of West Memphis, W. R. Norrell of Monticello, Oren Harris of El Dorado, Wilbur Mills of Kensett. (Senators J. William Fulbright and John McClellan also signed the manifesto.) *Courtesy of James W. Trimble Papers, Special Collections Division, University of Arkansas Libraries, Fayetteville.*

Little Rock police at Central High on September 23, 1957, after Governor Faubus had removed the Arkansas National Guard. *Photo by Larry Obsitnik, courtesy of the* Arkansas Democrat-Gazette *and Special Collections Division, University of Arkansas Libraries, Fayetteville.*

Little Rock police attempt to maintain order at Central High, September 23, 1957. *Photo by Larry Obsitnik, courtesy of the* Arkansas Democrat-Gazette *and Special Collections Division, University of Arkansas Libraries, Fayetteville.*

Classic Larry Obsitnik photo showing United States Army paratroopers arriving in Little Rock, September 24, 1957. *Photo by Larry Obsitnik, courtesy of the* Arkansas Democrat-Gazette *and Special Collections Division, University of Arkansas Libraries, Fayetteville.*

The Little Rock Nine enter Central High under armed escort, September 25, 1957. *Photo by Larry Obsitnik, courtesy of the* Arkansas Democrat-Gazette *and Special Collections Division, University of Arkansas Libraries, Fayetteville.*

Members of the "Screaming Eagles" of the 101st Airborne Division of the United States Army escorted the Little Rock Nine to and from school. *Photo by Larry Obsitnik, courtesy of the* Arkansas Democrat-Gazette *and Special Collections Division, University of Arkansas Libraries, Fayetteville*

Gov. Orval Faubus at a press conference in the capitol building in Little Rock, October 2, 1957. *Photo by Larry Obsitnik, courtesy of the* Arkansas Democrat-Gazette *and Special Collections Division, University of Arkansas Libraries, Fayetteville.*

Autographed photo of Harry Ashmore, editor of the *Arkansas Gazette*, whose editorials in favor of "law and order" won him a Pulitzer Prize but lost his paper millions of dollars in subscriptions and advertising. *Photo by Larry Obsitnik, courtesy of the* Arkansas Democrat-Gazette *and Special Collections Division, University of Arkansas Libraries, Fayetteville.*

Envelope bearing evidence of the widespread opposition to the *Arkansas Gazette*'s editorial policy and also to the use of federal force to achieve desegregation in Little Rock. *Courtesy of Virgil T. Blossom Papers, Special Collections Division, University of Arkansas Libraries, Fayetteville.*

THE WOMEN'S EMERGENCY COMMITTEE
TO
OPEN OUR SCHOOLS

_____

Policy and Purpose

The Women's Emergency Committee to Open our Schools is dedicated
to the principle of free public school education, and to law and order. We
stand neither for integration nor for segregation, but for education.

Our aim is:

to get the four free public high schools re-opened;
to get students back in their classes;
to retain our staff of good teachers;
to regain full accreditation by the North Central Association.

We know that the "school situation" at Little Rock is not simply a
local problem . . . and that Arkansas has been disgraced in the eyes of the
entire world. We realize that what has happened here is elsewhere
considered symbolic of "American Democracy" and so has made every
American citizen the object of distrust and even hate.
We believe that our free public school system is essential to the
future of our city and state.
It is our hope to say to the world that there are many of us here who
care enough to do something about this problem.

Women's Emergency Committee handbill from the spring of 1958. The WEC
ultimately devised the strategy that put an end to the crisis in Little Rock.
*Courtesy of Sarah A. Murphy Papers, Special Collections Division, University of
Arkansas Libraries, Fayetteville.*

Arkansas, the *Brown* Decision, and the 1957 Little Rock School Crisis: A Local Perspective

JOHN A. KIRK

T he U.S. Supreme Court's 1954 *Brown v. Board of Education* school desegregation decision met with a mixed reaction in Arkansas. On the one hand, in northwest Arkansas and in urban areas across the state, there was a general acceptance of the ruling. "Arkansas will obey the law," declared Gov. Francis Cherry in Little Rock, with the acknowledgment that the state would "not approach the problem [of desegregation] with the idea of being outlaws."[1] The *Arkansas Gazette* echoed the call for sensible handling of a potentially explosive issue by asserting that "Wise leadership at the upper levels" was needed and warning that "emotional excursions by the leaders of either race can do great harm." On the other hand, rumblings of discontent came from eastern Arkansas, where congressman E. C. "Took" Gathings condemned both the *Brown* decision and the Supreme Court for their interference with racial matters.[2] Although no groundswell of opinion advocating outright violent resistance to the law emerged, there were moves by some to formulate measures that would allow a legal circumvention preventing, or at the very least delaying, the implementation of the desegregation ruling.[3]

The regional division in attitudes toward the *Brown* decision was apparent in the actions of various school boards across the state. In northwest Arkansas three school districts immediately drew up plans to desegregate. Just four days after the Supreme Court ruling the Fayetteville school board announced that it would allow the nine black students in its district to attend the local high school with five hundred whites the following academic year. Previously, the nine black students had been bussed to segregated schools at Fort Smith and Hot Springs, a distance of 60 and 150 miles respectively, at a cost to taxpayers of five thousand dollars a year in order to preserve an all-white school system. Fayetteville's Superintendent of Schools Wayne White bluntly told reporters that "segregation was a luxury we could no longer afford." The school boards at Charleston and Bentonville, both in similar circumstances to Fayetteville, also voted to integrate.[4]

The one attempt to desegregate in eastern Arkansas aroused a storm of opposition. The incident occurred at Sheridan, a school district just a few miles outside the state capital of Little Rock, on the edge of the delta. Like the three school districts in northwest Arkansas, Sheridan bussed its nominal black student population to the nearest segregated schools. On May 21 the Sheridan school board voted unanimously to integrate its two black students with the six hundred whites at the local high school in order to alleviate the financial burden involved in maintaining segregation. The move led to an immediate protest from the white community that forced the school board to take a second vote the following night, resulting in a unanimous recanting of the plan to desegregate. Still not satisfied, three hundred parents held a meeting a week afterward and agreed to circulate a petition calling for the resignation of the entire school board. As a result of the meeting one school board member resigned followed by three others shortly thereafter. When the September school term began in Sheridan black students were still bussed twenty-seven miles to a black school in an adjoining county at an estimated yearly cost to taxpayers of four thousand dollars. No other school districts in the delta offered any signs of compliance with the Brown decision.[5] The pronounced regional difference in attitudes and approaches to school desegregation brought a deadlock over the issue at a state level. Although eastern Arkansas interests won concessions to prevent any major headway toward desegregation, they proved unsuccessful at imposing their agenda for a legal circumvention of the Brown decision. At the State Board of Education meeting in September 1954, Harold Weaver, chairman of the West Memphis school board, whose district bordered the banks of the Mississippi River, hysterically claimed that the Brown decision would "tear our school system all to pieces." Although members from outside of eastern Arkansas expressed sympathy with Weaver, and were prepared to assist in formulating a "go slow" gradualist approach to desegregation, there was little commitment to halting the process altogether. To mollify eastern Arkansas schoolmen, the State Board of Education advised school districts to work toward equalizing black and white school facilities and to wait for the desegregation implementation order from the U.S. Supreme Court before taking any action. Furthermore, the board voted to ask Arkansas Atty. Gen. Tom Gentry to file a friend-of-the-court brief with the Supreme Court, outlining the strong feelings that their decision had aroused in Arkansas, in an attempt to try to influence a lenient implementation plan. Gentry agreed to help, but sternly warned the board that the *Brown* decision was "the law of the land and we are going to have to abide by it," and that all he could do was to advise the Court on how, not whether, they wanted to desegregate.[6]

The stalemate between those resigned to compliance with the *Brown* decision and those who were calling for its circumvention was also evident in the election for governor in 1954. The victorious candidate, Orval E. Faubus, beat incumbent Francis Cherry without taking any firm position on the race issue. Faubus, who hailed from northwest Arkansas and cut his political teeth in the liberal Sid McMath administration, was generally inclined toward a moderate stance on the question of school desegregation. Yet the need to court votes in eastern Arkansas prevented Faubus from expressing unequivocal support for compliance with the Court ruling. What emerged instead was a convoluted and confused stance that pandered to racial conservatism by proclaiming that "Arkansas is not ready for complete and sudden mixing of the races in public schools," yet still left the way open for compliance and racial progress at a "local level with state authorities standing ready to assist in every way possible." The noncommittal approach of Faubus, which sought to satisfy all sections within the state, provided an interesting political barometer on the school desegregation question. The stance seemed to demonstrate that not even political campaigners could discern a popular mood in the state either strongly in favor of school desegregation or strongly opposed to it and were willing to wait for public sentiment to develop before committing themselves to any definite policy.[7]

The politically ambiguous role of the school desegregation issue was further in evidence at the biennial meeting of the Arkansas General Assembly, the legislative branch of state government, in January 1955. Halfway through the sixty-day session a bill aimed at circumventing the *Brown* decision was introduced into both Houses by east Arkansas state senators Fletcher Long, W. E. "Buck" Fletcher, and state representative Lucien C. Rodgers. The bill outlined a plan to appoint an assignment officer in each Arkansas school district who would then decide which schools students should be allocated to on a variety of criteria ranging from the "welfare and best interest of the child" to "geographical location." Essentially, the move was designed to preserve segregation by allowing for the assignment of blacks to black schools and whites to white schools without actually mentioning race as a factor.[8]

Opposition to the bill came from Max Howell, whose constituency covered the affluent white suburbs of Little Rock. In a delaying maneuver, Howell asked for the pupil assignment bill to be read in full. Next, Howell asked for the bill to be tabled, effectively killing its measures outright. By a narrow vote the Arkansas senate decided to retain the bill, but Howell won a delay in its implementation until after the U.S. Supreme Court had issued its directive of how school boards should desegregate. In an impassioned speech to the Arkansas senate Howell declared that "Just because some other dyed-in-the-wool southern state jumped in haste to preserve [segregation] doesn't mean that Arkansas should." The delay robbed eastern Arkansans of a preemptive strike against the Supreme Court's school desegregation implementation order and kept hope of constructive progress on the issue alive in the state.[9]

The finely balanced position of the state between a willingness to accept the 1954 *Brown* decision as the law of the land and attempts to circumvent the Supreme Court ruling served to heighten the importance of the Little Rock School Board's stance on desegregation. With the largest school system in the state, located on the geographical border between northwest and eastern Arkansas, Little Rock offered guidance and leadership for other communities in the state. The state capital, with a reputation for being a progressive upper South city, seemed adequately suited to that leadership role. The city was in the midst of an economic boom, guided by a dynamic business elite that had successfully managed the community's prosperity and well-being. An enlightened attitude to race relations accompanied the city's economic affluence with a notable absence of racial tensions, helped by a small but significant cadre of white liberals and the moderate *Arkansas Gazette* newspaper.[10] Even more militant members of the Little Rock black community conceded that its reputation as a progressive southern city was deserved.[11] Positive steps by the state capital for compliance with the *Brown* decision held the potential to weaken significantly the crusade for the circumvention of school desegregation in eastern Arkansas, while a posture of defiance would prove highly damaging for further progress.

Recognizing the pivotal importance that Little Rock would have on school desegregation throughout the state, the local branch of the NAACP had attempted to establish negotiations with the city's school board in the years prior to the *Brown* decision. Through the offices of an interracial group, the Little Rock Council on Schools, NAACP representatives, along with a handful of white sympathizers, petitioned the Little Rock School Board to consider a proposal for limited desegregation. The proposal, which outlined a plan for black students to use the print shop at Little Rock (later Central) High School, since Dunbar High did not have such a facility, was considered seriously by several board members. Only the presence of the Superintendent of Schools Harry A. Little, a committed segregationist, cast a shadow over the proceedings.[12]

The fact that the Little Rock School Board at least was prepared to give consideration to proposals for change gave heart to those who believed that Arkansas's capital city would lead the way for compliance with the *Brown* decision in the state. Certainly, this was the view of those in the black delegation who gathered to hear what the new Superintendent of Schools Virgil T. Blossom had to report about the plans of the Little Rock school board four days after the U.S. Supreme Court ruling was handed down. As he started to outline the school board's plans, however, Blossom noticed that the "high spirits" with which the meeting began soon transformed in a "rapid [loss of] enthusiasm." Blossom told the black delegation that the school board did not intend to move ahead with desegregation immediately. Instead, he stated, a decision had been taken to wait for the Supreme Court implementation ruling before instigating any further action. In the meantime, Blossom indicated that he would take on the job of drawing up plans for what might happen if the Little Rock schools were indeed eventually forced to desegregate.

After Blossom finished his speech, L. C. Bates, editor of the black Little Rock *State Press* newspaper, stormed out of the meeting in outright disgust at the school board's perceived lack of conviction to forge ahead with a desegregation program. Others stayed, but it was clear from their comments that disappointment with the school board's decision was widespread among those present. Rev. Fred T. Guy, pastor at one of Little Rock's largest black churches, told Blossom, "Next to the law of God the constitution of the United States means the most to me. When you start to tinker with the constitution it becomes awfully important to us." Blossom assured Guy that the school board was not proposing to "delay for delay's sake, but to do the job right."[13]

The initial disappointment at the school board's response to the *Brown* decision was quickly followed by attempts from the black community, spearheaded by the NAACP, to press for a definite declaration of plans for desegregation. At a meeting with Virgil Blossom, NAACP representatives were informed that before any desegregation could take place the school board planned to build two new schools, Horace Mann High in the predominantly black eastern part of the city and Hall High in the affluent white suburbs of the west. Blossom stressed that, although the two new schools were designated in black and white residential areas respectively, they would have no set racial designation. Rather, Blossom assured NAACP members, the school board planned to desegregate all three of the city's high schools, Horace Mann, Hall High, and Central High, along color-blind attendance zones in 1957, with elementary schools to follow some time around 1960.[14]

The so-called Blossom Plan met with a mixed reaction among members of the Little Rock NAACP. On the one hand, more militant members like L.C. and his wife, Daisy Bates, who was head of the Arkansas State Conference of NAACP branches, opposed the plan on the grounds that it was "vague, indefinite, slow-moving and indicative of an intent to stall further on public school integration." On the other hand, a clear majority supported the plan and cautioned against pushing the school board too hard. Most felt that Blossom and the school board should be given a chance to prove their good intentions, that the plan they had drawn up was reasonable, and that, importantly, the plan would be acceptable to the white community. The local branch therefore decided that it would await further developments before taking any action.[15]

In April 1955, in anticipation of the U.S. Supreme Court implementation order, Vernon McDaniels, a fieldworker for the NAACP who had spent six months in Arkansas assessing the school desegregation situation in various communities across the state, addressed a meeting of NAACP members in Little Rock. McDaniels admitted that different communities would offer different degrees of resistance to school desegregation, but insisted that with increased efforts by blacks at a grassroots level across the state to urge local school boards into compliance with the law, Arkansas represented "the brightest prospect among the southern states for integration."[16]

This upbeat assessment was based upon the encouraging developments of the past year. A few school districts in northwest Arkansas had already moved to desegregate, whereas in many other southern states no progress had been made at all. Also, unlike other states, no widespread, organized campaign of resistance to school desegregation had developed. Moreover, the one direct attempt to circumvent the *Brown* decision in the legislature had been delayed by a majority vote, indicating that there were law-abiding influences in Arkansas that could stymie dissenting voices of protest. Although the situation over school desegregation was still largely in the balance, there were grounds for cautious optimism that a definite time-table for desegregation would tip the scales decisively toward moderation and gradual racial change.

However, to those who held faith in the ability of the U.S. Supreme Court's implementation decision to clear a path for compliance with its previous school desegregation decree, the words of the justices on May 31, 1955, came as a major blow. Instead of following up on its initial convic-tion, the Court equivocated. The Supreme Court implementation order, which became known as *Brown II*, ambiguously told school boards that they must make a "prompt and reasonable start" to desegregate "with all deliberate speed." No definite deadline was set for when integration had to begin and no indication was given of what exactly constituted compli-ance with the *Brown* decision, for example, in terms of how many students were to be integrated and at what grades. Indeed, the Court even listed the "local problems" that might be given as reasonable excuses for delay. The task of administrating school desegregation was handed to federal district judges, who had no means of enforcing their rulings, and local school boards that could exert pressure to drag out the process of integration for as long as possible.[17]

The Supreme Court's implementation order proved a significant turn-ing point for school desegregation in Arkansas. One of the first indications of a change of mood in the state was the reaction of Virgil Blossom, who, shortly after *Brown II*, indicated that certain modifications were planned in his original school desegregation plan. The most notable development was the introduction of a transfer system that would allow students to move out of the school attendance zone to which they were assigned. Under the original Blossom Plan it was clear that schools were being geo-graphically gerrymandered to provide catchment areas that would ensure a majority black student population at Horace Mann High and a majority white student population at Hall High. The subsequent assignment of black students to Horace Mann High, even though they lived closer to Central High, had confirmed the intentions of the school board to limit the impact of desegregation as much as possible. Even so, the original plan meant that quite a substantial amount of integration would have occurred. The new plan, however, allowed whites to transfer out of Horace Mann

High, but did not give blacks the right to choose to transfer into Hall High. To encourage the shift of white pupils from Horace Mann High the school board clearly designated the school as a black institution by assigning an all-black teaching staff to it. Furthermore, the school board declared that it intended to open Horace Mann High as a segregated black school in February 1956, a move that would establish a precedent for black attendance just a year before the school was supposedly due to desegregate.[18]

The changes made to the original Blossom Plan indicated a subtle yet significant shift from a stance of begrudging compliance to active reluctance to implement the law. This in turn sent a signal to other school districts across the state that the capital city intended to stall on its desegregation plans. As a result, the three other largest school systems in the state, at Fort Smith, North Little Rock, and Hot Springs, all drew up desegregation plans that purposely delayed any action until Little Rock made the first move.[19]

The wavering of these school districts had far more serious consequences than simply drawing out the process of school desegregation. Their actions served to encourage the development of a massive resistance movement in the state among militant die-hard segregationists. This movement began in the unlikely place of Hoxie, a small settlement in northeast Arkansas. With a population of just over a thousand, Hoxie was close enough to the Arkansas delta to have a split school term to allow for the cotton picking harvest, yet it was atypical in that, with only fourteen black families living in the town, it did not reflect the density of the black population in other delta areas.[20] On June 25, 1955, the school board at Hoxie voted to desegregate, ostensibly on the same money-saving basis that had motivated other school districts to do so. On July 11, the first day of integrated classes, a small group of disgruntled local men gathered outside the school to witness proceedings. Some parents voiced their misgivings, with one, a Mrs. John Cole, worriedly telling newspapermen that her eight-year-old daughter, Peggy, "feared Negroes." But despite the apprehensions surrounding integration the general consensus of opinion was that "we have to obey the law." Although there was some tension in classes at first, teachers soon made black students feel welcome and normal school life quickly resumed. By noon recess black boys were being invited by whites to try out for the school baseball team and even the fearful Peggy was captured on film by photographers playing and walking arm in arm with black female students.[21]

Ironically, it was the very success of school desegregation at Hoxie that made it the rallying point for massive resistance forces in the state. *Life* magazine reporters were present to document the event and ran a story the following week under the title of "A 'Morally Right' Decision." The article included an extensive array of pictures showing black and white students attending classes and playing together with a pronouncement that desegregation could work successfully in the South.[22] Whereas other school boards were at pains to avoid the glare of publicity, desegregation at Hoxie became a national story, and as a result the town became a center of attention for segregationists throughout the region. With the help and encouragement of segregationists in other states, particularly the closely neighboring Mississippi, a meeting was held in Hoxie at which Herbert Brewer, a local soybean farmer and part-time auctioneer, was elected as chairman of the Citizens' Committee Representing Segregation in the Hoxie Schools.[23] Brewer and the Hoxie Citizens' Committee picketed and petitioned the Hoxie school board to try and persuade its members to reverse their decision to desegregate. Although the school board held firm in its conviction and rebuffed the demands of segregationists, in an effort to provide a cooling off period the board subsequently closed the schools two weeks before the scheduled end of term.[24]

The concession to close the schools early proved unfortunate, since it only served to encourage further disruption from the segregationists who stepped up their campaign of intimidation. The gathering storm also helped to draw support from other segregationists across the state. White America, Inc., which was formed in Pine Bluff in 1955, and, according to historian Neil McMillen, had hitherto "languished in obscurity," sent one of its leading spokesmen, lawyer Amis Guthridge from Little Rock, to tell Hoxie citizens that "integration will lead to intermarriage; they [blacks] want in the white bedroom." Next to arrive was James Johnson, head of the newly formed segregationist faction, the White Citizens' Councils of Arkansas, who continued to exploit incendiary interracial sex taboos by playing a recording of a speech allegedly made by "Professor Roosevelt Williams" of Howard University to an NAACP meeting in Mississippi which expounded the virtues of sleeping with white women. The fraudulent recording, manufactured by the Mississippi White Citizens' Council, became a regular feature at Arkansas rallies of which there were to be many more. The meeting of segregationist factions at Hoxie led to a pooling of resources in the formation of the Association of Citizens' Councils of Arkansas, which became the main vehicle for white resistance to school desegregation in the state after the Hoxie campaign.[25]

Significantly, in spite of the bluff and bluster which surrounded school desegregation at Hoxie, segregationists found only a long and protracted defeat there. The Hoxie School Board obtained a court injunction against segregationist interference with school desegregation that was successfully upheld through numerous appeals. A suit launched to harass school board members by claiming variously that they had broken the law by employing their spouses in the district, conducted business illegally, and refused to call a mass meeting to discuss the school budget, was dismissed out of hand by the courts. Likewise, a petition to the courts from the Hoxie Citizens' Committee to investigate the affairs of the school board was summarily dispatched.[26] A similar experience befell White Citizens' Council affiliates in Arkansas, Crittenden, Drew, Lonoke, and Jefferson Counties.[27] None of the White Citizens' Councils affiliates could boast a large membership comparable to that of other similar groups in the Deep South. Even the largest branch, the Capital Citizens' Council in Little Rock, counted only five hundred members at its peak, of which no more than three hundred actually lived in the city.[28]

Despite the fact that the Citizens' Councils lacked a strong standing and only spoke for a disgruntled minority in Arkansas, their loud voices echoed around the state and kept the sensitive issue of desegregation in the headlines. This only served to add to the unease among the populace at large, hitting at their deep-rooted and nagging fears that school desegregation would undermine white supremacy and the southern way of life, latent even in many of those who were unwilling to take an active stand to prevent desegregation from occurring.

Nowhere was the impact of the White Citizens' Council more apparent than in state politics. As Governor Faubus's reelection campaign began in 1956 his relatively benign stance on school desegregation slowly began to drift toward strong support for maintaining segregation. Fueling Faubus's fears was the emergence of Jim Johnson as a potential rival for the position of governor in the 1956 elections. Johnson hailed from Crossett in southeast Arkansas and had proved an effective political campaigner in the area for Francis Cherry in his successful 1952 bid for governor. Subsequently, however, Johnson had failed to translate his ability to foster regional support into a potent statewide force, as his unsuccessful bid for the position of state attorney general in 1954 demonstrated. The school desegregation issue helped to revitalize Johnson's political career. As head of the Arkansas White Citizens' Council, Johnson shored up local support in Arkansas's southeastern counties through his strong segregationist stance. As the issue began to gain political currency throughout the rest of the state his potential popularity grew. The highly publicized campaign to halt desegregation at Hoxie provided Johnson with further exposure in the state's media.[29]

In January 1956, the impact of Johnson's political maneuvering on Faubus's school desegregation stance first became apparent. In a written response to questions from *New York Times* reporter Damon Stetson, the governor revealed he had commissioned a poll which showed that 85 percent of people in Arkansas were against school desegregation. In his first unequivocal statement on the issue since his election in 1954, Faubus declared that in light of the results he could not "be party to any attempt to force acceptance of a change to which the people are so overwhelmingly opposed." The poll Faubus referred to was conducted by Eddie Newsom of Paragould, Arkansas, who was head of Mid-South Opinion Surveys. Under closer scrutiny the statistics provided far less conclusive evidence for widespread opposition to school desegregation than the governor claimed. Newsom polled only five hundred people, all from eastern Arkansas, which could hardly be taken as representative of the state as a whole. Moreover, 18 percent of the people questioned had expressed no opinion on the matter and were therefore excluded from the figures altogether. Nevertheless, the governor used the poll as a springboard for further pronouncements and policy decisions on the school desegregation issue.[30]

Another significant development following *Brown II* was the increasing alienation felt by the Little Rock black community, particularly as a result of the changes made to the Blossom Plan, a desegregation program which they had previously been willing to accept in good faith. Blossom's about-face led to a feeling of betrayal within the black community. Repeated approaches by the Little Rock NAACP in an attempt to find common ground with the Little Rock School Board resulted in failure. Finally, in December 1955, exasperated at having exhausted every other possible channel of action, the Little Rock NAACP voted to file a lawsuit against the school board to gain some indication that they intended to desegregate the city's schools sometime in the near future.[31] On February 8, 1956, local NAACP attorney Wiley Branton filed suit against the Little Rock School Board for desegregation on behalf of thirty-three students who had been refused entry into white schools by Virgil Blossom, under the title of *Aaron v. Cooper.* [32]

The team of top city attorneys hired by the school board to fight the case made little headway when depositions were taken in May 1956.

Attempts to intimidate NAACP representatives into admitting that they felt the Blossom Plan was a reasonable desegregation program failed. The real turning point came at the trial, held in August 1956, when a mix-up between the local NAACP branch and the regional NAACP attorney U. Simpson Tate of Dallas lost the suit. The local challenge to the Blossom Plan was based upon carefully selected plaintiffs who would face particular hardships under its revised terms. Without bothering to consult local NAACP members, Tate argued at the trial for the immediate desegregation of all schools. Such a position was untenable since the Blossom Plan clearly upheld the doctrine of "with all deliberate speed." The issue of the bad faith of the school board in reneging on earlier promises was therefore not even presented to the Court. Predictably under the circumstances, Judge John B. Miller upheld the revised Blossom Plan. An attempt to revive the case on appeal finally failed on April 29, 1957, when the Eighth Circuit Court of Appeals at St. Louis again upheld the legitimacy of the revised Blossom Plan.

Nevertheless, local NAACP lawyer Wiley Branton reported that in spite of the defeat he was pleased by "some aspects" of the decision, particularly the affirmation by the appeals court that desegregation must take place in September 1957. Branton felt that the ruling offered an important "cloak of protection against some die-hard, anti-integration groups who might still try to delay integration."[33] After much speculation in the Little Rock press about a possible further appeal of the case to the U.S. Supreme Court, on July 13, 1957, Branton announced that no appeal would be filed.[34]

The NAACP remained optimistic despite the court defeat. Continuing developments in Arkansas indicated that the state was still prepared to accept gradual racial change. In the schools, with Little Rock under federal court order to desegregate, four other major municipal school districts at Pine Bluff, Hot Springs, North Little Rock, and Fort Smith all drew up integration plans for September 1957.[35] By then, all of the state's publicly supported colleges and universities had begun to admit blacks. Alongside this were other significant developments. In politics, six blacks were appointed to the Democratic State Committee by Governor Faubus, two blacks were elected to the city councils of Hot Springs and Alexander, and two blacks were elected to school boards at Wabbaseka and Dollarway. Local groups and associations across the state made goodwill gestures promoting interracial harmony. For example, several religious groups integrated, with an interracial ministerial alliance formed in

Little Rock in 1956. Some county medical societies also integrated their memberships, along with the American Association of University Women in Conway and Fayetteville and the Little Rock League of Women Voters.[36]

The most striking development came in April 1956, when four municipalities at Little Rock, Hot Springs, Pine Bluff, and Fort Smith successfully desegregated their public transportation systems after a mis-understanding over a ruling issued by the Supreme Court. The mix-up involved a complicated ruling by the Court in the *Fleming* case, which had been incorrectly reported by many national newspapers as heralding the end of segregation in public transport. Amid the confusion several bus companies, not only in Arkansas but also in other upper South cities, took the initiative to desegregate.[37] The success of the policy in Arkansas led to its continuance even after the mistake was discovered, and subsequently all interstate waiting rooms for bus and rail transportation were desegregated without incident.[38]

A memo from the Arkansas Council on Human Relations to the offices of the SRC, written less than a month before Central High was due to desegregate, revealed that sentiment in Arkansas over school desegregation was still much as it had been just after the *Brown* decision—"mixed"—with "defying forces . . . [as] in other sections of the South" along with "progressive affirming forces." The memo concluded that "the defy-ing forces and the affirming forces just now seem squared off for a tussle." Prophetically it predicted, "In the matter of school desegregation this may prove a fateful year."[39]

Not until August 1957 did indications of a potential disaster at Little Rock begin to emerge. Over the summer of 1957 the Capital Citizens' Council ran a last gasp campaign of intimidation, taking out advertise-ments in the local newspapers criticizing the school board, disrupting school board meetings, calling in outside speakers to stir up racial antago-nism, and criticizing Governor Faubus for not invoking segregationist leg-islation to halt school desegregation. Yet all this still had minimal impact. Faubus off-handedly dismissed suggestions that he might intervene by pro-claiming, "Everyone knows no state law supersedes a federal law. . . . If any-one expects me to use them to supersede federal laws they are wrong."

By August, however, with school desegregation imminent, a flurry of lawsuits were filed in local courts to try to forestall the Blossom Plan, and there were highly publicized speeches by Georgia Gov. Marvin Griffin and the former speaker of the Georgia state congress Roy Harris, who told people in Little Rock that "every white man in Georgia," including the governor, general assembly, and the population at large, would rally to prevent school desegregation. Rumors of impending violence, escalating weapons sales, and caravans of armed whites bent on disrupting orderly desegregation, none of which were subsequently proved true, began to flood the city.[40]

Under intense scrutiny, the inherent flaws in the Blossom Plan began to show. Importantly, the Blossom Plan ignored the class tensions within the white community surrounding school desegregation. By building a white high school in the west of the city, to which the affluent members of the white community could send their children, while focusing desegregation on Central High School, which would affect predominantly working- and lower-middle class families, the Blossom Plan was open to criticism that it forced integration on one section of the community while sheltering others from its impact.[41] Since the main constituency of hard-core support for continued segregation emanated from the very people the Blossom Plan targeted, and at the same time the school board's plan distanced those in the white community who had an ability to help steer a course of acceptance and moderation, the plan appeared particularly vulnerable. The fact that only one school was to desegregate also proved an unfortunate logistical mistake since it played into the hands of the Capital Citizens' Council, who, working with only limited resources, could concentrate all their efforts of agitation and disruption at one particular site.[42]

Compounding these problems was the fact that in selling his plan to the community for acceptance Blossom spoke almost exclusively to high-profile white community groups, again consisting of those largely unaffected by his desegregation plans, while ignoring those directly involved.[43] As Blossom had mishandled preparations for successful school desegregation among the white community, he also alienated many in the black community with his concern for minimizing the impact of school desegregation while totally disregarding their feelings, concerns, and comments.[44]

Without even the barest involvement of influential community figures, the school board became increasingly isolated against the howls of segregationists who rallied support to halt the process of school desegregation.[45] Afraid to tarnish his carefully crafted image of confidence and competence with Little Rock's business community, Blossom increasingly looked to Faubus for help. The more that segregationists intensified their calls for defiance of the *Brown* decision as the date of school desegregation drew closer, the more frantic Blossom became.[46] Blossom's telephone calls and meetings with Faubus rapidly multiplied and were characterized by increasingly hysterical predictions that there would be violence if the governor did not intervene.[47]

Faubus finally entered the fray on August 27, 1957, when he testified in a suit filed by the segregationist group the Mother's League of Central High that he believed violence would occur if plans to desegregate went ahead. Chancellor Murray O. Reed granted the request for a restraining order prohibiting the school board from implementing its desegregation plan. With Faubus now apparently throwing the full weight of his office behind the segregationists, the situation in Little Rock rapidly deteriorated into a well-documented crisis.

What went wrong at Little Rock? Why did a community which seemed prepared to accept gradual racial change in 1954 so quickly descend into racial crisis in 1957? Issues of community responsibility seem central to the answer. Whereas the militant segregationist minority in the city was able to articulate its grievances effectively, those in the white community who acknowledged the need to obey the law and accepted gradual racial change offered no viable, active support to implement the process. A passive acceptance of school desegregation proved an inadequate response to a vital community issue.

Moreover, the procrastination, prevarication, and political maneuvering of those who held the ability to shape positively the course of racial change actually helped strengthen the hand of militant segregationists. No movement of resistance to school desegregation developed in Arkansas until after the U.S. Supreme Court appeared to waver in its conviction with the ambiguity of *Brown II*. No opposition to the Blossom Plan for gradual racial change came until after it had been watered down. No violence occurred in Little Rock until after troops had been called out to prevent it.

Only after two years of racial crisis did the Little Rock business community finally mobilize to defeat a segregationist stranglehold of the city. During that period the city's school system ground to a halt and its economy nose-dived. To onlookers in other parts of the South, the situation at Little Rock confirmed that, like it or not, racial change was going to occur and that the central question would now be at what cost. Some cities learned the lesson of the 1957 Little Rock school crisis and the need for a proactive management of the dismantling of Jim Crow if they were to avoid a similar fate. Others knowingly went through the turmoil rather than face the inevitable consequences. But after the events of September 1957 one thing became abundantly clear across the South: the issue of racial change could no longer be swept under the carpet and just simply ignored.

The White Reaction to *Brown*: Arkansas, the Southern Manifesto, and Massive Resistance

ANTHONY J. BADGER

W hen the Supreme Court handed down the *Brown* decision, knocking out the constitutional basis for segregated education, the justices were under no illusions about the enormity of the change they were asking of the South. The southern judges, notably Hugo Black, left their colleagues in no doubt as to the extent and pervasiveness of the white South's commitment to segregation. Black conjured up apocalyptic visions of blood in the streets and predicted the destruction of the forces of southern liberalism.[1]

That perception on the part of the Court of mass white segregationist sentiment in the region underpinned its decree in May 1955 laying down how *Brown* was to be implemented, how school desegregation was to be accomplished. The Court placed its faith in local community initiatives, monitored by local federal district judges. To avoid stirring up angry white popular resistance through immediate change imposed from outside, the Court placed its confidence in moderate, law-abiding leaders across the region who would be given the opportunity to lead their communities into voluntary and gradual compliance with the law of the land.[2]

Arkansas appeared to be just the sort of southern state to justify the Court's optimism. It boasted two of the leading practitioners of biracial politics in the region. Governors Sid McMath and Orval Faubus had combined liberal economic policies aimed at lower-income whites and blacks with the active solicitation of support from the steadily increasing black electorate. They had fought for increased appropriations for African American institutions, appointed African Americans to both state and Democratic party positions, and had taken public stands against both lynching and the poll tax. In 1948, 1950, and 1954 they had defeated segregationist opponents — in contrast to those southern states where race-baiting had already eliminated liberal politicians. McMath attributed neither of his defeats — for reelection as governor in 1952 and for the Senate against John McClellan in 1954 — to the race issue. McCarthyism and the role of labor unions he considered more important.[3]

In Washington, the state was represented by three of the most liberal southerners in Congress — Brooks Hays, James Trimble, and the fervent internationalist J. William Fulbright. Together with Harry Ashmore, editor of the leading newspaper in the state, the *Arkansas Gazette*, they had actually attempted in the years before *Brown* to establish the ground rules for a regional compromise on race, which they called the Arkansas Plan. According to this plan the South would make good its commitment to gradual racial change by eliminating lynching, removing the obstacles to full political participation by African Americans, and striving for genuine equality in the provision of black education. In return, the national government would be patient and back off counterproductive demands for immediate desegregation. To a certain extent, the administrations of McMath and Faubus had indeed been taking the steps to meet Arkansas's part of such a regional bargain. Even before *Brown*, the University of Arkansas had integrated both its medical and law schools.[4]

What went wrong? How did Arkansas become the southern state that resisted school desegregation so violently that federal troops were sent in to enforce court orders and impose school desegregation, precisely the outcome that Arkansas moderates, the president, and the Supreme Court itself so fervently hoped to avoid?

Little Rock white leaders at the time were both bewildered and surprised by the outcome. How had it happened here? as school superintendent Virgil Blossom put it. How could a city that was enjoying unprecedented economic growth, had quietly desegregated its buses, parks, and hospitals, and had received national acclaim for its own voluntary school desegregation plan become a symbol of massive resistance, the subject of national and international opprobrium?[5]

From the start, Little Rock leaders blamed outsiders — whites from outside Little Rock — for their troubles. But the most convenient scapegoat, who offered the Little Rock leaders the easiest way of absolving themselves of responsibility, was Governor Faubus, who, the leaders argued, undermined their own responsible position by stirring up the forces of mass popular resentment. In 1990 Sid McMath laid out this position bluntly in an interview with John Egerton:

You know custom dies hard. But there were people, intelligent people and educated people, and people in positions of leadership, that knew it [desegregation] was inevitable. The *Brown* decisions, you know, and that it's just a matter of time.... You know Virgil Blossom had this plan which he had taken to all the civic clubs and the labor organizations and various groups in Little Rock, and had their approval. It was an integration, but people were willing to accept, you know, people are law-abiding. They were willing to accept it as the law of the land. They didn't like it. 'Course, they would welcome an alternative, and Faubus gave it to them. The Virgil Blossom plan, if Faubus had stayed out of it, would have gone in and worked... if they'd had proper leadership at the time the Central High School thing never would have happened.[6]

It is not my concern at this point to argue how partial and self-serving this statement was. What I want to look at is the reaction to the *Brown* decision in white Arkansas up to the Southern Manifesto of March 1956, when the entire congressional delegation, liberals and conservatives, signed that blast of defiance at the Supreme Court and pledged to resist the *Brown* decision. What I want to argue is that there was no reason to be surprised by the Little Rock crisis in 1957: the political dynamics of the race issue, which inhibited an effective policy of compliance with desegregation, were already in place by March 1956. Specifically, I will argue (1) that Faubus was convinced by the events of early 1956 that it was political suicide to defy mass white segregationist sentiment; (2) that Faubus himself helped create that segregationist sentiment, which he later claimed to be the prisoner of in 1957; and (3) that racially moderate politicians at the national level had already displayed the fatalism and caution that rendered them ineffective when the crisis developed in Little Rock in 1957–58.

In March 1956 Sam Harris argued in the *Arkansas Gazette* that the state had, until recently, been fulfilling the hopes that moderate, responsible leaders would maintain a "balanced stand" on integration. He said that "despite the best efforts of extremists in the integration versus segregation argument" the volatile subject had not become an important item in the political field until a few weeks before.[7]

Up to the end of 1955, Arkansas did indeed look as if it was moving responsibly in the way the Supreme Court hoped. In 1954 conservative Governor Cherry announced simply that the law would be obeyed. By 1955 three of the state's school districts had desegregated; the university town of Fayetteville in northwestern Arkansas claimed to be the first community in the South to announce its intention of desegregating its schools, and desegregation followed peacefully in September 1954 under the leadership of Superintendent Virgil T. Blossom, who moved soon thereafter to Little Rock as Superintendent of the Little Rock School District. The Charleston School District, also in the west, had in fact opened its schools on an integrated basis the month before Fayetteville. Both school districts had very small black populations and the costs of busing blacks to all-black high schools were crippling. In northeastern Arkansas, Hoxie followed suit in 1955. The Little Rock school board announced its intention in 1954 of desegregating in the fall of 1957. Governor Faubus, perceived as a racial moderate, showed little desire to interfere in the decisions of these local school boards.[8]

The state legislature in 1955 failed to pass a pupil assignment law, which would have circumvented the *Brown* decision. Segregationist pressure groups like the White Citizens' Councils of Arkansas and White America, Inc., lacked, as historian Neil McMillen has showed, both the popular support and the elite leadership that characterized groups in states like Mississippi and Alabama. They campaigned against desegregation in Hoxie, but they failed in the face of determined court opposition and the refusal of Faubus to intervene.[9]

This picture of moderation has to be qualified. Undoubtedly most white Arkansans favored the continuation of segregation, if possible. Even those who now believed segregation to be wrong were in no hurry to give up the privileges that the system brought to whites. Some had undoubtedly come to the conclusion that segregation was wrong from a Christian and moral point of view, but such decisions were often uncertain and individual. State and regional church groups were more likely than local congregations to make such decisions public. More whites, including church people, put a premium on obedience to the law. Neither of these stances was going to produce a campaign or crusade for compliance with school desegregation. The *New York Times* surveying Arkansas identified the Arkansas Council on Human Relations, the churches, and lawyers as groups advocating compliance. But, the *Times* noted, "for the most part they speak softly."[10]

In eastern Arkansas in the areas of large black populations, the commitment to segregation was very different. In Hughes the school board had built two new black schools. "I would never let my two daughters," said one resident, "attend a school with two Negroes to one white. It will not work." Said the mayor, "There's just not going to be any nigger kids going to white schools here. They've got to come a long way first. We wouldn't be building these two nigger schools if we were going to integrate." "It will be twenty five years before widespread integration is undertaken in southern Arkansas," predicted the State Commissioner of Education.[11]

In eastern Arkansas segregation functioned as a source of labor control for Arkansas planters. It was also a source of negative stereotypes, for it was difficult for east Arkansas planters to view as equals a dependent and subordinate group whom they saw performing nothing but menial jobs. Finally, segregation functioned to ameliorate fears: what, whites worried endlessly, would African Americans do if they were not under the strict control of segregation?[12]

It was here in eastern Arkansas in early 1956 that white supremacy pressure groups appeared to be whipping up segregationist passion. In Hoxie, Little Rock attorney Amis Guthridge, a former opponent of Brooks Hays, and state Sen. James D. Johnson combined as attorneys for the Hoxie Citizens' Council. They then launched a campaign to secure enough petitions to put an interposition amendment on the ballot. A rally at England, on the edge of the delta, on February 24 drew an audience of two thousand. They heard Guthridge call for three hundred thousand signatures for the interposition amendment which, according to Johnson, would nullify the "illegal action" of the Supreme Court. Roy Harris reported on the steps Georgia was taking to avoid compliance.[13]

At the end of the England rally, former governor and Dixiecrat Ben Laney warned: "We have had some sanctimonious politicians in Arkansas who couldn't open their mouths on this issue before. After a few more meetings like this, they will reconsider." Jim Johnson was clearly planning to challenge Faubus, and there was speculation that Laney might challenge J. William Fulbright for his Senate seat. Faubus, for one, adjusted his position accordingly. In January he reported that "85 per cent of all the people in the state are opposed to integration of the races at the present time. I cannot be a party to any attempt to force acceptance of a change to which the people are so overwhelmingly opposed."[14]

Faubus also sent a committee of legislators with Chairman of the State Board of Education Marvin Byrd to Virginia to examine Virginia's massive resistance tactics. All the lawmakers were from eastern Arkansas; four had attended the England Citizens' Council rally. On their return, they reported that an emergency existed in Arkansas. Faubus endorsed their findings in favor of an interposition resolution in the state legislature (as distinct from a constitutional amendment) and a pupil placement law. While he left open the question of whether a special session of the legislature would be needed and still expressed faith in local efforts as the best way to handle the issue, the governor made it clear that he was "ready to resist all efforts to completely integrate Arkansas's public schools." Thus, Faubus moved to break Jim Johnson's monopoly on segregationist sentiments.[15]

What was happening in eastern Arkansas was not happening in a vacuum. Whites across the region in 1954 and 1955 might content themselves that school desegregation might never happen—that intimidation of black plaintiffs and the decisions of local white judges might delay integration indefinitely. But by early 1956 it was clear that determined black plaintiffs would eventually get to court and some school board would comply. Whites in the Deep South flocked to join the Citizens' Council. At the same time African Americans stepped up their activism: in Alabama, Montgomery blacks boycotted the buses and Autherine Lucy attempted to enter the state university; in Arkansas, the NAACP, impatient at the timetable allowed in the Blossom Plan, attempted to secure the admission of black schoolchildren at Little Rock Central High School on January 22, 1956, and, failing in this effort, filed suit in the federal district court in Little Rock on February 7.[16]

It was against this background that the document known as the Southern Manifesto pledged its signers from the U.S. Congress to "use all lawful means to bring about a reversal of this decision [Brown] which is contrary to the Constitution and to prevent the use of force in its implementation." The drafters of the manifesto were not marginal men but the most senior southern senators. They aimed above all to persuade white southerners that school desegregation could be prevented, for they were concerned that white southerners were too fatalistic on the race issue; they believed that if doubtful southerners could be convinced that the Supreme Court could be defied, then the North might be persuaded to go slow on the enforcement of desegregation.[17]

When the manifesto was proposed in February 1956, the majority of Arkansas congressmen welcomed the opportunity to reemphasize their segregationist credentials. Conservative Sen. John McClellan had already joined Rep. Howard Smith and Sen. Willis Robertson of Virginia in sponsoring legislation to restrict the appellate powers of the Supreme Court and to protect explicitly the right of states to operate segregated schools. Congressman E. C. "Took" Gathings from the Arkansas delta had recently demanded a congressional investigation of communist influence in the

NAACP, using the information on its officers and board members sup-plied by the House Un-American Activities Committee.[18]

Congressman William Norrell, whose district included England, Arkansas, was virtually incapacitated. Facing a tough reelection battle in 1956 but unable to return to his district to campaign, he was later advised to publicize his signing of the manifesto to bolster support in his constituency. Oren Harris in southern Arkansas was a political ally of McClellan and Ben Laney and had not been averse to using the race issue against challengers for his seat. He was the Arkansas representative on the committee chaired by William Colmer of Mississippi, which served to coordinate southern congressional resistance to civil rights legislation. In this role, Harris actually circulated the manifesto to his fellow Arkansas congressmen for their signatures.[19]

Wilbur Mills, as second-ranking Democrat on the Ways and Means Committee, was a close ally of Speaker Sam Rayburn, who, like Lyndon Johnson, saw the manifesto as a gratuitous airing of an emotional sec-tional issue that was bound to divide the national Democratic party and could not be brokered by the usual compromises. Mills also had the national leadership aspirations which prompted some other southerners to eschew the manifesto's extreme rhetoric. But Mills kept closely in touch with political developments in Hoxie and was in no doubt about the strength of segregationist sentiment in his district. He was also a close ally of Faubus. On this issue, unlike most controversial issues, he did not consult Rayburn:

> But I *had* to sign it, I felt like. I didn't talk to Mr. Rayburn about it but if I hadn't signed it, I'd have been beaten on that. That thing in Little Rock was so explosive that they would have beat me about the least, any little thing that you might have done or not done that indicated that you weren't on their side in maintaining segregation. So it helped me at the time, you see.[20]

The alacrity with which congressmen from southern and eastern Arkansas signed the manifesto testified to their own segregationist views and their perceptions of their constituents' commitment to traditional pat-terns of race relations. The test of the success, however, of the authors of the manifesto in obtaining "unity of action" in the South and bringing wavering politicians into line was not their capture of the conservative faithful but rather their ability to bring into the segregationist camp the internationalist, progressive Sen. J. William Fulbright and the two most liberal members of the House delegation, Brooks Hays from Little Rock and James W. Trimble, Fulbright's successor in Congress from his northwest Arkansas district.

The news that Fulbright had signed the manifesto disappointed many of those in the North and outside the United States who admired his internationalist politics and his courageous stand against Joe McCarthy. Many Fulbright scholars expressed their dismay at the damage done by the manifesto to America's image in the very countries to which the senator's international exchange program had sent them. Fulbright's initial response to critical correspondents was that the "matter is much too involved to treat adequately in a letter." But in the long run, his explanation, which he never disavowed, was first that he had signed reluctantly and only after securing changes to the manifesto that toned down the initial intemperate drafts; second, that he had no political alternative but to sign, otherwise he would have faced certain defeat; third, that he was no racist and that the manifesto was consistent with his doctrine of gradualism, promoting change in race relations through gradual economic and educational change, rather than through legislative or judicial fiat.[21]

Unlike the most respected southern liberal senator, Lister Hill of Alabama, who allegedly signed the manifesto without reading it, Fulbright was reluctant to sign the first draft presented to the southern senators. Indeed, his aides, who were keen that he not be associated with such a defiant document, prepared a statement explaining why he was not going to sign. The statement was cast very much in the same mold as the statements of southerners like Lyndon Johnson and Albert Gore, who did not sign. Like the public pronouncements of most southern political moderates in the 1950s, the aides' proposed statement did not indicate approval of the Supreme Court decision; indeed, it deplored attempts to force integration on the South. But it argued that intemperate pronouncements like the manifesto, by alienating nonsoutherners, would make the task of resisting forcible federal intervention more difficult.[22]

Fulbright's aides argued that the problem of school desegregation was best left to local officials. Their proposed statement expressed the view that Governor Faubus had been maintaining through 1955: that the wisest course for a state was to "give its local communities and school boards the widest possible discretion to do what they wish and what they can. For this is a problem which is peculiarly local in the strictest sense of that word. Local autonomous school boards can deal with it far more wisely and effectively than we, the Congress, or perhaps even the states." What was particularly disturbing about the manifesto to Fulbright's aides, as it was to all those who did not sign, was that it held out "the false illusion" to southerners that the Supreme Court decision could be overturned and gave a "false hope" that state measures designed to avoid the impact of the decision would be successful. Instead, the duty of southern leaders, the proposed Fulbright statement argued, was one of "candor and realism. It is simply unrealistic to say that a decision of the Supreme Court is 'illegal and unconstitutional' and to imply, thereby, that it can be overturned by some higher tribunal."[23]

Fulbright rejected the advice of his aides. Instead he worked with Senators Holland (Florida), Daniel (Texas), and Sparkman (Alabama) in a subcommittee to tone down the revised version of Thurmond's original draft that had been prepared by Richard Russell, John Stennis, and Sam Ervin. Moderates who had signed, like Lister Hill, were anxious not to be left out on a limb and put pressure on the nonsigners to come up with acceptable language that would ensure a united front. Indeed, as Price Daniel remembered it, Fulbright was one of those who had signed and he only worked to revise the draft when he realized that Holland and Daniel would not otherwise sign.[24]

The changes that Fulbright and the subcommittee secured were largely cosmetic. It was true that the *Brown* decision was no longer denounced as "illegal and unconstitutional," but it was still "unwarranted" and "a clear abuse of judicial power" and an exercise of "naked judicial power." The manifesto did promise to use lawful means to resist, and it appealed to southerners to refrain from disorder and lawlessness, but so did the Russell draft. It did eschew an explicit commendation of interposition, but the Russell draft had already eliminated an endorsement of interposition and it commended the motives of states "who have declared their intention to resist forced integration [as distinct from the *Brown* decision itself] by any lawful means."[25]

"I don't think anything has happened to shake my belief that I wouldn't have survived politically if I hadn't taken the course I did," Fulbright told his biographer, Randall Woods. This perception of overwhelming mass white segregationist sentiment had led Fulbright in the past to advocate voluntary and gradual racial change. He had supported the admission of a black graduate student to the University of Arkansas Law School, but he argued at the time against legislation in race relations which "may in fact create such antagonisms as to destroy much of the progress we have made during the last several years." Economic prosperity and education, not laws, he believed, would bring peaceful racial change in the South. This progress was now threatened by the *Brown* decision. As he stated after the manifesto was issued, "the whole theory of revolutionizing racial relations by fiat is wrong. You can't pass laws to make men be good to each other." The Supreme Court decision had confirmed his worst fears because it had merely stirred up groups like White America, Inc. Fulbright felt that the popular response left him no option but to sign the manifesto.[26]

Certainly Fulbright's friends in eastern Arkansas feared that Dixiecrat Ben Laney would exploit racial passions to run against the senator in 1956. When Fulbright signed the manifesto they felt, as Jim Hale in West Memphis told him, that Laney would not now run. Fulbright's aide John Erickson told him of a conversation between Liz Carpenter and *Arkansas Gazette* reporter Sam Harris: "Sam thinks your signing the Manifesto pretty well takes care of Laney."[27]

It is difficult to see that Fulbright needed to have been so cautious. John Erickson liked to drive off potential opposition by depriving potential candidates of possible sources of campaign funds in the fall before a reelection year. In 1956 Fulbright was already assured of the backing of the single most powerful source of funds in Arkansas, Witt Stephens, whose investment firm now controlled Arkansas Louisiana Gas Company. The senator remained on close terms with the Faubus administration. It did not seem that political necessity demanded that he sign the manifesto.[28]

Certainly, many of Senator Fulbright's Arkansas supporters were disappointed. Racial moderates in a state that prided itself on its progress in race relations felt that Fulbright had let them down and undercut their position. Nowhere was this felt more strongly than in his hometown of Fayetteville, where, after all, his brother-in-law, Hal Douglas, had been chairman of the school board that had presided over school desegregation. As Gordon McNeil from the university history department put it:

> Might not the man whose name is given to a scholarship program designed to win us friends abroad, and the former law professor who knows the possible consequences of intemperate attacks on the court, also have declined to sign?. . . You have given aid and comfort to the extremists who reject our fundamental democratic and Christian principles. Did you really mean to do this? Did you really want to stir up the die-hards here in your own community of Fayetteville, where the adjustments to more equal educational opportunities are being made peacefully?

As one among a number of Little Rock lawyers and churchmen noted, "You yourself know that Arkansas has experienced very little trouble during the outset of this program and surely as integration moves into the Little Rock system, the majority of the state will follow the pattern with little opposition." Fulbright, lamented the wife of a Little Rock teacher, could "have given encouragement to the mass of the people who are *not vocal*, but who want to see our state progress." Many were opposed to integration "but those people are law-abiding citizens and have only been waiting for the leadership from the right sources."[29]

The disappointment of racial moderates in Little Rock and northwest Arkansas might have been expected. What was especially poignant was the disappointment of churchmen in eastern Arkansas who now felt abandoned and isolated. As a West Helena minister noted, "I am not writing McClellan or any of the other representatives of our state for I more or less expected such from them. I am writing you only because your assent to this attitude is a truly disturbing thing. I would never have believed that you would be party to such."[30]

To the end, Fulbright argued that he had been right to sign the manifesto. He did, however, note wistfully that he did not "think that the gradualist school that I belonged to, looking back from now, will receive the approval of history." However, it was not Fulbright's gradualism that was flawed, but the fact that he did not speak up for gradualism at the time. As a perplexed former Fulbright scholar and Presbyterian minister in Jim Johnson's hometown of Crossett complained, the manifesto was not advocating gradualism: "I am fully aware of the difficulties that will accompany integration. But I look on it not as an evil to be avoided, but a good which is worth the price it costs. If you had said 'slow down' I could have understood your position even if I did not agree with it, but when you said 'stop' I am left wondering."[31]

It is difficult to avoid Randall Woods's stark conclusion that "indisputably" Fulbright was a racist. There are many gradations of racism, and certainly Fulbright was no race-baiting demagogue. But, unlike many of his correspondents, Fulbright had not come to see segregation as a moral evil or unchristian. Fulbright was not uneasy with the patrician prejudices of his eastern Arkansas planter friends, and he did not see desegregation as an important enough issue to stand up against what he perceived to be the deeply held sentiments of the mass of his constituents.[32]

Fulbright acknowledged the passion of the segregationists' beliefs— "You had a hell of a chance of persuading them that it's a good thing for their daughter to go to school with a black man"—but he had no similar feel for the impatience of his African American constituents. He had little personal understanding of the poverty and daily humiliation of their lives, and, like most liberal politicians in the South in the 1950s, he campaigned for black votes at a distance through his aides who dealt with particular community leaders. These leaders—"racial diplomats," as Numan Bartley calls them—were used to telling white politicians what those white politicians wanted to hear. As a result Fulbright was shielded from the growing sense of grievance in the Arkansas African American community. Leaders of that community, like Lawrence Davis and I. S. McClinton, whatever their private thoughts, reassured Fulbright that they understood the political realities of his position. Fulbright's signing of the manifesto, underpinned by his certainty of the strength of mass white segregationist sentiment, was entirely consistent with his political philosophy and with his later inaction during the Little Rock crisis.[33]

Fulbright never regretted signing the Southern Manifesto. Brooks Hays regretted signing almost immediately after he had done so. Hays had been a prominent moderate on racial matters and a prominent Baptist, a New Deal–style liberal on domestic policy, and a committed internationalist on foreign affairs, with many northern congressional contacts. In 1949 he had proposed, at the instigation of Fulbright and Harry Ashmore, the Arkansas Plan for racial progress: support for federal action on anti-lynching and against the poll tax in return for the South maintaining segregation. He described himself as a states' rights liberal who favored positive action by the southern states to fend off federal intervention. He did not approve the *Brown* decision, but he had initially refused to sign the manifesto because it approved interposition and because it had no appeal to the people to pursue legal and constitutional methods for change. He still held out even after the changes engineered by Fulbright, Holland, and Daniel had met those objections. But as more and more southern representatives signed, Hays found himself under pressure from other moderates not to break ranks.[34]

Orval Faubus was in Washington in the spring of 1956, and he set himself the task of securing the signatures of the two holdouts, the two most liberal members of the delegation: Hays and James W. Trimble. With Oren Harris, who was collecting the Arkansas delegation signatures, Faubus accompanied Hays to the Bethesda Hospital where Trimble was ill. Faubus spent three hours at Trimble's bedside persuading the two liberals to sign. As Hays recalled:

Faubus...confronted the two of us...with the idea that if we did not do something to allay the hysteria and the fears that had been generated of his being forced all of a sudden conceivably through military action on the part of the federal government, if we did not do something along that line to quiet the people down, that we would find what he called the Ku Klux Klan and the extreme Citizens' Council groups taking over the political life of the state, and that the racists and the radicals would displace the moderates. Faubus was known as a moderate.

When Trimble eventually agreed to sign, Hays felt that he was obliged to follow suit. He was not proud of his action: "in the present context I can see that I shouldn't have done it because it didn't spare us much. I think we could still have saved the political leadership of the state from those extremists but the threat was powerful enough that I was influenced."[35]

In 1976 John Ward, editor of the Conway *Log Cabin Democrat* brought together two of the principal actors in the Little Rock crisis: Orval Faubus and Brooks Hays. Hays had paid for his failed 1957 efforts to mediate between Faubus and President Eisenhower by losing his congressional seat in the general election of 1958, defeated after a last-minute write-in campaign by segregationist forces. Hays was always willing to believe the best of people and in the 1976 interview he appeared to accept Faubus's assurance that he "didn't do anything against Brooks" in that 1958 race, indeed that Faubus had "discouraged...everyway in the world" his secretary who masterminded the write-in campaign. Faubus was anxious to show that "a man in public life then" had to act pragmatically and was keen to argue that he and Hays had adopted much the same pragmatic stance. To make his point he turned the conversation to the Southern Manifesto, identifying it as

> the forerunner of our opposition...signed by every member of the Congress from all the Southern States except two...and one of them got beat and the other had strong opposition and the only way he saved himself, he said "I didn't sign it because it wasn't strong enough." And he survived. Do you see, in all that situation, for the federal government to issue an order like that and place all the burden on the state authorities or local authorities and say, "Go ahead, and (looking at it from the pragmatic standpoint) commit political suicide now. We're aloof from it." I didn't think it was proper. I didn't think it was honest. I didn't think it was courageous.[36]

In 1992 Faubus told John Kirk:

> So then up in Washington, they get the pressure. What do they do? They devise and proclaim the Southern Manifesto . . . even Fulbright, the great liberal, became the first man to sign it. Brooks Hays went up and signed it, all from Arkansas. So the handwriting was on the wall for everybody in that time, in that situation. So the congressmen, they'd say "Oh we've done all we can, now it's up to the state administration."[37]

Faubus believed that the mass white segregationist public opinion that forced people to sign the manifesto left him no alternative but to defy the courts in 1957. What he conveniently ignored was the role he himself played in creating that pressure. What Faubus and the conservatives were aiming to do was to stir up white public opinion, to convince the people that token compliance was *not* inevitable and that the Court could be defied. They then hoped that wavering politicians who might have accepted the inevitability of gradual change would be coerced back into the massive resistance camp.[38]

This conservative strategy worked in Arkansas. Fulbright and Hays appear to have been paralyzed by their conviction that the mass of white public opinion was overwhelmingly hostile to any desegregation. They were not prepared to campaign for the gradualism they espoused, nor were they prepared to campaign to persuade the people to accept the inevitable. Instead, Fulbright and Hays, egged on by Faubus, signed a document which, as Fulbright's aides acknowledged, gave the "false illusion" to white Arkansans that the Supreme Court could be successfully defied.

This fatalism by the state's leading politicians reflected a fatalism among southern moderates generally in the 1950s, a reluctance to attempt to build up public support for compliance. It was as if they believed that public agitation would unnecessarily stir up the forces of white popular racism, whereas if no fuss was made gradual racial change and desegregation could quietly be implemented almost unnoticed: a strategy seemingly followed by Little Rock community leaders in the summer of 1957.

What the Southern Manifesto demonstrated in Arkansas was that if you disavowed compliance with the Supreme Court, you were in no position to control the segregationist pressure groups that resolutely opposed any compromise with desegregation. Faubus's strategy in 1956 was predicated on the notion that concessions to segregationist pressure would enable moderates like himself to stay in office and defuse the extremist threat. Instead, he found that in a battle where one side is prepared to mount a righteous crusade to defy the Supreme Court, and the other wants to keep quiet, the segregationists were going to win.

Fulbright's moderate correspondents who were so disappointed by the senator in 1956, and who felt that their positions in their communities as advocates of compliance with the law of the land had been undermined, were right to be apprehensive. The experience of March 1956 suggested that if the choice came between obeying court orders and bowing to segregationist mob pressure, moderates at the community level could look in vain for help from leading politicians like Fulbright and Faubus. It was difficult to convince people that there was no alternative but to obey the law of the land, that they should accept the inevitable, when leading politicians in the state were proclaiming that there *was* an alternative, that desegregation could be avoided.

Reviewing the apparently polarized racial and political scene in March 1956, newspaperman Sam Harris predicted that fame awaited the Arkansas politician in the next two years who resisted demagoguery and exercised some courage. Fame would come to an Arkansas politician, as Harris foretold, but it was a demagogue who was to achieve it.[39]

The Contest for the Soul of Orval Faubus

ROY REED

One popular explanation for the 1957 crisis at Central High School is that Gov. Orval E. Faubus precipitated it for political advantage. The thinking is that he needed an issue to guarantee him a third two-year term in office and that, when the integration of Central loomed, he saw an opportunity and grasped it eagerly.

There is much in that explanation to make it appealing. But, like many easy theories, it is not the whole truth. The roll call of ambition, political opportunism, cowardice, and blame in the Central High crisis extends well beyond the name of Orval Eugene Faubus. It is conveniently forgotten in the shorthand versions of 1950s history that Orval Faubus did not start the segregationist resistance to school desegregation in his state or in his region. In fact, he was on the other side in the beginning. He himself was a target of the segregationist wrath.

Faubus grew up in a Socialist household in the backwoods of Madison County. His father, Sam, was an organizer for the Socialist party. He made sure that his seven children understood the evils of capitalism and racism. Some of the children, embarrassed by their father's reputation for radicalism, ignored the teaching. Orval took it in, molded it into a more politically practical shape, and used it to propel himself into the governor's office as a friend of the poor.

Until well into his second term, he talked and acted like a moderate on the race issue. He appointed a number of black people to state office. He helped integrate the state Democratic party's governing body. He oversaw the integration of several outlying school districts after the Supreme Court declared segregated schools unconstitutional in 1954. By 1957, Arkansas under his governorship had more desegregated schools than eleven other states combined—a statistic that he still remembered with pride until he died. During the early part of his tenure, he was suspected in certain circles of being a rampant integrationist, and, in the Red scare of the 1950s, that meant he was probably a communist. The more colorful elements of the white supremacist movement routinely portrayed him as a race-mixing scalawag, a secret sympathizer if not outright member of the National Association for the Advancement of Colored People, and a tool of the communist conspiracy.

How, then, did this friend of the liberals become a hero of the segregationist resistance? That almost certainly would not have happened had it not been for an accident of timing. It was Faubus's fate to be governor when several opposing forces of history collided in the capital of the state and he was offered a number of choices in dealing with the collision— none very palatable, politically speaking.

The Little Rock School Board, guided by its ambitious superintendent, Virgil T. Blossom, had planned for nearly three years to start a severely minimal process of desegregation in the fall of 1957. The idea was to choke down as little of the poison as the federal courts would approve. Desegregation would begin with a handful of Negro children at a single high school, then proceed slowly to the lower grades, a few pupils at a time. The plan was described openly as a scheme for continued segregation for the overwhelming majority of white and black students.

No one in the school district hierarchy or in the ruling establishment of the city ever uttered a public word suggesting that abolishing segregation —apartheid, if you will—was the morally correct thing to do. It was merely the legal thing to do, and large numbers of white people disagreed even with that tortured position. That was the position of not just the unlettered multitudes. The rich white men who ran Little Rock were for the most part committed segregationists. They also understood that racial violence was bad for business, so they reluctantly went along with the Blossom plan for slow desegregation.

It is difficult for young people today to understand the depth of southern resistance to the Supreme Court's 1954 school decision. The resistance was based on a supremely confident racism: a belief among millions of white people that black people were inferior and should be treated so under the law. Polls routinely showed in excess of 80 percent of southern whites opposing integrated schools. In the face of such attitudes, it would have taken a rare collection of unpaid school board officers to pursue integration as anything more than an unpleasant task required by an unbending federal court system. The Little Rock School Board was fortunate. Blossom, the man paid to do the school board's planning, understood well the public resentment against the federal court's demands and tried to make allowances for it.

Governor Faubus, of course, faced the same problem: how to stay out of the way of the growing public resistance. His personal attitude on race was not as simple as liberal or conservative. There is little evidence that he felt strongly one way or another except to include blacks, a little like an afterthought, among the downtrodden common folk he most identified with. In spite of occasional liberal actions and utterances, he had let it be known in private that he might be prepared to exploit the race issue. However, any exploitation he had in mind was to be consistent with his centrist politics. He had no taste for extremes. Not yet.

He made that clear in the election campaign of 1956 when he was running for a second term. He was blessed that year with an opponent of such extreme segregationist views that he could safely stake out the middle ground. Even so, he did not dare portray himself as a friend of black people. Indeed, he rather adroitly left the impression that he was as much in favor of segregation as his opponent, but without being radical about it—without having to "jump up and down and stomp on my hat," as he once put it. He won that election by a sizable margin.

But he read the signs of the growing storm. While those of us in the more detached trade of journalism continued to believe that Arkansas would obey the Supreme Court's ruling and not make a fool of itself, Faubus became more pessimistic. He saw James D. Johnson, his 1956 opponent, not as the colorful, bombastic clown portrayed in the newspapers but as a voice of dissent that would soon have to be heard and dealt with. Faubus understood that Johnson not only spoke for large numbers of angry people but also that his act of speaking aroused multitudes of others to an anger that they had not felt before. Johnson was one of the most eloquent champions that the segregationist movement could have had. He knew how to arouse the racist fear and loathing that many otherwise decent white people felt. Beyond that, he was able to turn those feelings to anger and to direct that anger toward the federal apparatus that was trying to cram this repulsive change down their throats. And if any Arkansas leader—a governor, a newspaper editor—appeared to be soft on the burning question, then Johnson did not hesitate to point the finger at him. With justification, Faubus considered himself a target of this growing anger.

Arkansas was not isolated. The storm was gathering across the South as political leaders, including many with more respectability than Jim Johnson, thundered against the Supreme Court decision and vowed to lead a resistance so massive that the federal government would have to back down and leave segregation intact. Those leaders pointed to state laws that had sanctioned a segregated society for generations. They noted that the Supreme Court half a century earlier had upheld the constitutionality of segregation. Why should it change its mind now? The Court was giving in to sentimental claptrap and academic hogwash. And what about the revered doctrine of states' rights? Didn't that count for anything any longer? Some thinkers went so far as to recommend that each state adopt laws or resolutions of interposition claiming power for the states to interpose their authority between the federal courts and local governing bodies. Several states, including Arkansas, did so with varying degrees of seriousness.

What the South saw during these years was a replay of the run-up to the Civil War. Moderates began to lose ground just as they did during the 1850s. Extremists, led and prodded by leaders from the historically reactionary Black Belt, began to dominate the debate. White Citizens' Councils sprang up across the South to lead the resistance. Dissent was seen in these circles as tantamount to treason, just as it was one hundred years earlier.

The resistance gathered such force that public officials, even those with no strong feelings on the race issue, were swept along with it. Perhaps the turning point toward madness was the Southern Manifesto, a document sired in the Black Belt and circulated in Washington, D.C., during the spring of 1956. It called the Supreme Court's desegregation decision an exercise of "naked judicial power" and challenged the Court in language so inflammatory that one scholar called it "a calculated declaration of political war against the Court's decision." The document was signed by all but a handful of the South's senators and representatives.[1]

The signers included all eight of Arkansas's delegation, even though some of them considered it pernicious and misguided. Gentlemanly old Jim Trimble, who had represented the Ozarks in Congress for many years and who was known as a center-to-left Democrat on social issues, was in the hospital when the manifesto was circulated. Grave illness was no excuse. Faubus and Rep. Brooks Hays, two of his best friends in politics, went with a delegation to his hospital bed and told him that his career was at risk if he failed to sign the document. He did it, angrily and reluctantly.

Hays signed the thing with the same misgivings and suffered a guilty con-science the rest of his life. Heading the list of Arkansas signers were Sen. John L. McClellan and Rep. Wilbur D. Mills, two of the state's most promi-nent men, both powerhouses in Congress, and Sen. J. William Fulbright, who was already famous around the world. Fulbright was being threatened by strong opposition in the next election back home.[2]

Faubus, himself increasingly vulnerable on the race issue, figured that if McClellan, Mills, and Fulbright could not withstand the growing pres-sure, he certainly could not. For a member of Congress refusing to sign would have been like painting a bull's-eye on his chest and inviting the angry troops of massive resistance to aim and fire. But congressmen at least had the comfort of knowing that once they signed they could forget it. As Faubus saw it, the congressmen had blustered and clamored from the safety of their Washington offices; then, having stirred up the folks back home, they retired from the fight and left the officeholders in their state capitals to deal with the problem. It is hard to disagree with that judgment.

The manifesto was a warning shot. Before the summer of 1956 was over, more than 83,000 voters in the Arkansas Democratic primary had marked the ballot for Jim Johnson, the governor's firebrand opponent. Faubus took further fright in the November general election. The voters, roused to growing anger, approved three anti-integration measures, includ-ing a Johnson-sponsored interposition amendment declaring the Supreme Court's school decision null in Arkansas. "That amendment was damned near a declaration of war against the United States," Johnson once told me. "It'd kill corn knee high."[3] One of the other ballot measures was Faubus's own resolution of interposition. Compared to Johnson's amendment, the resolution was little more than a statement of disagreement with the Court's decision. Faubus took little comfort from the fact that his innocu-ous resolution got a few thousand more votes than Johnson's "declaration of war."

The resistance intensified during the winter of 1957. The Arkansas legislature passed, and Faubus unenthusiastically signed, four laws aimed at obstructing integration. One established a state sovereignty commission to investigate the forces pushing for integration. Winthrop Rockefeller, a Republican and a known integrationist, said it sounded like an Arkansas Gestapo. Faubus showed his own distaste for the agency by ignoring the legal mandate to appoint the commission members. He might have pro-crastinated all year had a group of segregationists not filed a lawsuit and forced him to act.

By summer, the Capital Citizens' Council was making itself heard. It had only about five hundred members at the beginning of the summer, but as the impact of the Blossom Plan on working-class neighborhoods sank in, the council's message began to take hold. White people in the older part of town who had not been paying close attention suddenly saw what was happening. The new high school just built on the western edge of the city would be all white. That's where the rich and the upwardly mobile lived. The only whites directly affected by the first years of integration would be the humbler sort who lived in the Central High neighborhood. Looking ahead, certain real estate speculators who had invested heavily in western Little Rock could see the day when thousands of white people would flee westward to escape integration and would need the houses that the speculators were conveniently situated to supply. Those same speculators and their friends in the establishment had already started the population shift by using federal urban renewal funds to destroy black housing in the central city and move the inhabitants eastward. School integration would now finish the task of dividing Little Rock into two cities, black on the east and white on the west.[4] Even those blue-collar whites who mistrusted the extremism of the Citizens' Council began to find their voices as the date approached for the start of the Blossom Plan.

Johnson and the Citizens' Council focused on two main targets for their advertising and public statements: the governor and the school superintendent. Call them! Write to them! Demand that they stop the race mixing, the councilors cried. In addition to the advertising, noisy rallies, and press conferences, Johnson and his associates organized a secret telephone campaign to persuade Faubus and Blossom that caravans of armed men were prepared to descend on Little Rock to stop integration by force. Ten days before school opened, Gov. Marvin Griffin of Georgia flew to Little Rock and raised the temperature further. He told a Citizens' Council rally that integration would never occur in his state and that Arkansas did not have to have it, either. It could be stopped if the governor simply refused to obey the federal courts. His message was cheered far beyond the walls of the meeting place in Little Rock.

Faubus continued to maneuver for the political center even as it crumbled under his feet. He hit on the device of stanching the segregationist anger by delaying the start of integration. He knew that he could not stop it permanently, but he calculated that if he could stall it, even for a short time, he would have the cover he needed in the next election. It now seems clear that Faubus's first choice throughout the building tension was not dramatic confrontation but delay. He could not be sure whether confrontation would help or hurt him. Delay seemed to be a safer course.[5]

He learned that Blossom and some of his associates would also be happy to have a delay. Blossom was growing increasingly agitated over the possibility of violence. Johnson's telephone campaign had unnerved the superintendent and caused him to fear that integration would bring bloodshed. He cast about for help. His first impulse was to seek assurance from the Little Rock Police Department. But that force was under the command of a weak chief serving at the pleasure of a discredited city administration and a city council dominated by segregationists. He feared he could not count on the local policemen to protect the black students at Central. He then turned to Governor Faubus. In Blossom's view, the governor could forestall violence by issuing a strong plea for order, then, if necessary, backing that up with state law enforcement to protect the students. Here was still another pressure on Faubus as school opening approached. This one was easier to withstand. It was clear to Faubus, if not to Blossom, that providing state protection for the black students would amount to promoting integration. It was too late, he believed, for the governor of Arkansas to take such a course and survive. The anger of the resistance had become a roar. The lion was in the streets.

Faubus and Blossom did agree on one last-minute scheme for delay. They managed, in a shadowy dance of collaboration that would eventually be denied by Blossom, to have a lawsuit filed in Pulaski Chancery Court asking for an injunction to stop the integration of Central High. The suit succeeded, but only for a day. The injunction was nullified by a federal court before the benefits of delay could accrue.

Only then did Faubus opt for confrontation. When he did so, when he sent the National Guard to block the door in front of the black students, he secured his hold on the governor's office for the next decade. He also betrayed the better instincts of his state and his own nature, and he began his descent into the dark side of history.

What if he had clung to his course of moderation and refused to join the segregationists? He probably would have been defeated at the next election. We have numerous examples from across the South, beginning with Arkansas's own Brooks Hays in the election of 1958. Hays tried to preach reason and calm and was unseated by a hero of the extremists. There was to be no room for moderation until the lion was removed from the streets.

The Lesson of Little Rock: Stability, Growth, and Change in the American South

JAMES C. COBB

Scholars are fond of touting the constitutional significance of the Little Rock crisis as the first test of executive and judicial willingness to enforce the Supreme Court's ruling in the landmark *Brown v. Board of Education* decision. In terms of the immediate impact of the confrontation on other southern states and communities facing the prospect of school integration, however, some of the most influential decisions concerning Little Rock were made not in the Oval Office or the courtroom but in the corporate boardroom.

Prior to 1957, Little Rock had been enjoying considerable success in attracting new industry, but in the wake of the crisis, industrial executives opted to shy away from the racially troubled city, and it failed to capture a single new plant for the next four years. When officials of Jacuzzi Brothers of Richmond, California, announced in 1962 that they were finally breaking the drought by locating a plant in the Arkansas capital, the occasion was one of both celebration and somber reflection on what observers were already calling "The Lesson of Little Rock."[1]

In March 1958 as the outcome of the Little Rock crisis still hung in the balance, Oberlin College sociologists J. Milton Yinger and George E. Simpson were asking, "Can segregation survive in an industrial society?" Answering their own question, they assured readers that, the current difficulties down in Arkansas notwithstanding, "once a society has taken the road of industrialization, a whole series of changes begin to take place that undermine the foundation of the segregation system." Yinger and Simpson's position was noteworthy as a reflection of a long-standing tendency among social scientists to associate economic modernization with social and political democratization; but the question of whether segregation was incompatible with an industrialized society seems ironic indeed in light of the history of segregation itself. If it was legitimate to ask in the middle of the twentieth century whether segregation could survive in an industrialized South, in the late nineteenth century the question might have been turned on its head to inquire whether in fact industrialization could occur in the South *without segregation*.[2]

In recent years, several historians have pointed out that de jure segregation of the races actually emerged in the post-Reconstruction period in tandem with the so-called New South effort to industrialize the region and reintegrate it into the national economy. The racial system that would eventually become synonymous with the "southern way of life" may have been rooted in the slave-tended soil of Old South plantations, but it actually acquired its mature identity in the more dynamic industrializing and urbanizing New South, where it offered the promise of a stable and controlled living, labor, and investment environment.

Eric Hobsbawm has explained that the "invention of tradition" is likely to occur wherever and whenever "a rapid transformation of society weakens or destroys the social patterns for which 'old' traditions had been designed." Legally mandated segregation became one of the New South's "invented" traditions in response to a variety of factors, including not just the destruction of slavery, but the subsequent move of the population into the region's urban areas and industrial workplaces where the two races were most likely to come into contact—and conflict—without the controlling presence of slavery. Facilitating this population shift, the New South's expanding railroad network served as both the harbinger and agent of Jim Crow, because the close contact between the races required by rail travel quickly trapped the rail companies and, ultimately, their friends in the state legislatures between irate whites unwilling to share accommodations with blacks and determined blacks who refused to accept banishment to inferior quarters after paying for first-class accommodations. "Tough decisions forced themselves on the state legislatures of the South after the railroads came," wrote historian Edward L. Ayers, who pointed out that railroad expansion brought "the first wave of segregation laws that affected virtually the entire South in anything like a uniform way." Nine southern states enacted railroad segregation laws in the years between 1887 and 1891. Certainly, "railroad segregation was not," as Ayers wrote, "a throwback to the old-fashioned racism," but it became to whites, at least, "a badge of sophisticated, modern managed race relations."[3]

Likewise, studying the emergence of segregation in the late-nineteenth-century urban South, Howard Rabinowitz found southern cities at the vanguard of the region's move toward racial separation. Well before 1890, white urbanites had implemented most of the strategies and policies aimed at setting blacks apart from and generally behind whites. Although liberal theorists such as Simpson and Yinger would later insist that the modern urban-industrial environment was incompatible with segregation and other such obsolete traditions of the countryside, Rabinowitz's study indicated that, as John Cell observed, "Jim Crow...was not born and bred among 'rednecks' in the country. First and foremost, he was a city slicker." Rigid residential segregation had long since become a fact of life in the urban North, and because the New South's emerging cities were the locales where the races were most likely to encounter each other in new and unfamiliar surroundings and circumstances, they were the settings where the structure and order promised by segregation seemed most needed. Not surprisingly then, segregation made its greatest and most visible impact not in older, more racially "settled" cities such as Charleston or New Orleans, but in the upstart New South metropolises like Atlanta and Birmingham. By 1910, for example, indices of racially dissimilar residential patterns showed that Birmingham was approximately five times more segregated than Charleston. Far from a capitulation to the past, segregation was the wave of the future in the New South of the late nineteenth and early twentieth centuries.[4]

As they sought northern industrial capital, Henry Grady and his New South cohorts insisted that racial home rule for southern whites—in effect rolling back the tragically misguided policies of Reconstruction—was a prerequisite for the region's reintegration into the national economy. Accordingly, racial separation became a prominent theme in Grady's speeches as early as 1883, and by 1885 he was insisting that the doctrine of separate but equal should apply "in every theatre," as well as in "railroads, schools, and elsewhere." Segregation became a vital component of the New South Creed, because a stable racial climate was deemed essential to a stable investment climate, which, in the euphemistic rhetoric of New South boosters, actually meant an abundance of cheap, dependable, and docile workers. "Docile" in this case referred to the absence not only of labor militancy but also of interracial conflict occasioned by black-white competition for jobs and living space. Institutionalized discrimination helped to achieve both of these ends, keeping the southern workforce divided and politically weak and ensuring low wages for whites by imposing even lower wages on blacks.[5]

As the legacy of Reconstruction was being dismantled and the courts validated this process, segregation promised to ease tensions not just between southern blacks and southern whites, but between southern whites and northern whites as well, thus facilitating the flow of capital from North to South. Seen in a broader national, as well as regional, economic perspective, the emergence of the Jim Crow system surely reaffirms Ralph Ellison's observation that "Negro life does not exist in a vacuum but in the seething vortex of those tensions generated by the most highly industrialized of Western nations."[6]

Ellison's observation was also applicable to disfranchisement. By the end of the nineteenth century, some of the white South's ostensibly most advanced thinkers had embraced disfranchisement as an absolute necessity that would reduce both racial tension and electoral fraud and thereby facilitate the South's full and speedy return to full participation in national political life. Some New South intellectuals even saw disfranchisement leading to the rise of two-party politics, because, freed from the divisive and potentially threatening presence of the black vote, southern whites could calmly and soberly entertain the Republican party's platform and principles solely on their merits. After surveying its numerous potential benefits, President Edwin A. Alderman of the University of Virginia hailed disfranchisement as one of the "most constructive acts of Southern history."[7]

The overall impact of disfranchisement on southern and national politics hardly could have been more contrary to what its architects had promised. By keeping almost all blacks and many poor whites away from the polls disfranchisement effectively concentrated power in the tight grip of those who had the most to gain from perpetuating the Democratic party's conservative political hegemony. With the Democrats comfortably ensconced as Dixie's party of no other choice, electoral participation plummeted, but corruption still flourished as fierce intraparty factional struggles quickly became the order of the day.[8]

One-party elections forced all aspirants into a single Democratic primary featuring a huge field of candidates. Not surprisingly, victory often went to the candidate who managed to catch the electorate's attention by yelling "white supremacy" the loudest and generally acting the biggest fool. Such an atmosphere hardly seemed conducive to stability, but the politics of personality and faction seldom yielded an identifiable, articulated issue much less any substantive effort to translate that issue into a genuine alteration of policy.

By rewarding demagoguery, disfranchisement heightened rather than reduced racial tensions; but, as New South advocates had hoped, the white South reintegrated itself into national politics, and it did so on its own terms. Insulated from the masses of black and white voters, reactionary southern senators and congressmen eagerly did the bidding of Black Belt chieftains and corporate bosses, returning to Washington year after year to use their seniority on behalf of their white patrons and thwart any and all reform initiatives that might contradict their interests. When the civil rights agitation of the post–World War II years finally began, southern stalwarts in Congress could and did capitalize on their strategic, seniority-endowed committee chairmanships to defend the "southern way of life" against the onslaughts of black activists and whatever legislative or judicial assaults their liberal allies in Washington might mount.

Contemporary sensibilities make it difficult to understand how relatively enlightened southern whites could have accommodated themselves to the injustices catalogued here, but it is important to note that both segregation and disfranchisement were advanced by many proponents in an effort to reduce the horrifying frequency of lynching and defuse the tensions that permeated the violent, racially charged atmosphere that prevailed in the late-nineteenth-century South. As Cell reminds us, "the ideology of segregation was not the contribution of the most fanatical, ignorant unbending racists of the period." Rather, "it was developed and articulated by moderate men who...in a frightening atmosphere of widening extremes and apparent social disintegration...sought the middle ground of sanity and compromise." Describing what he and others of like persuasion were up against, Edgar Gardner Murphy deplored the "more radical spokesmen" who moved "from the contention that no negro shall vote, to the contention that no negro shall learn, that no negro shall labor and (by implication) that no negro shall live."

Confronting such sentiments, southern moderates made their peace with segregation and disfranchisement as immutable facts of life in the South, leaving themselves little option beyond ineffectual pleadings for fair and humane treatment of a race that had been socially stigmatized and legally and politically neutralized. For these moderate whites, the best hope of ameliorating what was widely identified as the "negro problem" seemed to be the economic progress promised by the advocates of the New South. Meanwhile, incoming industrialists readily accommodated their operations to prevailing regional mores, practicing discrimination by industry as well as by jobs within certain industries.[9]

Reflecting on the ease and speed with which the invented traditions of segregation and disfranchisement became synonymous with the "southern way of life," C. Vann Woodward described a Jim Crow system that "had reached its perfection in the 1930s and prevailed throughout the South in all aspects of life....Everywhere one was assured that this was the way things had always been, that it was because of Southern folkways, that colored people themselves preferred it that way, and anyway there was nothing that could be done to change it."[10]

As impregnable as the Jim Crow system may have seemed in the South of Woodward's youth, its very solidity and oppressiveness helped to sow many of the seeds of its own destruction. In the aftermath of World War I, massive out-migration shifted a significant segment of the black population from a part of the nation where they could not vote to a part where they could, thus encouraging the Democratic party's increasing attention to black concerns. The New Deal's centralized response to the South's socio-economic ills and President Franklin Roosevelt's appointments of Supreme Court justices more sympathetic to civil rights also proved crucial, as did the growing strength and increasing effectiveness of black activism and NAACP litigation efforts. Meanwhile, World War II focused increasingly critical attention on the South's racial practices and the irony of fighting for freedom abroad while acquiescing to subjugation and repression at home. Ralph Ellison produced a number of short stories suffused with the irony of black soldiers ostensibly fighting for democracy but unsure whether its greatest enemies were foreign or domestic, and Lillian Smith insisted that "fighting for freedom while tolerating Jim Crow" amounted to trying to "build a new world with Confederate bills." Suffice it say that American aspirations to free-world leadership in the cold war era only made southern style de jure segregation seem even more intolerable.[11]

On the economic front, New Deal farm programs aimed at acreage reduction had further stimulated the out-migration of farm labor, both black and white, by facilitating the mechanization and consolidation of southern agriculture. World War II greatly accelerated this trend, both pushing and pulling labor away from the land. The war also provided a massive injection of capital. Per capita income tripled in the region during the 1940s, and the South emerged from the decade with the attractive consumer markets whose absence had theretofore shackled it to a development strategy centered on the courtship of low-wage, low-value-added industries.[12]

World War II not only stimulated the South's economy as never before, but it also encouraged a more subtle if nonetheless important political transformation as well. In the short run, returning veterans spearheaded a series of "GI revolts" aimed at cleaning up political corruption and utilizing the resources of state and local governments to promote economic development on an expanded scale and at an accelerated pace. One such uprising came in Hot Springs, Arkansas, where Sid McMath led a political rebellion that eventually propelled him into the governor's mansion. As governor, McMath combined infrastructural improvements and image building with a vigorous campaign for industrial development. While they were committed to fiscal conservatism and pro-business policies, this new breed of political leaders remained staunchly segregationist, disclaiming only the race-baiting demagoguery of the Talmadges and Bilboes as potentially injurious to the mounting effort to recruit new and better industries to the South.[13]

Institutionalized racial segregation had emerged in tandem with the late-nineteenth-century crusade to build a "New South" by courting low-wage, low-value-added manufacturing firms and seeking thereby to integrate the region into the national industrial economy at the trailing edge. The New South strategy prevailed over most of the next three-quarters of a century, yielding a pattern of slow growth and a decidedly labor-intensive manufacturing economy. Spurred by the massive economic boost supplied by World War II, however, the leaders of the region's more dynamic metropolitan areas began to enjoy some success in courting more sophisticated, socially responsive companies, which operated nearer the vanguard of the national and global economy.

Meanwhile, the increased emphasis on industrial development quickly transformed the South's governors into supersalesmen for their states, and industrial recruitment soon ranked second only to the defense of segregation as a gubernatorial priority. Elected governor of Arkansas in 1954, Orval E. Faubus had entered state politics as a part of the reform-oriented McMath administration. As governor, Faubus supported a bill establishing the Arkansas Industrial Development Commission and appointed Winthrop Rockefeller to head what became one of the most aggressive and highly visible industrial recruitment agencies in the South. The governor also backed a constitutional amendment permitting local governments to buy land and build plants for incoming industries. Faubus readily affirmed his commitment to segregation but insisted repeatedly that school integration was a "local problem" and should therefore be addressed on "the local level."[14]

In the wake of the 1954 *Brown* decision and in the midst of the militant response to the desegregation threat mounted by members of the Citizens' Councils and other proponents of massive resistance, Faubus and other economic development-oriented southern politicians found it increasingly difficult to sidestep the question of whether they would actually defy any federal attempt to force integration of the public schools. Having failed in his efforts to shift responsibility for enforcing the integration decree to the White House or the courts, Faubus finally weighed the political consequences of his alternatives and chose to block integration, calling out the National Guard to enforce segregation and "maintain or restore order."[15]

Even before the Little Rock crisis, southern economic development leaders had expressed concern about the probable negative impact of racial strife on their efforts to recruit new industry. In response to the Montgomery bus boycott of 1955, a pro-business group known as "The Men of Montgomery" failed in their efforts to mediate the boycott dispute. Though ineffectual, their initiatives reflected their perception that racial conflict was injurious to a community's prospects for economic growth.[16] While this perception doubtless existed in Little Rock as well, it manifested itself too late to prevent the ugly, image-tainting scenes of hatred and violence that erupted in September 1957 and the school closings that came a year later. Business and industrial development leaders quickly discovered what the crisis had done to Little Rock's image when they found they could stir up little or no interest among industrialists in moving to Little Rock, cheap labor and tax concessions notwithstanding. One executive who was apparently on the verge of making the final decision to locate in Little Rock reversed himself, citing the "reluctance" of "key employees" and explaining that "the wives of these employees played a prominent part in their decisions not to move to Little Rock. The adverse publicity given your area on the 'school issue' was certainly no help to your cause." Yet another prospect simply asked to be removed from "consideration" because "our contacts with Arkansas have given us an unfavorable opinion of that state in comparison with Tennessee, Mississippi or Missouri. We have no desire to be involved in the segregation problems current in that state."[17]

Between 1950 and 1957, an average of five new plants per year had come to the city, and in the first eight months of 1957 eight more had chosen Little Rock locations, creating one thousand new jobs. In the wake of the integration crisis, however, not only did Little Rock's industrial growth screech to a halt, but statewide, new plant investment, which had totaled $131 million in 1956, fell to $44.9 million in 1957 and then $25.4 million in 1958. The only economic beneficiary of the Little Rock debacle, it seemed, was a local mover who admitted, "We are moving families away from Little Rock faster than ever before." The lesson of Little Rock, as one observer summed it up, seemed to be that "any environment which is unstable and in which public education is threatened is not conducive to business development or expansion."[18]

This lesson was not immediately apparent to everyone. In January 1959 Gov. J. Lindsay Almond Jr. promised to save Virginia from the "livid stench of sadism, sex, immorality and juvenile pregnancy infesting the mixed schools of the District of Columbia and elsewhere." Almond's stand against integration led to several school closings, however, and pressures from business and industrial development leaders forced lawmakers to back away from the state's massive resistance policies. Six months after his vow to preserve segregation at all costs, Almond reversed himself dramatically by insisting that "no error could be more grave, no mistake more costly, no travesty more tragic, no curse more productive of woe than to succumb to the blandishments of those who would have Virginia abandon public education and thereby consign a generation of children to darkness and illiteracy, the pits of indolence and dependency, and the dungeons of delinquency."[19]

Convinced that die-hard resistance to desegregation was economic suicide, groups supporting or at least willing to accept integration sponsored speaking appearances by Little Rock Chamber of Commerce representatives Boyd Ridgeway and Everett Tucker, who proceeded to spin their city's tale of woe throughout the South. Tucker invariably ended his talks by admonishing local audiences to "keep your public schools open. You will never regret it."[20]

Tucker's message dovetailed nicely with the Southern Regional Council's efforts to encourage businessmen to assume responsibility for bringing a speedy and nonviolent end to segregation and discrimination in their cities. The council's periodic "Leadership Reports" went to a thousand selected decision makers across the South between 1959 and 1961, providing data on the severe economic consequences of racial disturbances and citing prominent examples in which businessmen took the lead in promoting peaceful desegregation. One report, entitled "Businessmen Point the Way," cited the example of Raleigh, where directors of the Merchants Bureau challenged businessmen to "do these things that would further the human relations and continued growth of Raleigh." In the same report, a Knoxville Chamber of Commerce resolution affirmed that "what is morally right is economically sound."[21]

Nowhere did the lesson of Little Rock appear to have been learned more readily than in Atlanta. In fact, the lesson appeared to have been anticipated by Mayor William B. Hartsfield, who helped engineer peaceful desegregation of the city's golf courses in 1955 and masterminded the relatively uneventful transition to token school desegregation in 1961 that bolstered Atlanta's reputation as the "City Too Busy to Hate." The Atlanta business and financial community likewise played a key role in keeping the state's public schools and its state university open in the face of the integration threat. Chaired by Atlanta banker John A. Sibley, the General Assembly Committee on Schools took testimony and received petitions across the state before recommending, in apparent defiance of majority white sentiment in the state, that local communities be given the option of deciding whether their schools should be closed rather than integrated. Atlanta business interests also exerted crucial influence on Gov. Ernest Vandiver, who chose to back away from his vow that "No Not One!" black would attend schools with whites while he was governor, the result being that not one but two black students enrolled at the University of Georgia in 1961. The long arm of Atlanta also reached into the courts in support of the litigation that overturned Georgia's outrageously antiurban county-unit system, paving the way for the election of Carl E. Sanders, a development-oriented self-described "segregationist but not a damn fool," over former Governor Marvin "If You Ain't for Stealin', You Ain't for Segregation" Griffin, who had threatened to put Martin Luther King "so far back in the jail you will have to pipe air back to him."[22]

The lesson of Little Rock was more persuasive in some economic and sociopolitical contexts than others, however. After his defiant "segregation forever" inaugural speech in 1963, Alabama Gov. George Wallace received a letter from industrial location specialist Henry C. Goodrich, who was also the vice president of the Birmingham Rotary Club. Goodrich assured Wallace of his own segregationist sentiments but warned that Wallace's extremist position would lead to "economic disaster." In response, Wallace coolly reminded Goodrich of the need to maintain constitutional government and state sovereignty lest the United States degenerate into "a complete welfare state" with "Washington taking care of all of us." Wallace assured Goodrich that indications he had received from around the state and nation suggested that there would be "no major problem in bringing industry into Alabama."[23]

It would be difficult to imagine the governor of Georgia delivering such a rebuff to Goodrich's counterpart in Atlanta. Yet, with its politics dominated by the ultra-conservative Big Mules and its economy still in the grip of the steel industry, a static Birmingham was not a dynamic Atlanta. The president of the Birmingham Chamber of Commerce had assured Wallace that he was "unalterably opposed" to desegregation, and another supporter hoped that a means could be found to "stop these Yankee corporations from putting pressure on these third-rate Babbitts in these Chambers of Commerce to surrender to these Negroes!" Alabama Development Commission files indicate that a number of northern corporate leaders were reluctant to have their meetings with Wallace publicized, but Wallace remained a tireless and surprisingly effective industrial recruiter. He was particularly proud of his achievement in getting Hammermill Paper to announce plans to locate in Selma even as that city was providing some of the most striking examples of police abuse of demonstrators that occurred during the entire civil rights movement. Hammermill officials seemed undisturbed not only by this shocking display but by the disparity between a fifty/fifty black-white population mix and a 99 percent white to 1 percent black voter registration profile. Hammermill caught considerable flak for its decision, but the company's primary considerations were purely economic: cheap labor, cheap land, cheap water, a 50 percent property tax deduction, speedy approval of waste disposal plans, and the Wallace administration's pledge to begin the immediate construction of a new bridge to handle the expanded traffic flow created by the new plant.[24]

The foregoing contrasts between a setting in which state and local leaders appeared to learn the lesson of Little Rock and one in which they did not suggests a discernible if not entirely definitive pattern. In general, those states and communities with avowedly prodevelopment political and economic leaders and with relatively or potentially dynamic economies already in place appeared receptive to learning from Little Rock's misfortunes, while those with more status-quo-oriented leadership and less dynamic economies were less responsive. The former category included not only Atlanta but also Charlotte and Dallas, while the latter included not only Birmingham and Alabama at large, but also Oxford, Jackson, and Mississippi at large, as well as New Orleans, where the mob scenes accompanying school desegregation made even Little Rock appear to be a citadel of toleration and civility.

Our presumption to this point has been that learning the lesson of Little Rock was decidedly beneficial not only to public order but also to the state and local economy. In fact, however, aggregate job-growth rankings show that, while Arkansas fell rapidly after the Little Rock crisis and Mississippi remained at the bottom throughout the 1950s and 1960s, Alabama's standing remained relatively constant over the entire period, the antics of Governor Wallace, Bull Conner, and the bombers in Birmingham notwithstanding. Among the relatively more moderate states, Georgia made more rapid gains after 1960, but Texas, North Carolina, and Tennessee remained near the top both before and after the civil rights movement.[25]

In many cases, industrialists expressed more reluctance to locate in racially troubled areas than they in fact demonstrated, primarily because the prevailing climate of opinion demanded such statements lest adverse publicity or even boycotts or protests ensue. In a poll of manufacturers locating in Tennessee in the 1960s, only 4 of 308 respondents even claimed to have given any consideration to the community's actual progress toward racial adjustment as they made their location decisions. In fact, it was difficult to dispute Winthrop Rockefeller's assertion that "the industrial prospect doesn't give a hoot whether your schools are segregated or not, but he wants no part of disorder or violence." Many industrial development leaders apparently felt the same way. As Harry Ashmore explained, "It is not that the bustling gentlemen at the local Chambers of Commerce or the state Industrial Development Commissions are particularly concerned with race as a moral problem; on the contrary, they, like most of their fellow southerners, wish the matter of integration would quietly go away.... But they also recognize that sustained racial disorder would be fatal to their effort to lure new industries and new capital from the non-South, and that the existing level of tension isn't doing their handsomely mounted promotional campaigns any good."[26]

In many cases, developers worried less about the impact of violence on its victims than its effects on the community's image. In the aftermath of the seventeenth church bombing in the previous five years, a Birmingham Chamber of Commerce official complained in 1963: "Let a car load of riffraff throw a stick of dynamite and—boom—we're set back another five years." Perhaps with tongue in cheek, Ashmore quoted a booster who lamented, "One lynching and we've wasted two hundred thousand dollars in magazine advertising."[27]

Many development leaders showed less concern about addressing their community's problems than silencing those who were calling attention to these problems. Across the South, developers repeatedly warned civil rights demonstrators that their actions were likely to undercut efforts to promote economic growth. An angry Birmingham leader insisted in the wake of the violence and bloodshed of 1963 that "We're going to be all right if we can just get Martin Luther King, Governor Wallace and President Kennedy out of here and keep them out."[28]

An ardent proponent of industrial development, Tupelo, Mississippi, editor George McLean sized up the Ole Miss crisis in 1962 and warned that "if Gov. Barnett closes our schools, we no longer will be able to develop or attract new payrolls even if we slash the income tax on industry to zero and offer a cash subsidy to any firm which will come to our state." The real problem, McLean believed, was Barnett, who seemed to be intent on shoving the Magnolia State "into the national spotlight" and positioning himself "as a hero for saving the state from integration." McLean contrasted Barnett's bumpkinesque mishandling of the Meredith crisis with the skillful, praiseworthy manner in which Barnett's predecessor, J. P. Coleman, had quietly blocked two previous integration attempts at Mississippi colleges. In these cases, one would-be breaker of the color barrier wound up in a mental institution and for the other the final destination was the state penitentiary at Parchman.[29]

Elsewhere, in Augusta, Georgia, economic development leaders supported desegregation of lunch counters and theaters in order to stave off demonstrations during the Master's Golf Tournament in 1962. White leaders did little to promote racial harmony thereafter, however, and actively resisted the election of black officials. In the absence of continuing protests by blacks, racial tension simmered throughout the 1960s only to erupt in a bloody and destructive 1970 riot that left six blacks dead and injured a number of Augustans of both races.[30]

As the Augusta case illustrates, in communities where developers took an active role in facilitating desegregation, once the protests were over, there was often little in the way of the "follow through" needed to sustain further progress toward full-scale desegregation, equality of economic opportunity or many of the other goals that black activists sought. Black leaders consistently charged industrialists with "redlining" areas with large concentrations of blacks in the population. A 1985 survey showed that manufacturing employment grew twice as fast between 1977 and 1982 in counties where the population was less than 25 percent black as in those where it was more than 50 percent. This pattern reflected considerations other than race, such as educational and skill levels and the relative remoteness of most southern black belt locations. It also revealed, however, a concern about political stability in areas where black voter areas were often neutralized by representatives of less disadvantaged areas who usually succeeded in getting these provisions extended to their districts as well.[31]

It is difficult to summarize a century's worth of interaction between race and economic change in the South without repeated reliance on the word *stability*. The South's institutionalized system of segregation emerged concurrently with the New South move to industrialize the region. Segregation and disfranchisement promised the racial and political stability northern investors presumably sought. Rather than a stopgap measure, however, the institutionalized Jim Crow system quickly became a deeply ingrained tradition which survived for well over half a century and in fact became the fundamental and defining reality of southern life. The economic, demographic, and political changes wrought by the Depression, New Deal, and World War II seemed to pose a threat to the South's racial system, but it was not until aggressive legal activism and civil disobedience threatened to destabilize southern states and communities and derail an increasingly aggressive industrial development effort that southern white economic leaders began to rethink their commitment to segregation. The willingness of these leaders to counsel moderation was in direct proportion to their dedication to economic development and to the relative success they had already enjoyed in recruiting newer, more dynamic industries to their states and communities. Put another way, the cutting edge of acquiescence to desegregation fell at or near the cutting edge of economic advance.

Expectations that ongoing or accelerating economic expansion would push or pull racial progress along with it were only partially realized at best, however, for as soon as the potential for racial upheaval or conflict was diminished, development leaders frequently retreated to their traditional advocacy of the fiscally, socially, and politically conservative "good business climate" they believed essential to continued growth. In the 1990s, no less than the 1890s, racial stability was thought to be implicit in a good business climate, but the other elements of this climate—low taxes; low wages; low levels of union membership; low expenditures on public health, welfare, and human uplift—were largely antithetical to the interests and goals of working-class blacks seeking to claim a greater share of so-called Sunbelt prosperity. Although white business and development leaders were willing to support improvements in infrastructure deemed conducive to economic growth, as political scientists Earl and Merle Black pointed out, "in its emphasis on low rates of taxation, minimal regulation of business and reso-lute opposition to unions and redistributive welfare programs for have-nots and have-littles, the current political ideology retains important continu-ities with the traditionalistic political culture."[32]

Clearly, the campaign for industrial development played a significant role in facilitating the transition to desegregated schools and public facili-ties in the South. The desire for new industries afforded southern white leaders a vital escape route by which they could retreat from their uncom-promising defense of segregation. If many of those white leaders who took this route seemed less motivated by moral or social goals than economic ones, the states and communities where such leaders prevailed nonetheless fared considerably better in their initial integration experiences than those where they did not.

On the other hand, it is also evident that the catalyst for business and development leaders taking action was not so much the incompatibility of segregation with industrial development as the threat to community sta-bility and corporate images posed by demonstrations and confrontations over segregation. Well before the civil rights movement, generations of well-intentioned liberal observers had insisted that the South's racial prob-lems would be greatly ameliorated by economic development. Indeed, the belief in the social as well as economic benefits of capitalist expansion reveals itself in numerous contemporary initiatives encouraging invest-ment in economically, socially, and politically backward areas within the United States and throughout the world. The continuing insistence on the reciprocal relationship between capitalism and democracy not-withstanding, case after case from South Carolina to South America to Southeast Asia has demonstrated that when forced to choose, investors are likely to opt for stability over democracy. As Lawrence Goodwyn noted, "the popular aspirations of the people of the 'third world' in the twentieth century have easily become as threatening to modern Americans as the revolt of their own farmers was to gold bugs eighty years ago.... American foreign policy and American weapons have defended anachronistic feudal and military hierarchies in South America, Africa, and Asia, such actions being justified at home as necessary to the defense of 'democracy.'"[33]

As the twentieth century draws to a close, the South's economic leaders continue to exert a significant influence for stability. In South Carolina, agitation over the practice of flying the Confederate flag over the state-house seemed to reinforce the negative perceptions spawned by a raft of church burnings and other ugly racial incidents. Fearing that these developments might derail the state's highly effective industrial recruitment effort, development leaders stood squarely behind Gov. David Beasley's call for removing the flag.[34]

This example reminds us that the propensity of business and development leaders to seek stability can, in fact, have positive consequences, but the history of the interaction between race and economic modernization in the postbellum South likewise reveals that whether this propensity is positive or negative often depends on whether advocacy of change or support for the status quo seems to provide the best route to stability. Seen against the backdrop of what came before and what came after, the lesson of Little Rock might well be expanded to suggest that while racial conflict may be incompatible with economic progress, economic progress cannot guarantee racial progress unless those who seek a developed economy are equally committed to a developed society as well.

The Constitutional Lessons of the Little Rock Crisis

KERMIT L. HALL

oday we have the somewhat ironic task of gathering to commemorate the fortieth anniversary of the Little Rock crisis at the same
time that Proposition 209 becomes law in California. That constitutional initiative, known as the California Civil Rights Initiative (CCRI),
mandates an end to state-sponsored affirmative action in California and,
by example, in the nation as a whole. Its advocates assert that true equality
can only exist when there are no preferences granted based on race.[1] No
matter where one stands on the CCRI, its existence as part of the living
law of California underscores the enduring importance of constitutional
lessons of the Little Rock crisis, now some four decades in our past.[2] Those
lessons involve the most critical matters of American constitutional practice: federalism, separation of powers, equal protection of the laws, and,
perhaps most importantly, the role of the Constitution, courts, and judges
in both responding to and shaping legally binding social transformation.
Taken in parts and as a whole, the constitutional story of the Little Rock
crisis reminds us how much our constitutional world stays the same even
as it changes.

The attempt to integrate Little Rock's Central High School in 1957
generated a major constitutional confrontation that eventually made its
way to the Supreme Court. Today, accepted wisdom holds that the justices
are sovereign in their power to interpret the Constitution conclusively.[3]
The disputed CCRI, however, reminds us of the boldness of this assertion
of federal judicial supremacy. The U.S. Supreme Court in this instance
bowed before the majority of California voters, and on November 4, 1997,
removed the last significant hurdle to the state's ban on affirmative action

when it rejected a constitutional challenge by civil rights groups.[4] The justices refused to rule on the merits of the case and, instead, left standing without comment a ruling by the Ninth Circuit Court of Appeals that found the CCRI constitutional. Once again the Court demonstrated, as it had done in the now famous *Bakke* decision of 1978, an unwillingness to link racial preferences with equality.[5]

Forty years ago the authority of the Court to engage issues of race and equality was, if anything, even less certain than today. The American Bar Association at its 1957 meeting had openly snubbed Chief Justice Earl Warren because of his role in *Brown v. Board of Education*.[6] During the previous year, southern members of Congress published their Southern Manifesto denouncing the Court and, with the assistance of conservative northerners, urging a constitutional amendment to limit its jurisdiction.[7] As a matter of political reality, if not always constitutional understanding, the justices' claims to expansive powers of judicial review drew an even more hostile response than they do today. When approached in this way, the Little Rock crisis was notable for the important contribution that it made to the incremental growth of federal judicial authority. Much of the controversy over the Court stemmed from its two *Brown* decisions. In *Brown I* the justices unanimously invalidated racial segregation in public schools and discarded the separate-but-equal doctrine of *Plessy v. Ferguson* (1896).[8] In holding that in the field of public education "separate" could never be "equal," the Court revised the accepted understanding of the equal protection clause of the Fourteenth Amendment and asserted its authority to ignore a long-standing precedent with important social implications, especially in the South.[9] The following year, the justices announced in *Brown II* an ambiguous enforcement standard that required an end to desegregation with "all deliberate speed."[10]

Unanimity among the justices in *Brown* was purchased at the price of uncertainty about the scope of the Court's powers to mandate such profound social change. The issue was not just whether the Court should proceed but how it should do so. While the justices did not doubt their authority to rule on constitutional rights, the scope of their rulings raised a significant issue of separation of powers, since if they strayed too far into the realm of social engineering they ran the risk of usurping powers constitutionally assigned to the legislative and executive branches.[11]

Prior to the *Brown* decisions, the Court had normally addressed constitutional rights as "present and personal."[12] This term meant that a litigant who established a constitutional injury could get a remedy, including an injunction. During the late 1940s and early 1950s the Court had relied on this approach in dealing with segregation in higher education, but as *Brown* made clear the justices were reluctant to do so with primary and secondary education. They became preoccupied in settling *Brown* with the concept of gradualism, especially since the lawyers for the NAACP, notably Thurgood Marshall, insisted that the "present and personal" standard should apply to schools as it had to universities.[13]

A majority of the Court in *Brown* refused to accept such a standard. Justice Felix Frankfurter especially complained that strict adherence to the standard would generate social unrest in the South and put the Court in the uncomfortable position of making rather than deciding law. Frankfurter also insisted that neither the White House nor the Congress supported so bold a stroke as immediate desegregation.[14] Justices Hugo Black and William O. Douglas, however, believed that immediate action was both constitutionally appropriate and politically sound. Immediate implementation would emphasize the Court's unwillingness to compromise on principle while stiffening the resolve of moderate elements in the South to support change. They did recognize that even if the Court issued an opinion calling for immediate desegregation, none was likely to be forthcoming. Yet they also calculated that for moderates a direct statement would affirm that they enjoyed the support of the highest federal court, one that would encourage the executive and legislative branches to uphold the new constitutional standards of equal protection.[15]

Frankfurter's view, of course, prevailed. In the end, what he had to contribute to the debate was the concept of gradualism, a concept rooted less in social policy than in a view of separation of powers that assigned law making to the political branches and constitutional interpretation to the courts. Frankfurter believed that judicial review was such a powerful instrument that it had to be applied on a limited basis in order for the Court to retain its legitimacy.[16] The concept of "all deliberate speed" in *Brown II* effectively separated the practice of treating constitutional rights as requiring "present and personal action" from the immediate need to help people the law was supposed to help. It also put the Court in the position of proclaiming rights but doing so without much vindication, or at least with vindication so far removed into the future that it no longer had the urgency required to support those rights effectively.[17]

President Dwight Eisenhower and his Department of Justice were also implicated in these separation of powers questions. Ike criticized the Court's invocation of judicial review and condemned what he believed was needless meddling by the justices in social policy. The president thought the *Brown* decisions a mistake, but he and his Department of Justice were thankful for the time that the "all deliberate speed" wording promised.[18] While revisionist scholarship has attempted to portray Eisenhower as aggressive on civil rights, the evidence to support that position remains problematic, especially when measured by moderates or civil rights leaders in the South.[19]

President Eisenhower believed in the rule of law and the necessity of obeying the Supreme Court, but his public and private pronouncements indicated that he believed he had a duty to check judicial excesses. For example, Eisenhower viewed the judicial appointment process as one way of prospectively controlling the bench, although his selections of Earl Warren and William J. Brennan Jr. remind us of how little success he ultimately had in attempting to do so.[20] Moreover, when Eisenhower did address the connection between law and civil rights, he invariably did so in the narrowest possible terms, advocating slowness to the point of glacial movement and urging the judiciary to go neither further nor faster than social realities permitted.[21]

Eisenhower's approach to issues of separation of powers, just as was true of the Court's, also had important social and political implications. Thus, any person who pressed a southern school board or a county commission for greater action, no matter how limited, quickly found him- or herself framed as an extremist on the race issue by segregationists and with little countervailing pressure from the White House.[22] When Gov. Orval E. Faubus and other segregationists suggested that southerners could decide through their elected representatives whether they wanted Arkansas to obey the federal Constitution, they effectively cut the democratic ground out from under moderate proponents of desegregation. For example, it was politically unrealistic to expect a southern school board member to take a more advanced position on school integration than the president of the United States. Hence, Ike's failure to support the Court played directly into the hands of segregationists.[23] The separation of powers issues, therefore, were not just about whether the Court alone could interpret the Constitution conclusively, but whether the president could modulate the Court's decisions in keeping with his understanding of political reality.

Eisenhower argued that the essential issue in Little Rock was law versus lawlessness, not one of segregation versus desegregation. Yet that position created severe problems for the budding black civil rights movement and for white moderates. Maintaining ordered liberty was critical to the

moderates and to Eisenhower, but the latter essentially abandoned the former by ordering his Department of Justice not to aid those occupying the
critical center in moving the national agenda forward on the race issue.
Instead, Eisenhower adopted the view that *Brown* had to be implemented
at the local level and along lines that would permit a gradual change in
peoples' views. Desegregation could not be forced because doing so would
only foster resistance and rob the federal system of its mainspring of local
action and majoritarian democracy. Such an approach nonetheless left
southern white moderates feeling betrayed by the president, since he alone
was the one national figure capable of challenging the credibility of the
segregationists.[24]

 Ike's view of the separation of powers issues also played directly into
the hands of segregationist lawyers, whose goal was not so much to get
Brown overturned as to convince the nation that desegregation, like the
prohibition of liquor during the 1920s, was a bad policy because it was
unenforceable. The goal of desegregation rested on the faulty assumption
that social change flowed from rather than preceded legal change. Even
when urgent requests came from places such as Nashville and New Orleans
for federal assistance, Ike's Department of Justice faltered.[25]

 It was in this conflicted environment of separation of powers that the
Little Rock School Board planned for desegregation. Superintendent
Virgil Blossom's scheme was nothing if not deliberate in its speed, providing for integration over a period of some six years.[26] The constitutional
oversight of that plan fell to the lower federal courts in Arkansas, as it did
in the rest of the nation. Even here the separation of powers' issue appeared,
although in a less obvious way.

 A considerable body of scholarship credits the heroic actions of lower
federal court judges in implementing *Brown* in the South.[27] While certainly appropriate, there is reason to ask whether this particular glass, at
least at the time of the Little Rock crisis, was half full or half empty. A
minority of southern federal judges in 1956 were segregationists. Judge
William H. Atwell of Dallas, for example, twice defied the Supreme Court's
rulings. When asked to comment on events in Little Rock, Judge Atwell
eagerly told the *Dallas Morning News* that "the real law of the land is the
same today as it was before May 16, 1954 [the date of the *Brown* deci-
sion]."[28] He even went on to give his opinion, before the issue ever
reached the Supreme Court, that President Eisenhower lacked the constitutional authority to use troops to enforce federal court orders arising
under *Brown*.

While most southern federal court judges were not as openly hostile as Atwell, as a group they had a mixed view of the constitutional wisdom of *Brown*, both as a matter of social policy and of constitutional law. Many were social and political moderates, which meant that they did not treat segregation as a sacred principle and they did subscribe to the belief that their oath of office required them to uphold the federal Constitution.[29] There is also no doubt that these judges often pressed the constitutional cause for desegregation with courage and personal sacrifice. For example, once the litigation to desegregate the New Orleans schools began, Judge J. Skelly Wright observed: "I don't see a lot of people anymore."[30] To these judges fell the real task of breathing life into "all deliberate speed"; to these same judges the political moderates in Little Rock and elsewhere turned for support in easing the demands for faster-paced desegregation pushed by the NAACP. In the case of Little Rock, however, a visiting federal judge, Ronald N. Davies from North Dakota, not Arkansas, granted the injunction against Governor Faubus that forced the withdrawal of the National Guard from around Central High School.[31]

Considerable tension existed within the federal judiciary over the implementation of *Brown* and the definition in action of "all deliberate speed." While bound to uphold the law, these lower federal judges also realized, as did Judge Davies, that the close assistance of the Department of Justice and the FBI was crucial.[32] What was most important, however, was that at the outbreak of the Little Rock crisis there was uncertainty about the breadth of judicial power and corresponding questions about the willingness of the executive branch and Congress to implement desegregation.

The separation of powers issues were ultimately framed against Frankfurter's standard of "all deliberate speed." The White House eluded much of its responsibility to overcome entrenched local majorities; the NAACP and white moderates suffered from the federal government's unwillingness to vindicate civil rights fully; and segregationists calculated that through massive resistance they could prevent a divided federal government from implementing the "present and personal" remedies associated with previous civil rights litigation.[33] As a result, in Little Rock the words "all deliberate speed" produced resistance to *Brown I* far greater than the Court had anticipated. Conflicts over separation of powers complemented constitutional ambiguities over the distribution of powers in the federal system. Gov. Orval Faubus and his segregationist allies insisted that based on principles of local control and majoritarian democracy southerners could decide for themselves whether they wanted to obey the Constitution.[34] No matter one's estimation of Faubus, he could plausibly conclude, given how the separation of powers issues divided the president and the Court, Ike would not act to prevent him from keeping black students from attending Central High. Such thinking took a particularly heavy toll on moderates, since they kept telling the public that change was inevitable and that desegregation would come. When an already divided federal government let Faubus's initial defiance go unchallenged, segregationists drew the predictable conclusion that they had everything to gain by resisting rather than cooperating.[35]

Governor Faubus, of course, sought to confront federal judicial power directly, taking the seemingly extreme step of calling out the Arkansas National Guard to prevent the entry of the Little Rock Nine into Central High School. Faubus based his actions on a wildly overstated threat of violence that he hoped would shift decision making away from himself and back to Eisenhower and the courts. Given the political calculus of Arkansas, Faubus wanted to prevent the segregation issue from swallowing up his populist reform agenda of better schools and better state services. To that extent, his behavior can be understood as posturing of the worst kind, since the governor knew that should he lend his leadership to the desegregation effort it stood a far better chance of succeeding.[36] There was, of course, no political incentive for Faubus to do so based on the actions of the federal government.

Faubus's claims also rested on his vision of majoritarian democracy and local control, themes that Eisenhower himself often sounded. Faubus quite properly claimed that a majority of the population of Arkansas and Little Rock had voted in 1956 to clothe the governor and the state courts with additional powers to resist *Brown*. When Faubus used the Arkansas National Guard, moreover, he did so based on a constitutional claim that as governor he was sworn to maintain not only order but to enforce the Arkansas Constitution and laws.[37] As Faubus explained in 1957, the crisis was "a classic confrontation between a state's right to govern and federal power, . . . a great constitutional question in which the actions of the national government were regarded by millions of citizens as another illegal encroachment of federal power into a field of state government."[38]

The NAACP subsequently brought suit claiming that Faubus's powers were constrained by the federal Constitution and courts. The result was the case of *Cooper v. Aaron*, the first significant legal test of the enforcement of *Brown*, a fact often missed in the discussion of the Little Rock crisis.[39] The facts in *Cooper* merged the issues of federalism and separation of powers together and asked the justices to reconcile them in a way that had not been done in the *Brown* decisions. In this instance, with the specter of Governor Faubus's use of the National Guard before them, the theoretical question of what would be required to implement desegregation was evident: a lot more than the Court had anticipated when it adopted "all deliberate speed" three years earlier.

Cooper posed two important issues of federalism. First, was it possible for a locality to postpone on a good-faith basis a desegregation program that threatened to produce racial unrest and that lacked majority support? Second, could the governor and the legislature of a state ignore the decisions of the Supreme Court of the United States and of the lower federal courts as well?[40]

The Court addressed these issues with greater clarity than it had ever done before. All nine members of the Court signed the opinion written by Chief Justice Warren. They held, first, that even postponing plans for desegregation in good faith and in the interest of preserving public peace violated black students' rights under the Fourteenth Amendment's equal protection clause. There could be no delay; "all deliberate speed" meant action not evasion.[41]

Second, governors and state legislatures were bound under the supremacy clause of the Constitution to uphold decisions of the Supreme Court just as they were bound by oath to uphold the Constitution itself. What the Court said the Constitution meant, therefore, was not subject to second-guessing by the states, no matter that the voting majority in a state bitterly opposed the Court's decision. The federal rule of law required, if nothing else, that majority will had to yield before the constitutional pronouncements of the justices. In essence, the justices concluded, the states could not make war on the federal government by refusing to enforce the decisions of that government's ultimate constitutional interpreter—the Supreme Court.[42]

Today, we tend to view with contempt those who made the arguments in opposition to these principles, such as Faubus and Governors George C. Wallace and John Patterson of Alabama, and Gov. Ross Barnett of Mississippi. Nevertheless, we can learn something from them about the persistence of constitutional values still very much alive, most notably in California.

A quarter century after *Cooper*, Orval Faubus explained his actions. Like Wallace, Patterson, and Barnett, Faubus wanted to reconstruct his reputation after the tides of history had rolled over him. Faubus insisted that he was only trying to preserve peace by turning the nine black students away from Central High School. Far from being an instigator, he argued, his role was actually one of peacemaker, a role that the national government denied him despite the fact the powers that provide for the health, safety, morals, and welfare of the public had historically vested in the state rather than national government. "There are some that still want to classify me," he observed, "as a prejudiced bigot. But that is the time-honored tradition of fighting unfairly."[43] Faubus claimed that he alone stood for constitutional order.[44]

Faubus cannot (and should not) escape accountability for his earlier choices. His actions appropriately made his name a byword for racism around the world. Still, even if admitting that Faubus was the embodiment of race baiting and political expediency, there are two parts of his conduct in the Little Rock crisis that require our attention. First, Faubus attributed the crisis to the city's moderates and to President Eisenhower.[45] According to Faubus, prominent Little Rock moderates had hypocritically trumpeted the school board's desegregation plan as a model for the South while moving their own children out of the city's public schools. Had they been more circumspect in their claims and noble in their actions, Faubus insisted, the nation never would have become interested in events in Little Rock. Faubus complained that the moderates had misrepresented the majority of the city and stood in direct opposition to the wishes of the people of the state. "You have," he explained in 1981, "to take into consideration what the feelings of the people were at the time, what beliefs were at the time. Because you don't deal with situations the way you like them to be; you deal with them the way they are."[46] Faubus asserted that he had no other choice as governor than to follow the constitutional mandate of his office to uphold the Arkansas Constitution and its laws, including four recently passed anti-integration laws approved by a majority of voters a year before.

Faubus also portrayed himself as the victim in what was supposed to be a federal system of distributed powers. From his perspective, the federal system ran from the bottom up and not the top down. If the officials of the national government, most notably Eisenhower and the Department of Justice, had been willing to enforce the ensuing federal court order that integration must proceed, then Faubus argued he would never have had to act as he did. What the federal government wanted, he complained, was a constitutional scheme in which it could dictate to the states but shirk responsibility for implementing its decisions and ignore the wishes of the majority of their citizens.[47] Today, similar arguments are echoed in the debate over the CCRI. "They knew it was going to be unpopular," he explained, "and they knew it was going to be difficult, and federal agents would have been the ones that were the object of invective and scorn. They were a bunch of hypocritical cowards, is what it boiled down to."

What troubled Faubus most was that federal officials "sat back with their idle hands" and called upon the governors and judges of the states of the South to go against their own people and their own constitutions.[48] They effectively stripped them of their sovereign authority and then expected that they would comply with the dictates of the Supreme Court. "I was asked," Faubus concluded, "to go against...[our] own laws and the sentiment of [our] own people to enforce a court order most people thought was unconstitutional anyway and illegal."[49] The rule of law, for Faubus, meant adherence to the wishes of the people that elected him and the legislature with which he shared power and whose laws he was bound to enforce. Faubus, then, connected his concerns about moderates with a disdain of the Eisenhower administration and utter contempt for the justices on the Supreme Court, who usurped the peoples' power in order to satisfy their own social agendas.[50]

As a constitutional matter, Faubus, as did many other contemporary southern demagogues on the race issue, treated the concepts of state sovereignty and states' rights as if they were interchangeable terms. They were not. As the historian Arthur Bestor Jr. has argued, the Little Rock crisis involved tensions present in the American constitutional system over the doctrines of state sovereignty, states' rights, and national power since the nation's founding. State sovereignty was a doctrine of power; states' rights, on the other hand, was a doctrine of right. While Faubus often used the latter, he invariably meant the former.[51]

The generally accepted wisdom of our constitutional history holds that the Civil War by force of arms and then the Thirteenth, Fourteenth, and Fifteenth amendments by constitutional fiat extinguished the doctrine of state sovereignty.[52] Yet nothing could be further from the truth, as both the words and actions of Faubus, his fellow southern governors and legislators in the 1950s and 1960s, and the supporters of the CCRI today make clear. The constitutional arguments in favor of the CCRI relied heavily on the belief that the majority of voters in a state acting independently of the national government can resist its mandates.[53] The notion that the doctrine of state sovereignty perished after the Civil War tells us more about what happens when winners write the history than it does about the constitutional contingencies that emerged in the century following the Civil War. No group, moreover, better appreciated this reality than the NAACP's Legal Defense Fund as it sought to redraw the nation's constitutional map of race relations by diminishing the police powers of the states as a way of providing national protection for minority rights against entrenched local majorities.[54]

As a constitutional matter, therefore, the Little Rock crisis cannot be dismissed solely as a resort by ardent segregationists, such as Faubus, to a discredited constitutional theory. That theory was alive, if in eclipse, then, while it shows signs of revival today. Faubus's position was real and legitimate, so much so that the Supreme Court in *Cooper* felt compelled to reject it vigorously, a sure indication of its vitality. In that vein, *Cooper* is best understood as the justices' fullest statement in favor of the doctrine of national power and the mutually supporting concept of federal judicial review while at the same time rejecting the notion of state sovereignty. Yet as the CCRI reminds us, a substantial constitutional claim based on principles of state-based majoritarian democracy can still be raised by the states against the federal government.

The Eisenhower administration on political grounds was also eager to maintain more than just a semblance of local control and autonomy over race matters. For example, as Tony Freyer so ably demonstrated, in September 1957 the Department of Justice engaged in secret talks designed to persuade the NAACP to withdraw its suit on behalf of the nine students.[55] The Court, of course, knew nothing of this maneuvering, and in this context the language used in *Cooper* was a bolder affirmation of the national government's authority in the federal system than the executive branch contemplated. As important, the justices also affirmed once again their power to interpret the Constitution and to do so in a way that bound the other branches and state officials. The breadth of the Court's holding and the fact that it was signed by all nine of the justices reminded not just Governor Faubus and southern segregationists of its powers but the executive branch of its constitutional obligations.[56] The high court decision also gave the NAACP the signal it required to move litigation forward knowing that all of the attempts by the states to invoke interposition and with it massive resistance would likely fail as a matter of constitutional law. The issue then became whether the legal mandate could be turned into meaningful political action; whether the executive branch and the Department of Justice would fulfill their responsibilities to implement desegregation in the federal system.[57]

In retrospect, of course, we now understand how the Court's bold pronouncements on federal powers and judicial sovereignty—on federalism and separation of powers—were as much rhetorical as real. *Cooper* put the weight of the federal government clearly on the side of desegregation. That development was perhaps more important in providing constitutional cover for the subsequent sit-in and nonviolent civil rights movement of Martin Luther King Jr. than it was in bringing the power of the national government to bear in support of racial equality.[58]

Cooper and the Little Rock crisis also amplified the scope of equal protection of the laws under the Fourteenth Amendment. The social and political implications of both *Brown* decisions were truly significant. Yet as statements of social policy and intended governmental purpose, they were, as matters of constitutional law, moderate in the claims they made about the scope of the federal government's powers to require the states to promote equality. Equality before the law, according to *Brown*, was to be gradually realized through the oversight of lower federal court judges.[59] This vision of equal protection did have benefits for moderates in places like Little Rock, since gradualism seemed the best way of producing change without the embarrassment, economic costs, and resistance to civil authority associated with swifter and more decisive action. Some of the more extreme segregationist voices in the South inadvertently supported the logic of Justice Frankfurter's position by arguing that the gradualism of *Brown* would lead to greater racial equality. Mississippi Sen. James Eastland, for example, complained bitterly: "If the Southern states are picked off one by one under the damnable doctrine of gradualism I don't know if we can hold or not."[60]

The Little Rock crisis exploded most of those notions. What the Court acknowledged in *Cooper* was that the equal protection issue and its own powers could not be left ambiguous, as they had been in *Brown*. The *Brown* decisions, we should remember, were suffused with uncertainty over the constitutional responsibilities of the states to bring about equal protection of the laws.[61] One reading of the case could produce the view that, on balance, it required only that state and local governments not make decisions about school assignments based on race, an approach not altogether different from that associated with supporters of the CCRI. This view was, while not altogether supportive of the idea of state sovereignty, hardly fatal to it. Thurgood Marshall, the future Supreme Court justice and NAACP counsel, responded squarely when he was asked during the oral argument in *Brown I* about the purported problem of the differences in ability between African American and white children. "Simple," he said, "put the dumb Colored children in with the dumb White children, and put the smart Colored children with the smart White kids."[62] In this scenario, using test performance to assign students to schools would not violate the Constitution, even if the classrooms were not racially balanced. This constitutional vision of color-blind equal protection in *Brown* required only desegregation, not integration. Moderates could view this side of *Brown* as validating the idea of neighborhood schools in circumstances of residential segregation and a relatively limited expenditure of the judiciary's authority to bring about change without massive social reengineering.

There was a second vision of equal protection in *Brown*, however, one that held important ramifications for judicial review, federalism, and social change through law. This expansive approach was also one that Marshall suggested to the Court in the context of trying to understand the ways in which the success of "all deliberate speed" would be measured. It interpreted *Brown* to mean that students of different races would attend the same school, rather than simply adopting the position that future decisions about student placement would be free from any direct concern with race. This position placed far greater demands on existing theories of separation of powers, judicial review, and state sovereignty. It anticipated a more active role for the federal government in general and federal judges in particular. The Court was to measure success based not on whether race had entered into the decision about assigning students but whether, instead, the schools were truly integrated based on a national standard of performance directly linked to race. In short, this vision of equal protection asked the federal judiciary and the executive branch to become social engineers. The constitutional standards required to measure that success would be different, but so, too, the political will necessary in federal and state governments to realize such an ambitious mandate on a day-to-day basis. The debate, in essence, prefigured the present conflict over affirmative action.

This double understanding of equal protection framed the differing responses of southern politicians, business leaders, the NAACP, school board officials, and others to the two *Brown* decisions. Lower federal court judges in attempting to implement *Brown* immediately encountered a profound difference in upholding a law requiring an end to segregation while measuring success in doing so. The Court, of course, had apparently hoped that the "all deliberate speed" formulation would complement the practice of "personal and present" remedies. Such a strategy would provide time for adjustments to powerful social realities with minimal resistance and substantial accommodation. To that extent, the Little Rock crisis was a remarkable harbinger of the same issues of state versus national power that are shaping the debate over the CCRI and affirmative action generally.[63]

Yet the events in Little Rock hardly developed in a way anticipated by most of the parties caught up in the crisis. As Governor Faubus pointed out, moderates received surprisingly little support from the national government. As a result, what had begun in *Brown* as a scheme to integrate gradually the schools on a "present and personal" basis without regard to race became transformed in Little Rock into a contest over the scope of separation of powers, federalism, and federal judicial supremacy. The justices found that faced with outright military resistance from the state of Arkansas, its governor, legislature, and courts, they could only elevate their own powers by broadening the scope of the equal protection clause to make it fit more readily with Marshall's second, more aggressive position.[64] Neither members of Congress nor the Eisenhower administration approved of this part of *Cooper,* but it remains one of the most important constitutional results of the Little Rock crisis.

Justice Oliver Wendell Holmes Jr. in *Buck v. Bell* (1927), remarked that in the course of constitutional litigation the resort to an equal protection claim is the sign of a desperate cause.[65] Such was certainly the case given the legacy of *Plessy,* but such was much less the case following *Cooper,* which brought in its wake a quickened understanding that equality before the law with regard to race had to become a pillar of American constitutional liberty.

Because the lesson was taught in *Cooper,* it did not follow that it was immediately or completely learned. While the justices in *Cooper* affirmed the notion that measuring success by race was essential to meeting the goal of equal protection of the laws, they offered no guidance about what measures mattered or how the counting was to take place. In these circumstances, first segregationists and now opponents of affirmative action find in the twin concepts of state sovereignty and majority rule the bases to challenge the assumptions of *Cooper.* In *Cooper* the high court selected the more powerful of the two views of equal protection anticipated in *Brown.*[66] Since then the justices have extended equal protection in varying degrees to other groups, notably women, the aged, the handicapped, and the gay.[67] Yet the federal judicial power and the concept of measurable impact on equality affirmed in *Cooper* have been invoked for surprisingly limited purposes, as the constitutional ambiguity associated with affirmative action reminds us.

As a result, the *Cooper* decision and more generally the Little Rock crisis worked a slower and smaller change in the social order of the South than might have otherwise been the case. Southern federal judges knew they had the power and support of the high court, but how they were to measure the transformation they were assigned was left entirely vague. As a result, when taken together, *Cooper* and the earlier *Brown* decisions altered in the South the meaning of constitutional moderation on the race issue. Indeed, in some ways no change was more important. Most white southerners in 1954 preferred segregation; but after *Brown* separate but equal was no longer a tenable moderate position, and after *Cooper* opposition to the federal courts was equally problematic and hopes of restoring separate but equal were also unrealistic.

New constitutional realities did produce new political and social realities. One of these was the opportunity for the civil rights movement to break local law while remaining legal within the larger federal constitutional system. Another was that the position of segregationists hardened and narrowed. To be a segregationist after *Brown* and *Cooper* was to oppose racial change no matter how limited or how gradual, no matter whether ordered by a judge or not. Compromise on the race issue dropped out of the segregationist lexicon entirely. The admission of African Americans to a white school was unacceptable—period. In Houston, Texas, for example, segregationists objected when the Houston School Board published its teacher directory without any designation of race. The following year the board reverted to its old practice of segregating the directory into "colored" and "white" sections.[68] Segregationists insisted on the one hand that law could never produce meaningful social change; on the other hand, they consistently worked to articulate a vision of law and society designed to preserve existing social arrangements. Segregationists did not deny the power of law, but they did dispute the idea that law could precede social change. It had, instead, to flow from it, and on the matter of race there was little chance that the majority of whites would ever embrace change.

Moderates, for their part, accepted that law could produce change, but that too much law could produce too much change. An order by a judge, whether state or federal, posed something of a dilemma for moderates. Judges were figures revered in southern society as the embodiment of the rule of law, and moderates were by and large committed to relying on the rule of law to curb traditional populist excesses.[69]

These differences inside the white community on the role of law were important because they rested on differing social bases for political action. The South as a whole and Arkansas in particular was not one place. They were instead many places, with competing social class and economic divisions. The sentiment for segregation had strong class tones and geographical roots, although in rural areas it also had a considerable following among the educated and the elite.[70] Governor Faubus certainly understood the class dynamics. He described his followers as "the good, honest, hardworking people of the lower and middle classes" while portraying white proponents of desegregation as "the high-collar city crowd," the "Cadillac brigade" of wealthy and prominent Little Rock leaders.[71] It largely held true for Little Rock, where recently arrived whites from the rural areas and the lower class sections of town opposed desegregation. Little Rock's leaders, on the other hand, prided themselves on building a model of progressive government that merged better public education and enhanced economic opportunities, including using a host of federal and state programs to attract new business to the state. Moderates composed, therefore, a critical part of the social, cultural, and economic leadership of Little Rock, one that subscribed to the theory that if the law were changed society would be served.[72]

Yet in the increasingly polarized politics of the South, one was a moderate because he or she was not something else. Unlike segregationists, moderates accepted some degree of school desegregation as the price for obeying the rule of law, maintaining the public schools, building the economy, and keeping anarchy at bay. The last essentially meant throttling the Klan and similar groups, such as the White Citizens' Councils. If there was a choice to be made between limited desegregation or no public schools, between peaceful desegregation and flouting the Supreme Court, then such was the case. In Little Rock, as elsewhere in the South, this position had sufficient backing to move the school districts from segregated to desegregated but not integrated. Moderates then were happy to adopt the race-blind view of *Brown* on equal protection issues, but they had far greater difficulty with the formulation of measurement and oversight by the federal judiciary promised in *Cooper*.[73] Such concerns, of course, have now spread from the South throughout the nation from the debate about desegregation to the quarrel over affirmative action.

Moderates, then, had little choice but to search for solutions that attenuated the boldness of the high court's ruling in *Cooper*. For example, some school leaders ignored *Cooper* and simply latched on to the first vision of *Brown* by developing elaborate schemes of student assignment in which race was not an explicit ground for making the decision. In the lexicon of affirmative action today, there were no quotas only opportunities.[74]

The Little Rock crisis affirmed the significance of the rule of law as a core principle for ending segregation and the broad power of the Supreme Court to interpret the meaning of the Constitution conclusively. Yet the Little Rock crisis also reminds us of the importance of separation of powers, the controversial character of judicial sovereignty, the resilience of the idea of state sovereignty, and the persistence of our disagreements over the relationship between law and social change and of the meaning of equality, on the one hand, and of equality of opportunity on the other. Events in Little Rock tested the principle of "all deliberate speed" and found it wanting. What the phrase implied was that relief could be delayed and might not ever come to individual litigants. It would never be "private and personal." As the Court saw the matter in *Cooper*, because the group to which the litigant belonged might never benefit from desegregation the historic constitutional restrictions on federal judicial power specifically and federal authority generally had to be reexamined. Recall that in the wake of Little Rock resistance actually grew, in part because the underlying issues were so acute and in part because the assertion of federal power in *Cooper* blasted the region's practice of associating white majority rule and state sovereignty. Tensions also grew because despite the invitation to action on the part of the executive branch that *Cooper* extended, the White House remained slow to respond, so much so that in many instances southern moderates found themselves isolated and unsupported in the national government.

The *Cooper* decision was an important weigh station on the road to what some have called the imperial judiciary, but it is perhaps even better understood as a singular moment in affirming the power of law to transform social evil. What the Court defended in *Cooper* was a process, albeit somewhat flawed in retrospect, by which the supremacy of federal law would permit local minorities to address through the federal judicial system social concerns beyond their reach. More than a decade passed before the justices made a genuinely bold enforcement move toward an integrationist model, finally doing so in *Green v. County School Board* (1968), which embraced busing as a tool to bring about integration.[75] At that juncture, the issue of school integration attained fully the character of public law litigation.

Public law litigation is an invitation to aggressive judicial intervention to right social conditions and repair constitutional wrongs beyond the compass of politics as usual. Some of the contemporary animus held toward the federal courts, toward court-supported affirmative action, and toward disbelief in the power of the federal law to solve social ills had its origins in the Little Rock crisis and the era of public law litigation that followed.

Finally, *Cooper* and *Brown*, taken together, transformed constitutional law by disconnecting the right that had been violated from the remedy to redress it. The *Cooper* Court interpreted *Brown* in such a way as to make it much more an instrument to accomplish socially valuable goals, not a commitment to the immediate vindication of present and personal rights, as was the case with the desegregation of higher education.[76] Not surprisingly the federal courts began to see themselves as managers of programs of social transformation rooted in a constitutional obligation to meet the terms of the *Brown* decisions.

Southern resistance had the ironic consequence of limiting the possibility that the moderate desegregation vision in *Brown* would prevail. First the Supreme Court and then the lower federal courts, backed by *Cooper*, shifted to the social engineering vision of *Brown* and with it a greatly enhanced role for the judiciary in modern American life. It was just such actions that restored energy to the idea of state sovereignty and prompted the CCRI. Equally ironic, the moderation that Frankfurter had preached in the use of constitutional power failed in Little Rock and that failure became, for the remainder of the civil rights movement, license from the federal courts for the activism that he and moderates feared. It also became clear, as the struggle over the CCRI reminds us, that even with forty years of constitutional and social change, the traditional notions of limited judicial power and national authority retain an impressive degree of vitality.

The Past As Future: The Little Rock Crisis and the Constitution

TONY A. FREYER

Constitutional values underlying public school desegregation operate in relation to popular opinion. A comprehensive report analyzing the Little Rock School District's (LRSD) troubled state as of 1997 prepared by a task force at the University of Arkansas at Little Rock (UALR) suggested this connection. *Plain Talk: The Future of Little Rock's Public Schools* demonstrated that in 1997 Little Rock community attitudes and claims of constitutional rights had meaning most visibly and immediately as ongoing federal court intervention and the controversial remedy of busing.[1] This report also suggested that these rights claims possessed a symbolic content that transcended the immediate agents of enforcement, a content that empowered groups and legitimated their values and interests.

The UALR task force report does not provide statistical data comparing Little Rock public opinion toward desegregation at either the enforcement or symbolic level in the 1950s and 1990s. Such a comparison would suggest, viewed from 1957, *whose* vision of desegregation had prevailed after forty years. This essay makes such a comparison: it argues that any remedy for the LRSD's current problems could benefit from understanding the extent to which a moderate constitutional vision of public school desegregation prevailed in the Little Rock crisis of 1957–59.[2]

The UALR task force report's survey data gave a clear picture of the city's public opinion in the mid-1990s. Among white households, 56 percent supported "sending my child to a racially integrated school"; African American households approved of that statement by a margin of 68 percent. But interracial popular approval of desegregation in principle disintegrated when considered in terms of particular outcomes. The only specific desegregation program a white majority supported was magnet schools, which 52 percent of whites attending *private schools* favored. African Americans, by contrast, were divided in their response to this question: Has desegregation had a positive, negative, or no effect on the quality of education in the LRSD? Thirty-three percent perceived a positive effect, 22 percent a negative effect, 24 percent no effect, and 22 percent were not sure. White opinion was more clear-cut: 18 percent replied that desegregation had a positive effect, 14 percent saw no effect, and 18 percent were undecided. The proportion of whites, however, who responded that the effect was negative was 50 percent. Regarding busing as a constitutionally sanctioned tool for bringing about compliance with federal court desegregation orders, the difference between each group's response was still more pronounced: 68 percent of white opinion stated that cross-town busing was not effective, while only 16 percent stated that it was effective. By contrast, 43 percent of African American households considered such a remedy effective. On questions that asked whites and African Americans whether creating *one-race* neighborhood elementary, junior high, and high schools was acceptable, whites approved of such an outcome by an average 72 percent; whereas African Americans disapproved of such a result by 39 percent and favored it by 40 percent.[3]

This divided public opinion reflected enormous challenges facing the LRSD. Intractable complexity arising from ongoing federal court intervention at all levels of the school system's administration delayed implementation of security measures needed to address discipline and safety concerns. State law that sanctioned an incongruity between the school district's boundary and the city's limits contributed to financial instability and potential bankruptcy. Ultimately, however, these issues were symptomatic of a fundamental reality: white flight. The task force report's quantitative and qualitative data showed that a return of between five and eight thousand white students to the city's public schools would alleviate the system's financial woes and likely bring unitary status, a level of racial integration permitting an end to federal judicial supervision. These changes in turn would invigorate administrative decision making and facilitate maintaining effective security measures.[4]

An inherently moderate desegregation policy nonetheless encouraged more problematic outcomes. The struggle for equal educational opportunity is rarely conceived of as a triumph of moderation. Yet if we think of moderation defined by the interplay of protest politics, constitutional symbolism, and judicial process we see that from the Little Rock crisis on, racism, persistent and damaging as it is, did not take, at least in public discourse, the blatant form espoused by the extreme segregationists of the past. Instead, public officials articulated a moderate discourse in which surrogate racial images equated constitutional rights claims with federal compulsion. Thus because successful defense of constitutional rights became synonymous with coercion, progress was limited and ambiguous, vulnerable to the social and economic forces identified with white flight. This victory of moderation was the enduring legacy of the Little Rock crisis and the Constitution.[5]

As it would be forty years later, Little Rock's public opinion in 1957 regarding school desegregation was divided. Concerning the issue as a matter of principle, of course, popular support for maintaining racially segregated public schools seemed overwhelming, with 85 percent favoring Jim Crow and only 15 percent against it. Nevertheless, several factors indicated that the popular consensus preferring segregation was ambiguous. Little Rock's most informed white and African American opinion leaders agreed that a majority of the city's whites opposed the most extreme segregationist views, which not only espoused violence to achieve their goals if absolutely necessary but also equated the Supreme Court's sanction of desegregation with the intention "to rule against states' rights to ban intermarriage of whites and non-whites."[6] Admittedly, at several different points prior to or during the crisis a majority of the city's voters endorsed an extreme segregationist program which, though rooted in racial feelings, was publicized in terms of a states' rights theory known as interposition. The program centered on passage of a constitutional amendment and state laws that would authorize local school districts to "assign" white and African American children to separate schools. But, if this effort failed, said one local segregationist leader, resistance must be carried "even to the point of destroying the public school system" by electing school board members who would "reduce the millage rates to nothing . . . [and thereby destroy the] public status of the schools, permitting the buildings to be rented, leased or sold to private corporations to operate [on a racially segregated basis]."[7]

Ultimately, however, Little Rock voters consistently rejected this extreme interposition program, favoring instead a moderate desegregation stance. After state and local majorities supported passage of interposition measures in a November 1956 election, a voter coalition of more affluent whites centered in Pulaski Heights and Little Rock's enfranchised African Americans narrowly elected in March 1957 moderate white school board members publicly committed to implementing the token desegregation program subsequently known as the Blossom Plan after school superintendent Virgil T. Blossom. Two years later, following the Supreme Court's decision of *Cooper v. Aaron* in September 1958, the same interracial coalition defeated the interposition program Faubus and extreme segregationists used to close the city's schools and "purge" school teachers and officials.

Adolphine Fletcher Terry and the Women's Emergency Committee, in conjunction with a campaign pushed by the Little Rock Chamber of Commerce, rallied moderate voters to win a special recall election on May 25, 1959, ending de facto segregationist control of the school board. The moderates employed the same pragmatic rationale for their campaign that the school board had relied on when publicizing the Blossom Plan prior to the crisis: the constitutional supremacy of federal power. The chamber's campaign resolution expressed sympathy for the segregationist position: "We think the [*Brown*] decision was erroneous and that it was a reversal of established law upon an unprecedented basis of psychology and sociology." Still it concluded that resistance to a Supreme Court order, "however much we dislike it," was futile, and therefore local resistance, however justified, was pointlessly destructive. In a brilliant stroke, the chamber planted a compensating hope in its argument for compliance, saying the Court might be outdone by a "correcting constitutional amendment" or, if left alone, might in time "correc[t] its own error."[8]

The Little Rock NAACP's stand on school desegregation contrasted markedly with the moderates' constitutional position. The desegregation plan school superintendent Blossom first developed immediately following the 1954 *Brown I* decision received the local NAACP branch's approval. After seeing it for the first time, Wiley Branton, the local branch's lawyer, told the school board's attorney that the plan was a reasonable one and... [the] NAACP might go along with it." [9] The local NAACP raised the court challenge, styled at trial as *Aaron v. Cooper*, only after Blossom and the school board retreated from a commitment to genuine desegregation of Little Rock's public schools.

In response to the Supreme Court's *Brown II* decision of 1955, which established the vague compliance standard epitomized by the phrase "with all deliberate speed," this revised Blossom Plan allowed, beginning in September 1957, only token desegregation of Central High School by a small number of African American students, now known to history as the Little Rock Nine. Further token desegregation of the city's lower grades would occur over an undetermined number of years. Accordingly, the city's NAACP changed its position only after it became clear that the new Horace Mann High School would open in February 1956 as a segregated institution. Later, the new Hall High School in Pulaski Heights would open on the same basis. In addition, permitting only token desegregation of Central meant that most African American children living near the high school would have to walk past it to reach Horace Mann, some two miles away. Finally, no dates were set for further desegregation of the city's schools.

Underscoring further the moderate character of the Blossom Plan was the NAACP's defeat in *Aaron v. Cooper*. The African American litigants lost in the federal trial court on August 28, 1956, and again upon appeal to the Eighth Circuit in April 1957.[10] Assessing the initial court decision, the *Arkansas Gazette* noted that "extremists" both for and against desegregation were "fated" to "attack" the Blossom Plan because it provided "a minimum of integration" spread over a period "that may run as long as 10 years." But despite this "extremist" criticism the *Gazette* observed that the moderate desegregation "program has the support of a considerable majority of the citizens of Little Rock of both races, who accept it as a practical solution to a difficult problem." The paper also generally approved the judicially sanctioned plan because it "takes into account the social problems inherent in any such transition, and the emotional climate in which school officials must function. But it turns away from the futile course of defiance of the legal process... which [in the form of interposition and racist violence was] being urged across the Deep South."[11]

The Little Rock NAACP was initially divided over whether testing the moderate plan was advisable. The Little Rock branch of the NAACP, led by Daisy Bates and her husband, L.C., was the organizational center of a local African American protest tradition reaching back at least to Reconstruction. Most notably, from 1889 to 1944 Scipio A. Jones was prominent among a small number of African American lawyers whose practice included challenges to racially discriminatory jury selection, voting, and criminal justice administration.[12] One of the lawyers Daisy and L.C. Bates and the local NAACP relied on was J. R. Booker, an associate of Jones's from the 1920s. Prior to *Brown I*, the city's NAACP had won, in conjunction with the Legal Defense Fund (LDF), teacher salary equalization cases. The Little Rock NAACP decided to challenge the revised Blossom Plan solely out of a determination to improve the educational opportunity of African American children; neither the initiative for nor the direction of the case came from the NAACP's or the LDF's national offices. Even so, the city's NAACP branch hired Branton (who was from Pine Bluff) in 1956 to bring a suit only after Booker and two of Little Rock's other African American lawyers had declined. Although these three lawyers were local NAACP members who usually handled the branch's legal work, they did not support the decision to bring *Aaron v. Cooper* because they believed the Blossom Plan was sufficiently moderate that federal judges in and outside of Arkansas might readily uphold it and thus establish a bad precedent for the desegregation cause. Subsequent events proved this view to be correct.

The wider African American community within which the local NAACP operated was also divided. In the post–World War I era, labor radicals associated with the Communists tried to organize Arkansas sharecroppers, resulting in the establishment of Commonwealth College, which Orval Faubus attended briefly as a young man. In urban areas like Little Rock and Pine Bluff, some of the more affluent African Americans carried on the accommodationist tradition of Booker T. Washington.

Between the ideological extremes of accommodation and tenuous labor radicalism was the NAACP branch, whose leaders combined the strong black church tradition, represented by Rev. J. C. Crenchaw and Daisy Bates, with the legal tradition of Scipio Jones, represented by J. R. Booker, Jackie Shropshire, and Thad W. Williams. The branch also included two white teachers and their wives at the predominantly black Philander Smith College, Georg and Wilma Iggers, and Lee and Grace Lorch. Unlike their fellow branch members, the Lorches quietly espoused radical ideas. Thus the local NAACP's interracial leadership supported challenging the moderate desegregation plan, while for different reasons neither the branch's own lawyers nor the African American accommodationists did so. After the crisis broke in September 1957, the Little Rock Nine's courage in the face of racist opposition helped silence dissension within the city's African American population about Daisy Bates's effective activist leadership. Ironically, African American voters in the city (apparently including even some members of the local NAACP) and throughout Arkansas continued to vote for Faubus, not only before but during and after the crisis of 1957–59.

The NAACP's court-centered protest strategy cultivated African American community support for constitutional rights. In keeping with episodic successes identified with the Scipio Jones activist record, the local NAACP had won some triumphs. But such modest victories did not promote broad-based African American demand for more assertive claims of racial justice. The desegregation litigation strategy growing out of *Brown* did, by contrast, foster the local African American community's greater struggle to gain constitutional rights, which ultimately prevailed over Faubus's strategic maneuvers. Thus the stand of Little Rock's African Americans confirmed what Julian Bond observed about the civil rights struggle generally. It was, he said, "a great testament to the Constitution's strength. Although ... that code of law had ... been bent and twisted to deny black Americans their rights, it also provided the basic tool used by the movement to win justice." Like so many other members of the civil rights movement, African Americans in Little Rock "knew that segregation was wrong on the basis of the nation's highest law. People were willing ... to fight through the legal system for change, because the Constitution was their ultimate shield."[13]

The local NAACP's promotion of constitutional rights claims was also consistent with Martin Luther King's nonviolent philosophy. Faubus's subsequent exploitation of interposition measures to confuse the white public's understanding of *Brown* conformed to King's distinction in "Letter from Birmingham Jail" between "*just* laws and ... *unjust* laws." Thus, he said, "I can urge men to obey the 1954 decision of the Supreme Court because it is morally right, and I can urge them to disobey segregation ordinances because they are morally wrong." The Little Rock branch's "civil disobedience" relied upon federal court litigation, a form of protest King condoned because "as federal courts have consistently affirmed ... it is immoral to urge an individual to withdraw his efforts to gain his basic constitutional rights because the quest precipitates violence. Society must protect the robbed and punish the robber."[14]

Faubus's standing among African American voters was consistent with his early acceptance of the Blossom Plan. The moderates' victories in the *Aaron v. Cooper* case and the school board election in March 1957 encouraged Faubus to maintain an accommodationist stance, acknowledging the constitutionality of school desegregation in the face of the interposition measures advocated by extremists like Jim Johnson. As late as August 1957, Faubus told the *Southern School News*, "Everyone knows that state laws can't supersede federal laws."[15] This embrace of the moderates' minimalist constitutional rationale underlying the Blossom Plan grew out of a political trade with east Arkansas legislators (his tax increase for their interposition laws) and a complex series of secret meetings in late summer 1957 involving, at different points, Faubus, school board members, representatives of the U.S. Justice Department, an Arkansas federal judge, and, peripherally, some extreme segregationists.

By the time Faubus set off the crisis in September, he had a new strategy in mind. He skillfully exploited the "popular mandate" represented by the interposition laws, widespread assertions about the state's police powers, and public confusion on what bearing these had on the "supremacy" of federal laws and the Constitution itself. His sponsorship of an attempt to challenge the Blossom Plan in state court apparently had a similar motive. Privately, a well-informed official in Little Rock stated that Faubus's reason for encouraging court intervention was "to keep people guessing" as to his own stance on desegregation.[16] More specifically, in a private conference with Justice Department official Arthur B. Caidwell the day before the state court hearing and a few days before he ordered the National Guard to Central, Faubus expressed hope that the federal government would intervene with a court order.

These considerations suggest that Faubus's overriding goal was to shift accountability for enforcing desegregation to federal authorities. Understanding this goal helps explain why Faubus changed from moderation to demagogic obstruction after August 1957. The usual explanation relies upon the narrow opportunism involved in Faubus's efforts to win a third gubernatorial term in 1958. As Faubus's own recollections suggest, however, the political cost-benefit calculus was quite murky: the public and private pressures building up among powerful white moderates in Little Rock in favor of token "compliance" as a way to avoid more thoroughgoing integration suggested that there were great political risks in opposing the Blossom Plan, to say nothing of the legal entanglements. This was before the political formula of massive resistance had been tested—Faubus was the first southern politician to do more than talk about resistance— and he hesitated greatly before throwing down the gauntlet. One member of the Arkansas NAACP, in a private memorandum on the eve of the crisis, confirmed the view that while Faubus would probably not defend integration and might even promise to delay it legally if that were the "will of the people," the "fact remains that he is not against integration and he is fairly certain that there is no legal means of preventing integration in the long run." Moreover, he would "certainly do everything within his power to keep down violence."[17]

Throughout the crisis Faubus acknowledged a constitutional obligation to obey "final" federal court orders. In each case, rather than risk a formal contempt charge, he complied. The most conspicuous instance of this occurred after federal Judge Ronald N. Davies finally ordered Faubus to withdraw the National Guard from Central on September 20. Neither in court nor afterward did Faubus ever provide evidence supporting his claim that he had blocked the Little Rock Nine's admission to the school on September 3 because of impending violence. And he never formally admitted the established constitutional doctrine that the duty of all elected officials, when confronted with possible or real defiance, was to defend and enforce constitutional rights rather than allow such rights to be subverted. Yet once he could effectively shift direct responsibility for implementing Davies's court order to federal officials he readily did so: Faubus had made a show of defiance and had made it appear that his retreat was being forced by federal authority. He employed this strategy throughout the crisis. As a result, he was the only player in the drama who creatively left himself enough room for maneuver and therefore emerged with unqualified political gain.

Thus the September confrontation shaped Faubus's third-term reelection bid in ways not generally understood. Faubus learned three important lessons from the secret negotiations with the school board, segregationists, and representatives of the U.S. Department of Justice in late summer 1957. First, the school board's moderates were willing to negotiate to encourage either the governor or the federal government to enforce a desegregation order, but they would not seek such an order themselves. In other words, they were not willing to lead or to take bold initiatives. Second, Faubus learned that the school board's sole emphasis on "compliance"—that is, deference to the Supreme Court rather than any desegregation principle for which they would stand up and be counted—encouraged the defiance associated with Jim Johnson's interposition measures.

Finally, and most important, Faubus learned that the federal government would intervene on behalf of a desegregation order only in the most extreme circumstances. The Eisenhower administration's repeated willingness to negotiate secretly may have seemed politically reasonable under the circumstances, but it conveyed to Faubus what Eisenhower and his advisers agreed upon privately: as long as the governor ultimately complied with federal court orders he should be given as much leeway as possible for what Eisenhower called an "orderly retreat."[18] The Department of Justice was sufficiently committed to this view that it attempted—unsuccessfully—to convince Branton to withdraw the court suit defending the Little Rock Nine's rights.

The administration's general policy coincided with the advice Faubus's legal adviser, William J. Smith, gave him during the crisis: he could, in effect, get all the political benefits of going to the brink before retreating. Meanwhile, the federal government's refusal to use the evidence the FBI had gathered for the trial before Judge Davies and in subsequent investigations to prosecute segregationist rabble-rousers, including those who provoked Eisenhower's September 24 dispatch of paratroopers, must have reinforced Faubus's understanding of the administration's reluctance to act against segregationists.

This reluctance encouraged Faubus to link his reelection bid in 1958 to federal court tests of new state "interposition" laws. Faubus used these laws to close Little Rock's high schools, even after what seemed the definitive decision from the Supreme Court in *Cooper v. Aaron* in September 1958. Though that decision favored the African American litigants by denying the school board's request for a two-and-a-half-year delay, it did not address directly as a matter for the Court's formal decision the constitutionality of interposition and other states' rights measures. Those measures required separate litigation, which ultimately led to lower federal court decisions rejecting the constitutionality of interposition (confirming Faubus's observation from just before the crisis, that no state law superseded a federal law).

The important thing was not Faubus's ultimate legal defeat in these decisions but the considerable delay before they were handed down. The delay encouraged further segregationist resistance (part of it surely carried on in the hope that Faubus would come up with yet a new subterfuge once the one pending in the courts fell through, and part of it in the hope that the black protesters would grow weary and quit). For Faubus, the delay lasted through his 1958 reelection campaign, so it did not really mater that he ultimately lost the decision in June 1959. Nor were there adverse political consequences when Little Rock's newly elected moderate school board surprised him by opening the city high schools early on the basis of token desegregation embodied in the Blossom Plan. The crisis was over.

After forty years, Little Rock sought a new desegregation remedy. Echoing President Bill Clinton's call for national interracial reconciliation, the UALR task force report urged the community to embrace a heightened consciousness grounded on trust. Whites had to understand the alienation African Americans felt as a result of their history of discrimination; African Americans needed in turn to have faith that their children would continue to receive material resources from the white tax-paying majority if federal court intervention ended. The Little Rock Nine's courage and determination continued to inspire hope that such a change of mind was possible. "We're all a work in progress," said one of the nine, Melba Pattillo Beals, in August 1997. "We just have to not lose faith and keep trying."[19]

Impeding the fulfillment of hopes such as Beals's, however, is a contrary consciousness that justifies desegregation primarily in terms of deference to the constitutional supremacy of federal power. The public discourse which reflects this consciousness rejects appeals to both blatant racism and the intrinsic worth of racial justice itself. Instead, a discourse of pragmatic moderation prevails which makes claims of constitutional rights contingent upon federal compulsion. A new consciousness of trust requires transcending this minimalist constitutional symbolism. Even so, remember the Gospel says: "But when ye shall hear of wars and commotions, be not terrified: for these things must first come to pass; but the end is not by and by." Such a transformation would mean after all that Little Rock's future was at last freed from its past.

The Documentary Heritage
of the Central High Crisis:
A Bibliographical Essay

MICHAEL J. DABRISHUS

In the state of Arkansas more than forty manuscript collections contain materials that pertain to the 1957 crisis at Little Rock Central High School. The interested student or researcher may obtain copies of the relevant inventories at each repository, or they may obtain photocopies of these inventories by mail for a nominal fee. Researchers and students may also examine inventories for many of the collections that exist on the Fayetteville campus of the University of Arkansas through the university library's website at www.uark.edu/libinfo/speccoll/. In addition, Linda Pine, head of the Special Collections Department at the University of Arkansas at Little Rock, has prepared a selective bibliography of published monographs, periodical articles, and pamphlets on the subject of the Little Rock crisis; copies of this bibliography can be obtained through UALR's Special Collections Department. Another useful source of information is the Little Rock Central High Fortieth Anniversary website (www.centralhigh57.org), which contains background information; a chronology; issues of the 1957–58 edition of the student newspaper, *The Tiger*; photographs; and more.

Special Collections Division, Mullins Library, University of Arkansas, Fayetteville

By far the most consulted of the Central High crisis collections are the papers of Orval E. Faubus (1910–78; 504 linear feet). As governor, Faubus had at his disposal a staff that maintained his official records. The collection includes two significant series: "Records Pertaining to Little Rock Integration Crisis" and "Records Pertaining to Race Relations in Arkansas."

Other components of the collection worth noting include clippings, scrapbooks, photographs, subject files, and sound recordings. What might be considered his private papers, many of which have been received since his death, provide insight to his personal life. In 1994 the division acquired a copy of the Federal Bureau of Investigation file (1935–64; 1 linear foot) on Faubus, part of which deals with Central High.

The Virgil T. Blossom Papers (1952–60; 13 linear feet) represent a recent major acquisition relative to the Central High story. As superintendent of Little Rock Public Schools from 1953 to 1958, Virgil Blossom occupied a crucial position in the controversy. His papers include correspondence files, opinion mail from all over the country, Little Rock Board of Education minutes, Central High School daily bulletins, segregationist pamphlets, and drafts of It Has Happened Here.

The Arthur B. Caldwell Papers (1912–75; 8.5 linear feet) include materials from Caldwell's work with the U.S. Department of Justice, where he held positions as chief of the Civil Rights Section and then assistant to the assistant attorney general for the Civil Rights Division. This collection contains much material on Central High, including a chronology of events; texts of remarks and statements by President Dwight D. Eisenhower, Gov. Orval E. Faubus, Warren Olney III, and others; correspondence with L. Brooks Hays, Archie F. House, and William H. Hadley; and periodical articles.

The Federal Bureau of Investigation maintained a file (1 linear foot) on the Central High crisis, and in 1990 the Special Collections Division received a copy. It includes interviews concerning people traveling by motor caravan from east Arkansas allegedly to demonstrate against integration at Central High; information on Governor Faubus's use of the National Guard amidst charges of potential violence at Central High; and an investigation concerning protests to restrain the 101st Airborne from operating at Central High.

The L. Brooks Hays Papers (1915–81; 93 linear feet) are a valuable source of information about the crisis in Little Rock. Congressman Hays served in the U.S. House of Representatives from 1943 to 1959, losing his seat to Dale Alford as a result of his position on Central High. There are many letters, clippings, photographs, and articles associated with integration, as well as sound recordings and transcripts of interviews with Hays and Faubus. (There is also an important collection of Brooks Hays Papers [1928–66; 134 boxes] at the John F. Kennedy Library; it contains extensive correspondence files, speech files, subject files, political files, and scrapbooks.)

The J. William Fulbright Papers (1931–94; 1,400 linear feet) also include Central High crisis materials, consisting primarily of letters expressing the views of his constituents. In August of 1958 Senator Fulbright filed an amicus curiae brief with the U.S. Supreme Court, urging a delay in desegregation, in which he expounded on his views on Little Rock. This collection also includes materials on the Southern Manifesto.

The Oren Harris Papers (1926–66; 165 linear feet) also include pertinent materials relating to the Little Rock crisis. Congressman Harris served from 1941 to 1966. His collection includes folders on civil rights and integration.

In 1986 Daisy Bates donated a group of her materials (1948–86; 8 linear feet) to the Special Collections Division at Fayetteville. While much of this collection centers on her work after the Central High crisis, it also includes pertinent photographs and sound recordings relating to the events at Central High. (In 1966 Daisy and L.C. Bates donated the bulk of their papers [1946–66; 6 boxes] to the State Historical Society of Wisconsin. This collection includes correspondence files, speeches and statements, clippings, and subject files, much of which pertains to the Central High crisis; it also includes drafts of Mrs. Bates's book, *The Long Shadow of Little Rock.*)

The Elizabeth P. Huckaby Papers (1957–63; 1 linear foot) consist of journals, correspondence, notes, school bulletins, memoranda, reports, transcripts, and other materials that Huckaby collected during her career as a teacher and vice principal for girls at Central High. The collection also includes drafts of her book *Crisis at Central High: Little Rock, 1957–1958.*

The Velma and J. O. Powell Papers (1958–79; 1 linear foot) consist of materials of J. O. Powell, vice principal for boys at Central High and his wife, Velma, one of the founders of the Women's Emergency Committee to Open Our Schools (WEC). Included is an account of the crisis by Mr. Powell. The collection also includes a copy of Vivion Brewer's manuscript "The Embattled Ladies of Little Rock," a transcript of an interview of Brewer by Elizabeth Jacoway, and a photocopy of a diary kept by Adolphine Fletcher Terry in 1958.

The Arkansas Council on Human Relations (1954–68: 18 linear feet) was an affiliate of the Southern Regional Council. The ACHR records include correspondence, memoranda, reports, minutes of proceedings, pamphlets, bulletins, newsletters, clippings, programs, sound recordings, and other materials created or received by the organization. These materials document the ACHR's work on the legal, political, educational, religious, social, and economic aspects of race relations in Arkansas. After 1957 the integration of public schools in Little Rock became central to the organization's mission.

The Colbert S. Cartwright Papers (1954–65; fourteen scrapbooks on microfilm) represent the work and interests of Cartwright when he was minister of the Pulaski Heights Christian Church in Little Rock. The scrapbooks include Cartwright's sermons, correspondence, and clippings. Taken together they document his support for human relations and improved racial understanding.

The Sara A. Murphy Papers (1924–95) were donated in 1995. Murphy joined the Women's Emergency Committee to Open Our Schools as a way to express her firm conviction against racial prejudice. She served as a WEC board member in 1962 and 1963. After the WEC disbanded she became a member of the Panel of American Women, a multiethnic, multiracial group that promoted racial cooperation and understanding. She later joined with Betty Bumpers in founding Peace Links. Her collection includes materials that she accumulated as an activist, as well as research materials that she obtained while conducting research for *Breaking the Silence*, which describes the role of the WEC during the integration crisis. Murphy conducted over forty taped interviews that are part of the collection, including interviews with Harry Ashmore, Daisy Bates, Orval Faubus, Ernest Green, Sammie Dean Parker, Elizabeth P. Huckaby, Ozell Sutton, Henry Woods, and Adolphine Fletcher Terry.

The Herbert L. Thomas Papers (1899–1979; 10 linear feet) contain correspondence, speeches, pamphlets, clippings, and other materials accumulated during Thomas's long career as a businessman and civic leader in Fayetteville and Little Rock. Thomas served as chairman of the University of Arkansas Board of Trustees when the University of Arkansas School of Law was integrated. He was also the author of "The Arkansas Plan," a plan of voluntary progress toward integration of public schools that he proposed as a way to end the crisis in 1958.

The Larry Obsitnik Papers (ca. 1941–79; ca. 10,000 items) is a collection that consists primarily of photographic negatives taken by Obsitnik during his lengthy career as chief photographer of the *Arkansas Gazette*. Obsitnik witnessed many of the events as they unfolded at Central High because he was there to document them. His collection includes photographs of Little Rock School Board members, federal troops arriving in Little Rock and then stationed at Central High, crowd scenes around the school, students, and notable politicians and other public figures.

The Robert A. Leflar Papers (ca. 1925–95; 25 linear feet) include significant materials on racial integration in Arkansas during the 1950s and 1960s. Dr. Leflar served as dean of the University of Arkansas School of Law when it was integrated in 1948. Later he served as chairman of the Arkansas State Advisory Committee to the U.S. Commission on Civil Rights. His collection includes a great deal of material on the legal aspects of integration in public schools in the United States.

The Henry Woods Papers (1952–96; 10 linear feet) were acquired in 1998. In 1957 Woods was a partner with the firm of McMath, Leatherman, and Woods. The collection includes a transcript of an oral history conducted in 1972 by T. Harri Baker on behalf of Columbia University; the collection also includes transcripts of the 1984 lawsuit the Little Rock School District introduced in U.S. District Court against the Pulaski County Special School District No. 1, et al.

The Harlan Hobbs Papers (1927–97; 12 linear feet) were acquired in 1997. Hobbs was a 1927 graduate of Central High. In the 1950s he was a business and civic leader in Ohio, where he became active in the state Republican party and a friend of President Eisenhower; on behalf of the White House, Hobbs made two trips to Little Rock in October and November of 1957 in an effort to seek a resolution to the crisis. His collection includes a file that contains his itinerary, correspondence with those that he met, and drafts of a letter purportedly from the students of Central High to President Eisenhower. The collection also includes an oral history interview.

The Roy Reed Papers (1985–93; ca. 100 cassette tapes) contain recordings and transcripts of interviews that Reed obtained during research for his book *Faubus: The Life and Times of an American Prodigal.* Tapes and transcripts exist for nearly all of the interviews, including Harry Ashmore, Bill Becker, Herbert Brownell, Orval E. Faubus, Jim Johnson, Sidney S. McMath, William J. Smith, Ozell Sutton, and Henry Woods. Access to some of the interviews is restricted.

The Henry Macmillan Alexander Papers (1933–1969; 31 linear feet) consist primarily of the research files Alexander accumulated while he was a professor at the University of Arkansas, Fayetteville. Recognized as an authority on Arkansas state and local government, Alexander served as a consultant to many governmental agencies during his long career. Selected files within this collection contain printed materials associated with the Central High crisis.

The Citizens' Councils of America Collection (1947–69; 110 items) consists of books, pamphlets, newspapers, leaflets, reprints, and other materials that the Citizens' Councils published and distributed from their Jackson, Mississippi, headquarters. Much of the material promotes the organization's political and social views on communism and segregation. The subject of the integration of Central High, which ran counter to the organization's views, received considerable treatment in their publications.

The University of Arkansas library also contains a collection of Little Rock Desegregation Crisis Transcripts that Columbia University's Oral History Program conducted in 1972–73 as a part of its Eisenhower Administration Project. It consists of the transcripts of oral interviews with J. Bill Becker, Orval E. Faubus, Nathaniel R. Griswold, Archie F. House, Elizabeth P. Huckaby, R. A. Lile, Sidney S. McMath, Terrell E. Powell, Everett Tucker Jr., and Wayne Upton.

Special Collections Department, Ottenheimer Library, University of Arkansas at Little Rock

The Harry S. Ashmore Papers (1947–61; 9 boxes) contain correspondence, printed materials, speeches, and clippings. Ashmore served as executive editor of the *Arkansas Gazette* from 1948 to 1959; his editorial writing in connection with the Central High crisis resulted in the paper receiving two Pulitzer prizes. Because Ashmore was a respected member of the community, business, professional, and political leaders sought his opinion on a variety of matters, and his papers reflect that stature.

The Bishop Robert R. Brown Papers (1957–64; 2 boxes) include letters, telegrams, printed materials, clippings, and speeches. Bishop of the Episcopal Diocese of Arkansas during the crisis, Brown was among those religious leaders who voiced strong disapproval of Faubus's handling of the situation. His views were published in *Bigger Than Little Rock*.

The Vivion Brewer Papers (1888–1982; 3 boxes) include correspondence, clippings, printed materials and family papers. Brewer was a founder and chair of the Women's Emergency Committee to Open Our Schools, and the collection contains some of the records of that organization, such as membership lists. Also included is a copy of Brewer's manuscript entitled "The Embattled Ladies of Little Rock."

The Elizabeth Huckaby Papers (1952–92; 12 boxes) include correspondence, clippings, handbills, scrapbooks, an oral history transcript, and a diary. Huckaby taught English at Central High and was vice-principal for women during 1957–58. In 1980 she published a book about her experiences at Central High entitled *Crisis at Central High*. Her collection also contains materials pertaining to the film of the same title that starred Joanne Woodward, including photographs from the set.

The Harry J. Lemley Papers (1956–61; 1 linear foot) consist of letters and scrapbooks. As federal judge of the Western District of Arkansas, Lemley issued an opinion in 1958 calling for a temporary halt to integration at Central High, a ruling that the Eighth Circuit Court of Appeals overturned. The vast majority of the materials in the collection pertain to Lemley's ruling.

The Little Rock School Board Minutes (1956–64; 9 boxes) provide a detailed view of the day-to-day operations of the Little Rock School District. The collection contains information on personnel, operating budgets, salaries, disciplinary actions, and much more. An index is included.

The Little Rock School Crisis Collection (1957–65; 2 boxes) contains printed materials that J. N. Heiskell, owner of the *Arkansas Gazette*, collected. Articles from major weekly magazines such as *Time, Saturday Review, Saturday Evening Post, Life,* and *Look* are included, as well as pamphlets, broadsides, and news clippings.

The Fletcher-Terry Family Papers (1826–1976; 31 boxes) is a large collection of the family papers of John Gould Fletcher III and his daughter, Adolphine Fletcher Terry, who was a community activist for women's rights and education. One box of the collection pertains to Adolphine's work during the Central High crisis. Her diary for 1958 is also part of the collection.

The E. Grainger Williams Papers (1958–60; 1 box) contain correspondence, telegrams, brochures, and newspaper articles pertaining to the work of Williams and other community leaders during the Central High crisis. Williams served as president of the Little Rock Chamber of Commerce from 1958 to 1959, and he was a member of the Board of Trustees of Little Rock University from 1959 to 1969.

The Bill Shelton Papers (1954–68; 4 boxes) include copies of the newspaper *Southern School News* and news reports about the Central High crisis and racial conditions in Little Rock. Shelton began working as the city editor of the *Arkansas Gazette* in 1957, a position that he held for many years thereafter.

The Dorothy Morris Scrapbooks (1957–66; 1 roll of microfilm) are composed primarily of clippings and other printed materials, with some correspondence. Morris served as secretary of the Women's Emergency Committee to Open Our Schools and also of the Arkansas Council on Human Relations.

The Osro Cobb Papers (1928–80; 2 boxes) include correspondence, speeches, published materials, photographs, clippings and scrapbooks pertaining to Cobb's life and work. Appointed U.S. attorney in 1954, Cobb served in that capacity until 1961. Faubus appointed him associate justice of the Arkansas Supreme Court in 1965, a position that he held until 1967. His collection includes a copy of his unpublished manuscript *"United States v. Gov. Orval E. Faubus."*

The Bill Graham Cartoon Collection (1945–85; ca. 4,700 drawings) contains the original rough drawings, art, clippings, and other materials of Graham as editorial cartoonist for the *Arkansas Gazette*. His daily editorial cartoons during the Central High crisis became a fixture at the newspaper for nearly three years.

The Georg Iggers Papers (1952–91; 32 items) contain correspondence, printed materials, clippings, articles, and reminiscences relative to the integration of Little Rock schools and other public facilities in Arkansas. Iggers was a professor at Philander-Smith, a black college in Little Rock.

The Joseph Crenchaw Papers (1955–79; 22 items) contain correspondence, memos, and printed materials pertaining to the crisis. Reverend Crenchaw was a leading figure in Little Rock's black community, especially in the affairs of the NAACP.

The Central High Museum, Inc., Collection (1996–97; 2 boxes) contains photographs the museum acquired during the course of its work to develop an exhibit about the desegregation crisis.

The UALR library holds a number of individual interviews that contain information about the Central High crisis; these include interviews with Lucie McDonnell Davis, Archie House, Pat House, Kathryn Lambright, Brownie Ledbetter, Dottie Morris, and Mary Sandlin Fletcher Worthen.

Arkansas History Commission, Little Rock

The Women's Emergency Committee to Open Our Schools Collection (1958–63; 8 linear feet) includes correspondence, membership lists, booklets, pamphlets, clippings, and other printed materials. Adolphine Fletcher Terry, Vivion Brewer, and Velma Powell founded the WEC in response to Faubus's decision to close the public schools of Little Rock. The stated purpose of the WEC was to inform the people of Little Rock and the state of the necessity of maintaining public schools and the enormous consequences if the schools remained closed.

The James R. Eison Papers (1954–94; 2 boxes) consist of letters, articles, clippings, and other materials associated with the crisis when Eison was a student at Central High. Eison and others were suspended after they participated in a walkout on October 3, 1957, and the collection includes some material on that subject.

The Little Rock Central High *Tiger*, the student newspaper, is also available at the history commission for the years 1928 to 1958.

Archives and Special Collections Department, Torreyson Library, University of Central Arkansas, Conway

The Richard C. Butler Papers (1956–84; 1.5 linear feet) contain correspondence, legal records, and printed materials for 1957–58. Butler, a native of Little Rock, served as special counsel for the Little Rock School Board during the Central High crisis, in which capacity he argued the case of *Cooper v. Aaron* before the U.S. Supreme Court.

Special Collections Department, Riley-Hickingbotham Library, Ouachita Baptist University, Arkadelphia

The John L. McClellan Papers (1942–77; ca. 1,000 linear feet) contain correspondence, clippings, published articles, and other materials relative to segregation and the Central High crisis in files specifically identified for those subjects.

NOTES

Understanding the Past: The Challenge of Little Rock
ELIZABETH JACOWAY

1. Everett Tucker III, "Remembrance and Reconciliation," conference speech, University of Arkansas at Little Rock, September 27, 1997.

2. Jacoway notes, Little Rock Central High Museum, Inc., Planning Committee, June 6, 1995, handwritten notes in the possession of the author.

3. The Central High Museum Program Plan, Draft, August 14, 1995; Bylaws of Central High Museum, Inc., distributed to the Planning Committee August 29, 1995; documents in the possession of the author.

4. The best brief overview of the Little Rock crisis is in Numan V. Bartley, *The Rise of Massive Resistance: The Deep South during the 1950s* (Baton Rouge: Louisiana State University Press, 1969), 251–69 ff; another useful overview of the Little Rock crisis is J. W. Peltason, *Fifty-Eight Lonely Men: Southern Federal Judges and School Desegregation* (New York: Harcourt Brace and World, 1961), 161–207; Virgil T. Blossom, *It Has Happened Here* (New York: Harper and Brothers, 1959).

5. For an excellent brief overview of the activities of the Capitol Citizens' Council, see Neil McMillen, *The Citizens' Council: Organized Resistance to the Second Reconstruction, 1954–64* (Urbana: University of Illinois Press, 1971), 267–85; for the text of *Cooper v. Aaron* see Wilson Record and Jane Cassels Record, eds., *Little Rock, U.S.A.: Materials for Analysis* (San Francisco: Chandler Publishing Co., 1960), 19–27.

6. Elizabeth Jacoway, "Taken by Surprise: Little Rock Businessmen and Desegregation," in *Southern Businessmen and Desegregation*, ed. Elizabeth Jacoway and David R. Colburn (Baton Rouge: Louisiana State University Press, 1982), 15–41.

7. Harry S. Ashmore, *Arkansas: A History* (New York: W. W. Norton, 1978), 153–54.

8. Roy Reed, *Faubus: The Life and Times of an American Prodigal* (Fayetteville: University of Arkansas Press, 1997).

9. Orval Eugene Faubus, *Down from the Hills* (Little Rock: Democrat Printing and Lithographing Co., 1980), 197–98.

10. Orval Faubus Interview, Eisenhower Administration Project, Columbia University Oral History Program, Eisenhower Presidential Library, Abilene, Kansas.

11. Peltason, *Fifty-Eight Lonely Men*, 165–66.

12. Ibid., 163–64.

13. For the theory of a "manufactured crisis" see ibid., especially 165.

14. Brooks Hays, *A Southern Moderate Speaks* (Chapel Hill: University of North Carolina Press, 1959).

15. Jacoway, "Taken by Surprise," 24–28.

16. Ibid., 25.

17. Ibid.

18. Blossom, *It Has Happened Here*, 147–75.

19. Melba Patillo Beals, *Warriors Don't Cry* (New York: Simon and Schuster, 1994); Daisy Bates, *The Long Shadow of Little Rock* (New York: David McKay, 1962; reprint, Fayetteville: University of Arkansas Press, 1987); Elizabeth Huckaby, *Crisis at Central High: Little Rock, 1957–58* (Baton Rouge: Louisiana State University Press, 1980). Virgil Blossom estimated the number of white tormentors to be fewer than fifty; Blossom, *It Has Happened Here*, 156.

20. Jacoway, "Taken by Surprise."

21. Harry S. Ashmore, *Civil Rights and Wrongs: A Memoir of Race and Politics, 1944–1994* (New York: Pantheon Books, 1994).

22. Tony Freyer, *The Little Rock Crisis: A Constitutional Interpretation* (Westport, Conn.: Greenwood Press, 1984), 145–46.

23. Irving Spitzberg, *Racial Politics in Little Rock, 1954–1964* (New York: Garland Publishing Co., 1982).

24. Freyer, *Little Rock Crisis*, 145–54; see also Peter Irons and Stephanie Guitton, eds., *May It Please the Court: Transcripts of 23 Live Recordings of Landmark Cases As Argued before the Supreme Court* (New York: New Press, 1993), 249–61.

25. Sara Alderman Murphy, *Breaking the Silence: The Women's Emergency Committee to Open Our Schools* (Fayetteville: University of Arkansas Press, 1997), 77–78; see also Vivion Lenon Brewer, "The Embattled Ladies of Little Rock," unpublished manuscript, Sophia Smith Collection, Smith College, Northhampton, Mass.

26. Murphy, *Breaking the Silence*, 84–90; Brewer, "Embattled Ladies of Little Rock," chap. 2.

27. Brooks Hays, *Politics Is My Parish* (Baton Rouge: Louisiana State University Press, 1981), 179–98; Dale and L'Moore Alford, *The Case of the Sleeping People (Finally Awakened by Little Rock School Frustrations)* (Little Rock: Democrat Printing and Lithographing Company, 1959).

28. Record and Record, *Little Rock, U.S.A.*, 119–27.

29. Murphy, *Breaking the Silence*, 91–108.

30. Ibid., 112; Jacoway, "Taken by Surprise"; see also Elizabeth Jacoway, "Civil Rights and the Changing South," in Jacoway and Colburn, *Southern Businessmen and Desegregation*.

31. Brewer, "Embattled Ladies of Little Rock," chap. 6; Murphy, *Breaking the Silence*, 160–80.

32. Ibid.

33. Ibid.; Joel E. Anderson et al., "Plain Talk: The Future of Little Rock's Public Schools," University Task Force Report on the Little Rock School District, University of Arkansas at Little Rock, 1997.

34. *Arkansas Democrat-Gazette*, September 21, 1997.

35. Ibid.; Hazel Bryan Massery Interviews, by Elizabeth Jacoway, January 26, 1996, August 19, 1998; notes and transcripts in the possession of the author.

36. Gov. Mike Huckabee, speech at Little Rock Central High School, September 25, 1997; copy in the possession of the author.

Little Rock and the Promise of America
SHELDON HACKNEY

1. Robert Bellah, Richard Madsen, William M. Sullivan, Ann Swidler, and Steven M. Tipton, *Habits of the Heart: Individualism and Commitment in American Life*, Updated Edition with a New Introduction (Berkeley: University of California Press, 1996), xi, xxx. The original edition was published in 1985.

2. Robert Putnam, "Bowling Alone: America's Declining Social Capital," *Journal of Democracy* (July 1995): 65–75; and "The Strange Disappearance of Civic America," *American Prospect* (winter 1996): 34–48. For an intelligent discussion and summary, see Scott Heller, "'Bowling Alone': A Harvard Professor Examines America's Dwindling Sense of Community," *Chronicle of Higher Education* (March 1, 1996). A scholarly exchange appeared in *American Prospect* (March/April 1996). See, for instance, Robert J. Samuelson, "'Bowling Alone' Is Bunk," *Washington Post*, April 10, 1996; Richard Stengel, "Bowling Together," *Time*, July 22, 1996; and Nicholas Lemann, "Kicking in Groups," *Atlantic Monthly*, April 1996. Seymour Martin Lipset, "Malaise and Resiliency in America," *Journal of Democracy* (July 1995). For a different judgment, see Everett C. Ladd, "The Data Just Don't Show Erosion of America's 'Social Capital,'" *Public Perspective* (June/July 1996). A similar optimistic reading with regard to a single city is reported by The Pew Research Center for The People and The Press in *Trust and Citizen Engagement in Metropolitan Philadelphia: A Case Study* (April 1997).

Segregation and Racism: Taking Up the Dream Again
DAVID R. GOLDFIELD

1. David Goldfield et al., *The American Journey: A History of the United States* (Upper Saddle River, N.J.: Prentice Hall, 1998), 579.

2. Kenneth W. Goings and Gerald L. Smith, "'Unhidden' Transcripts: Memphis and African American Agency, 1862–1920," *Journal of Urban History* 21 (March 1995): 372–94.

3. Both quotes from Goldfield, *American Journey*, 580.

4. Scholarship on southern women from the Civil War through the early twentieth century has added significantly to our understanding of that era of southern history. For some good and recent examples, see Drew Gilpin Faust, *Mothers of Invention: Women of the Slaveholding South in the American Civil War* (Chapel Hill: University of North Carolina Press, 1996); Evelyn Brooks Higginbotham, *Righteous Discontent: The Women's Movement in the Black Baptist Church, 1880–1920* (Cambridge, Mass.: Harvard University Press, 1993); Mary

Martha Thomas, *The New Woman in Alabama: Social Reforms and Suffrage, 1890–1920* (Tuscaloosa: University of Alabama Press, 1992); Marjorie Spruill Wheeler, *New Women of the New South: The Leaders of the Woman Suffrage Movement in the Southern States* (New York: Oxford University Press, 1993).

5. Quoted in Elizabeth Hayes Turner, "'White-Gloved Ladies' and 'New Women' in the Texas Woman Suffrage Movement," in *Southern Women: Histories and Identities*, ed. Virginia Bernhard et al. (Columbia: University of Missouri Press, 1992), 135.

6. Pauli Murray, *Proud Shoes: The Story of an American Family* (New York: Harper, 1956), 269–70.

7. Ernest J. Gaines, *A Lesson before Dying* (New York: Knopf, 1993), 47.

8. William Faulkner, *The Sound and the Fury* (New York: Random House, 1929), 107.

9. On the etiquette of race, see Bertram W. Doyle, *The Etiquette of Race Relations in the South: A Study in Social Control* (Chicago: University of Chicago Press, 1937).

10. All quotes appear in Dewey W. Grantham, *The South in Modern America: A Region at Odds* (New York: HarperCollins, 1994), 34–35; on this point, see also Edward L. Ayers, *The Promise of the New South: Life after Reconstruction* (New York: Oxford University Press, 1992), 423.

11. Quoted in Goldfield, *American Journey*, 584.

12. Maya Angelou, *I Know Why the Caged Bird Sings* (New York: Random House, 1969); Mary Mebane, *Mary* (New York: Viking, 1981); Richard Wright, *Black Boy: A Record of Childhood and Youth* (New York: Harper and Bros., 1945).

13. Wright, *Black Boy*, 216.

14. Mary Mebane, "Mary," in *Growing Up in the South: An Anthology of Modern Southern Literature*, ed. Suzanne W. Jones (New York: Penguin, 1991), 452.

15. Lillian Smith, *Killers of the Dream* (New York: W. W. Norton, 1949), 39.

16. Quoted in Tom Gilmore, "The South Is Rising Again—In Living Colors," in *The Rising South: Issues and Changes*, ed. Donald R. Noble and Joab L. Thomas (Tuscaloosa: University of Alabama Press, 1976), 54–55.

17. Pat Watters, "It's Been 20 Long Years," *Southern Voices* 2 (May–June 1974), 5.

18. Henry Louis Gates, *Colored People: A Memoir* (New York: Knopf, 1994); Raymond Andrews, *The Last Radio Baby* (Atlanta, Ga.: Peachtree Publishers, 1990).

19. Saul Friedlander, *Nazi Germany and the Jews: The Years of Persecution, 1933–1939* (New York: HarperCollins, 1997), 6.

20. For a discussion of the political limits of the civil rights victories of the 1960s, see David Goldfield, *Black, White, and Southern: Race Relations and Southern Culture, 1940 to the Present* (Baton Rouge: Louisiana State University Press, 1990), 238–44.

21. Steele quoted in Marvin Caplan, *Farther Along* (Baton Rouge: Louisiana State University Press, 1998), 320; Douglass quoted in Randall Kennedy, "My Race Problem—and Ours," *Atlantic Monthly*, May 1997, 56.

22. Jacob Heilbrunn, "Speech Therapy," *New Republic*, July 1, 1996, 22.

23. Peter Beinart, "New Bedfellows," *New Republic*, August 11, 18, 1997, 24.

24. Lewis quoted in Sean Wilentz, "The Last Integrationist," *New Republic*, July 1, 1996, 22.

25. Lewis quoted in ibid.

26. Douglass quoted in Kennedy, "My Race Problem—and Ours," 66.

Arkansas, the *Brown* Decision, and the 1957 Little Rock School Crisis: A Local Perspective

JOHN A. KIRK

1. *Southern School News*, September 1954, 2.

2. *Arkansas Gazette*, May 18, 1954.

3. *Southern School News*, October 1954, 3.

4. Ibid., September 1954, 2; October 1954, 3; December 1954, 8.

5. Ibid., September 1954, 2.

6. Ibid., October 1954, 3.

7. Ibid., March 1955, 2. On the reactions of liberal southern politicians to *Brown* see Tony Badger, "Fatalism, Not Gradualism: Race and the Crisis of Southern Liberalism, 45–65," in *The Making of Martin Luther King and the Civil Rights Movement*, ed. Brian Ward and Tony Badger, 67–95 (London: Macmillan, 1996).

8. *Southern School News*, March 1955, 2.

9. Ibid., April 1955, 7. Pupil assignment laws were the most common response by southern legislatures to *Brown*, with virtually every state adopting them in some form by 1955. However, the measures were moderate compared with the litigation that accompanied them in some states, which variously proposed the use of police power to stop integration, financing litigation opposing desegregation, investigation of pro-integration organizations, and leasing public schools to private corporations in an attempt to avoid federal orders to desegregate. Not until much later did Arkansas engage in such extremist measures (see Benjamin Muse, *Ten Years of Prelude: The Story of Integration since the Supreme Court's 1954 Decision* (Beaconsfield: Darwen Finlayson, 1964), 64–72.

10. Tony Freyer, *The Little Rock Crisis: A Constitutional Interpretation* (Westport, Conn.: Greenwood Press, 1984), 18–24.

11. Daisy Bates, *The Long Shadow of Little Rock: A Memoir* (New York: David McKay Company, 1962; reprint, Fayetteville: University of Arkansas Press, 1987), 2.

12. Georg C. Iggers to Tony Freyer, September 17, 1980. Supplied courtesy of Professor Iggers.

13. Virgil Blossom, *It Has Happened Here* (New York: Harper, 1959), 11–13.

14. Georg C. Iggers, "An Arkansas Professor: The NAACP and the Grass Roots," in *Little Rock, U.S.A.*, Wilson Record and Jane Cassels Record (San Francisco: Chandler Publishing Co., 1960), 286.

15. Ibid., 286–87.

16. *Southern School News*, May 1955, 2.

17. David R. Goldfield, *Black, White, and Southern: Race Relations and Southern Culture, 1940 to the Present* (Baton Rouge: Louisiana State University Press), 81.

18. *Southern School News*, July 1955, 3; Iggers, "An Arkansas Professor," 287.

19. Ibid., July 1955, 3; August 1955, 15; September 1955, 10.

20. Mildred L. Bond to Roy Wilkins, August 6, 1955, box 4, folder 10, Daisy Bates Papers, State Historical Society of Wisconsin, Madison (collection hereinafter cited as DBPW).

21. "A 'Morally Right' Decision," *Life*, July 25, 1955, 29–31.

22. Ibid.

23. Cabell Phillips, "Integration: Battle of Hoxie, Arkansas," *New York Times Magazine*, September 25, 1955, 12, 68–76.

24. *Southern School News*, September 1955, 10.

25. Neil R. McMillen, "The White Citizens' Council and Resistance to School Desegregation in Arkansas," *Arkansas Historical Quarterly* 30 (summer 1971): 97–100; Jerry Vervack, "The Hoxie Imbroglio," *Arkansas Historical Quarterly* 48 (spring 1989): 22.

26. Ibid., 28–33.

27. McMillen, "The White Citizens' Council," 100.

28. Ibid., 95–122.

29. Freyer, *Little Rock Crisis*, 68–70.

30. *Southern School News*, February 1956, 11.

31. Iggers, "An Arkansas Professor," 289.

32. *Southern School News*, March 1956, 4.

33. Ibid.

34. Ibid., June 1957, 9.

35. Ibid., July 1957, 10.

36. "What Is Happening in Desegregation in Arkansas," January 1957, box 29, folder 302, Arkansas Council on Human Relations Papers, Special Collections Division, University of Arkansas Libraries, Fayetteville, Arkansas.

37. Catherine A. Barnes, *Journey from Jim Crow: The Desegregation of Southern Transit* (New York: University Press of Columbia, 1983), 118–19.

38. "What Is Happening in Desegregation in Arkansas," 2.

39. "A Request to the Southern Regional Council," September 1957, reel 141, box 4, folder 219, "Arkansas, grants-in-aid, July 11, 1957–October 17, 1961," Southern Regional Council Papers (microfilm), Library of Congress, Manuscripts Division, Washington, D.C. (collection hereinafter cited as SRCLC).

40. McMillen, "The White Citizens' Council," 104–7.

41. Numan V. Bartley, *The Rise of Massive Resistance: Race and Politics in the South during the 1950s* (Baton Rouge: Louisiana State University Press, 1969), 253–54; Elizabeth Jacoway, "Taken by Surprise: Little Rock Business Leaders and Desegregation," in *Southern Businessmen and Desegregation*, Elizabeth Jacoway and David R. Colburn (Baton Rouge: Louisiana State University Press, 1981), 21.

42. Bartley, *Rise of Massive Resistance*, 256.

43. Ibid., 254–56.

44. Bates, *Long Shadow of Little Rock*, 51–52.

45. Bartley, *Rise of Massive Resistance*, 259.

46. Ibid., 259–60.

47. Ibid., 3–7; Freyer, *Little Rock Crisis*, 94–95.

The White Reaction to *Brown*: Arkansas, the Southern Manifesto, and Massive Resistance
ANTHONY J. BADGER

1. In working on this article, the author has been very fortunate to receive advice and assistance from Carolyn Abel, Brent Aucoin, Betty Austin, Andrea Cantrell, David Chappel, Robert Frizzell, Willard Gatewood, Elizabeth Jacoway, John Kirk, William E. Leuchtenburg, Elaine McNeil, and Randall Woods. The author also wishes to thank the editors of the *Arkansas Historical Quarterly* for granting permission to use a portion of the article they published entitled "'The Forerunner of Our Opposition': Arkansas and the Southern Manifesto of 1956." Richard Kluger, *Simple Justice* (New York: Random House, 1975), 593–94.

2. Ibid., 716–47.

3. Jim Lester, *A Man for Arkansas: Sid McMath and the Southern Reform Tradition* (Little Rock: Rose Publishing Co., 1976), 82, 157–59, 162–66; Roy Reed, *Faubus: The Life and Times of an American Prodigal* (Fayetteville: University of Arkansas Press, 1997), 85–127, 168–69; Sidney McMath Interview, by John Egerton, September 8, 1990, Southern Oral History Program, University of North Carolina, Chapel Hill.

4. Brooks Hays Interview, Columbia University Oral History Program, Lawrence Brooks Hays Papers, Special Collections Division, University of Arkansas Libraries, Fayetteville, Arkansas.

5. Virgil T. Blossom, *It Has Happened Here* (New York: Harper and Brothers, 1959).

6. McMath Interview, University of North Carolina.

7. *Arkansas Gazette*, March 4, 1956.

8. Julianne Lewis Adams and Thomas DeBlack, *Civil Disobedience: An Oral History of School Desegregation in Fayetteville, Arkansas, 1954–1965* (Fayetteville: University of Arkansas Press, 1994), 1–11.

9. Neil McMillen, *The Citizens' Council: Organized Resistance to the Second Reconstruction, 1954–64* (Urbana: University of Illinois Press, 1971), 94–95.

10. *Arkansas Gazette*, March 16, 1956.

11. Ibid.

12. Ibid.

13. *Arkansas Democrat*, January 8, February 25, 1956; *Arkansas Gazette*, February 26, 1956.

14. *Arkansas Democrat*, January 29, 1956; *Arkansas Gazette*, February 25, 26, 1956.

15. Reed, *Faubus*, 176–78; *Arkansas Gazette*, February 25, 26, 1956.

16. *Arkansas Democrat*, January 23, February 8, 1956.

17. Anthony J. Badger, "The Southern Manifesto of 1956," paper delivered at the annual meeting of the Southern Historical Association in Orlando, Florida, 1993.

18. *Arkansas Gazette*, February 7, 18, 24, 1956.

19. *Arkansas Gazette*, July 22, 1956. Typed sheet in 1956 scrapbook, Papers of William F. Norrell, Special Collections Division, University of Arkansas, Fayetteville. Oren Harris to Gus Jones, May 22, 1944; Harris to Rev. H. Nabors, June 25, 1942; Campaign File Loc. 1370, 13-4-12, Paul Geren; Oral History transcript, University of Texas, Oral History Project, Papers of Oren Harris, Special Collections Division, University of Arkansas, Fayetteville.

20. Wilbur Mills Interview, Papers of Sam Rayburn, Barker Center for American History, University of Texas. Brooks Hays Interview (1975) with Walter Brown and Bruce Parham, Brooks Hays Papers; Wilbur Mills Interview, Former Members of Congress Oral History Project, Library of Congress, Washington, D.C. I am greatly indebted to William E. Leuchtenburg for this reference. The Wilbur Mills Papers at Hendrix College, Conway, Arkansas, contain clippings suggesting that Mills's signing of the manifesto (and his later efforts to seat Dale Alford when Alford's defeat of Brooks Hays was challenged) harmed his long-term efforts to become Speaker of the House of Representatives.

21. Miss Alice Santamaria to J. William Fulbright, March 12, 1956; Miss Anne Ferrante to Fulbright, March 15, 1956; Mrs. E. T. Meijer, March 21, 1956; Fulbright to Dr. J. Kenneth Shamblin, March 14, 1956; Papers of J. William Fulbright, Special Collections Division, University of Arkansas, Fayetteville, Arkansas.

22. *Washington Post*, April 9, 1956; typed statement [n.d.], Fulbright Papers; Anthony J. Badger, "Southerners Who Did Not Sign the Southern Manifesto," paper delivered at the annual meeting of the Organization of American Historians in San Francisco, Calif., 1997.

23. Typed statement [n.d.] Fulbright Papers.

24. Randall B. Woods, *Fulbright: A Biography* (Cambridge, Eng.: Cambridge University Press, 1995), 207–11. The original Thurmond draft is in the Papers of J. Strom Thurmond, Clemson University. Fulbright's and Thurmond's papers contain both the Russell draft and the revisions by Fulbright, Holland, Sparkman, and Daniel. I am very grateful to William E. Leuchtenburg for providing me with the reference to the Price Daniels Oral History Interview, University of North Texas, Denton. John Sparkman to John Nolen, June 23, 1956, Papers of John Sparkman, W. S. Hoole Library, University of Alabama, Tuscaloosa. Typed commentary on the manifesto drafts, box 17, Thurmond Papers.

25. Final draft, Thurmond Papers.

26. Randall B. Woods, "Dixie's Dove: J. William Fulbright, the Vietnam War, and the American South," *Journal of Southern History* 9 (1994): 541; Fulbright to Mrs. Walter Bell, August 31, 1948; Clipping *Washington Post*, April 8, 1956, Fulbright Papers.

27. Jim Hale to Fulbright, March 14, 1956; Memo from John Erickson to Fulbright [n.d.], Fulbright Papers.

28. Woods, *Fulbright*, 202–4.

29. Gordon McNeil to Fulbright, March 19, 1956, Fulbright Papers. Gordon McNeil is the husband of sociologist Elaine McNeil who was very active in desegregation in Fayetteville; Adams and DeBlack, *Civil Disobedience*, 149–57. Elaine McNeil, "Policy-Maker and the Public," *Southwestern Social Science Quarterly* 39 (1958): 95–99. Jeff Packham to Fulbright, March 13, 1956; Mrs. J. O. Powell to Fulbright, March 15, 1956, Fulbright Papers.

30. W. Johnson to Fulbright, March 13, 1956, Fulbright Papers.

31. J. William Fulbright and Seth Tilman, *The Price of Empire* (New York: Pantheon Books, 1989), 94; Donald K. Campbell to Fulbright, March 12, 1956, Fulbright Papers.

32. Woods, "Dixie's Dove," 538, 541.

33. Ibid., 540–41; Numan Bartley, *The New South, 1945–1980* (Baton Rouge: Louisiana State University Press, 1995), 175–76; Woods, *Fulbright*, 211.

34. Brooks Hays Interview, 1970, 26–28, Columbia University Oral History Program, Brooks Hays Papers.

35. Ibid., 26–28; Brooks Hays Interview, 1971, 26, Lyndon Baines Johnson Library, Brooks Hays Papers.

36. John Ward Interview with Orval Faubus and Brooks Hays, June 4, 1976, in the Brooks Hays Papers. Faubus was referring to the two (not one) North Carolina congressmen who were defeated in primaries less than two months after refusing to sign the manifesto; Harold Cooley was the Tar Hell congressman who race-baited the race-baiter to keep his seat. In addition to the three North Carolina representatives, three senators and nineteen (seventeen from Texas) congressmen from the southern states also refused to sign; none of these others was defeated.

37. Orval Faubus Interview, by John Kirk, December 3, 1992, Newcastle University Oral History Program.

38. My analysis differs slightly from Roy Reed's in his indispensable biography of Faubus. Reed sees Faubus, like the moderates, responding to mass segregationist sentiment. I argue that Faubus helped create the sentiment to which he and the moderates claimed to be prisoners. Reed, *Faubus*, 356–57.

39. *Arkansas Gazette*, March 4, 1956.

The Contest for the Soul of Orval Faubus
ROY REED

1. Roy Reed, *Faubus: The Life and Times of an American Prodigal* (Fayetteville: University of Arkansas Press, 1997), 166. Much of the background for this paper is from the same source.

2. Orval E. Faubus, *Down from the Hills* (Little Rock: Democrat Printing and Lithographing Co., 1980), 119.

3. Reed, *Faubus*, 175.

4. Sara Alderman Murphy, *Breaking the Silence* (Fayetteville: University of Arkansas Press, 1997), 30, 60.

5. Nat Griswold, *The Second Reconstruction in Little Rock,* unpublished manuscript in possession of the author, 13.

The Lesson of Little Rock: Stability, Growth, and Change in the American South
JAMES C. COBB

1. James C. Cobb, *The Selling of the South: The Southern Crusade for Industrial Development, 1936–1980* (Urbana: University of Illinois Press, 1993), 125.

2. J. Milton Yinger and George E. Simpson, "Can Segregation Survive in an Industrial Society?" *Antioch Review* 18 (March 1958), 16.

3. Eric Hobsbawm, "Introduction" in *The Invention of Tradition*, ed. Eric Hobsbawm and Terence Ranger, 4 (Cambridge, Eng.: Cambridge University Press, 1983); Edward L. Ayers, *The Promise of the New South: Life after Reconstruction* (New York: Oxford University Press, 1992), 137–45.

4. John W. Cell, *The Highest Stage of White Supremacy: The Origins of Segregation in South Africa and the American South* (Cambridge, Eng.: Cambridge University Press, 1982), 134, 124, 135.

5. Ibid., 181.

6. James C. Cobb, *The Most Southern Place on Earth: The Mississippi Delta and the Roots of Regional Identity* (New York: Oxford University Press, 1992), 299.

7. Bruce Clayton, *The Savage Ideal: Intolerance and Intellectual Leadership in the South, 1890–1914* (Baltimore, Md.: Johns Hopkins University Press, 1972), 159.

8. J. Morgan Kousser, *The Shaping of Southern Politics: Suffrage Restriction and the Establishment of the One-Party South, 1880–1910* (New Haven, Conn.: Yale University Press, 1974).

9. Cell, *Highest Stage of White Supremacy*, 179–80.

10. C. Vann Woodward, *Thinking Back: The Perils of Writing History* (Baton Rouge: Louisiana State University Press, 1986), 87.

11. Ralph Ellison, "In a Strange Country," "Flying Home," in *Flying Home and Other Stories*, ed. John F. Callahan (New York: Random House, 1996), 137–46, 147–73; Morton Sosna, *In Search of the Silent South: Southern Liberals and the Race Issue* (New York: Columbia University Press, 1977), 186, 191.

12. James C. Cobb, *Industrialization and Southern Society, 1877–1984* (Lexington: University of Kentucky Press, 1984), 51–52.

13. Ibid., 102.

14. Numan V. Bartley, *The New South, 1945–1980* (Baton Rouge: Louisiana State University Press, 1995), 216–18.

15. Ibid., 228.

16. Cobb, *Industrialization and Southern Society*, 110.

17. Helen Hill Miller, "Private Business and Public Education in the South," *Harvard Business Review* 38 (July–August, 1960): 77–78.

18. Helen Hill Miller, "The Price of Defiance," *Business Week*, October 6, 1962, 31; Cobb, *Industrialization and Southern Society*, 111.

19. Miller, "Private Business," 80–84, 88.

20. Ibid., 77–78.

21. Cobb, *Selling of the South*, 129–30.

22. Ibid., 127–29.

23. Henry C. Goodrich to George C. Wallace, January 31, 1963; Wallace to Goodrich, February 7, 1963, in George C. Wallace correspondence, Alabama Department of Archives and History, Montgomery.

24. Cobb, *Selling of the South*, 138–40.

25. Ibid., 144–45.

26. "Business Citizenship in the Deep South," *Business Horizons* 5 (spring 1962): 62; Harry S. Ashmore, *An Epitaph for Dixie* (New York: W. W. Norton, 1958), 118.

27. Ibid.; Joe David Brown, "Birmingham, Alabama: A City in Fear," *Saturday Evening Post*, March 2, 1963, 13, 17–18.

28. "The Economic Fallout over Alabama," *Louisville Courier Journal*, September 22, 1963.

29. Editorial, *Tupelo Daily Journal*, September 18, 1962.

30. Cobb, *Selling of the South*, 147–48.

31. Ibid., 274; Stuart A. Rosenfeld and Edward M. Bergman, *After the Factories: Changing Employment Patterns in the Rural South* (Research Triangle, N.C.: Southern Growth Policies Board, 1985), 27.

32. Earl and Merle Black, *Politics and Society in the South* (Cambridge, Mass.: Harvard University Press, 1987), 296–97.

33. Lawrence Goodwyn, *The Populist Moment: A Short History of the Agrarian Revolt in America* (New York: Oxford University Press, 1978), 320.

34. *New York Times*, November 28, 1996.

The Constitutional Lessons of the Little Rock Crisis

Kermit L. Hall

1. Also known as Proposition 209, the California Civil Rights Initiative amended the California Constitution to eliminate affirmative action. On the conflict surrounding the adoption of the initiative, see California Catholic Conference of Bishops, "Statement Opposing California's Proposition 209," *Notre Dame Journal of Legal Ethics and Public Policy* 11 (1997): 95; Gerard V. Bradley, "A Case for Proposition 209," *Notre Dame Journal of Legal Ethics and Public Policy* 11 (1997): 97; and L. Darnell Weeden, "Affirmative Action California Style— Proposition 209: The Right Message While Avoiding a Fatal Constitutional Attraction Because of Race and Sex," *Puget Sound Law Review* 21 (fall 1997): 281.

2. The best treatment of the constitutional issues raised in the Little Rock crisis remains Tony Freyer, *The Little Rock Crisis: A Constitutional Interpretation* (Westport, Conn.: Greenwood Press, 1984).

3. The scope of judicial authority remains a subject of intense political and legal debate. The full range of these matters is addressed in Kenneth L. Karst, "Judicial Power and Jurisdiction," in *The Oxford Companion to the Supreme Court of the United States*, ed. Kermit L. Hall, 456–64 (New York: Oxford University Press, 1992).

4. See *Coalition for Economic Equity v. Wilson*, 110 F. 3d. 1431 (9th Circuit, 1997); 66 United States Law Week 3177 (August 29, 1997), cert. denied November 4, 1997 (No. 97–369).

5. See *Regents of the University of California v. Bakke*, 438 U.S. 265 (1978). In *Bakke*, the justices by a narrow margin addressed the unconstitutional use of racial quotas in admissions to state supported schools. On the general issues raised in this case and their relationship to school integration generally, see J. Harvie Wilkinson, *From Brown to Bakke: The Supreme Court and School Integration* (New York: Oxford University Press, 1979).

6. Ed Gray, *Chief Justice: A Biography of Earl Warren* (New York: Simon and Schuster, 1997), 339–41. The *Brown* decision is reported at *Brown v. Board of Education*, 347 U.S. 483 (1954) and 349 U.S. 294 (1955). The first decision dealt with the constitutional issues raised in *Brown*; the second treated the question of relief.

7. The Southern Declaration on Integration was adopted March 12, 1956. It can be found in Kermit L. Hall, William M. Wiecek, and Paul Finkelman, eds., *American Legal History: Cases and Materials*, 2d ed. (New York: Oxford University Press, 1996), 513–15.

8. *Plessy v. Ferguson*, 163 U.S. 537 (1896). The history of *Plessy* and of its constitutional fate is examined in Charles A. Lofgren, *The Plessy Case* (New York: Oxford University Press, 1987).

9. Charles L. Black Jr., "The Lawfulness of the Segregation Decisions," *Yale Law Journal* 69 (1960): 421–30. The standard work on *Brown* is Richard Kluger, *Simple Justice* (New York: Simon and Schuster, 1975).

10. As quoted in Dennis L. Hutchinson, "*Brown v. Board of Education*," in Hall, *Oxford Companion to the Supreme Court of the United States*, 94.

11. See Gerald Rosenberg, *The Hollow Hope* (Chicago: University of Chicago Press, 1991).

12. Mark Tushnet, "*Brown* and the Transformation of the Constitution," *Fordham Law Review* 61 (October 1992): 25.

13. These themes are fully developed in Mark Tushnet, *Making Civil Rights Law* (New York: Oxford University Press, 1994). Tushnet analyzes the role of Thurgood Marshall in attempting to help the Court understand that its aggressive policy in dealing with the desegregation of universities could be applied to elementary and secondary schools as well.

14. Tushnet, "*Brown* and the Transformation of the Constitution," 27.

15. Ibid., 26.

16. James F. Simon, *The Antagonists: Hugo Black, Felix Frankfurter, and Civil Liberties in Modern America* (New York: Simon and Schuster, 1989).

17. Tushnet, "Brown and the Transformation of the Constitution," 28.

18. Freyer, *Little Rock Crisis*, 105–9.

19. These issues are summarized in Michael R. Belknap, *Federal Law and Southern Order: Racial Violence and Constitutional Conflict in the Post Brown South* (Athens: University Press of Georgia, 1987), 33–34, 263 n. 2.

20. Gray, *Earl Warren*, 246n, 247–53, 262, 266, 289–90.

21. Ibid., 292, 296, 314, 337–38.

22. Jack W. Peltason, *Fifty-Eight Lonely Men: Southern Federal Judges and School Desegregation* (New York: Harcourt, Brace and World, 1961), 50–51.

23. Ibid., 54–55.

24. Harry S. Ashmore, *Civil Rights and Wrongs: A Memoir of Race and Politics, 1944–1994* (New York: Pantheon Books, 1994), 83, 101, 103, 104–5, 116, 128.

25. Peltason, *Fifty-Eight Lonely Men*, 51.

26. Freyer, *Little Rock Crisis*, 41–59.

27. See, for example, Jack Bass, *Unlikely Heroes: The Dramatic Story of the Southern Judges of the Fifth Circuit Who Translated the Supreme Court's Brown Decision into a Revolution for Equality* (New York: Simon and Schuster, 1981).

28. Peltason, *Fifty-Eight Lonely Men*, 9.

29. Charles V. Hamilton, *The Bench and Ballot: Southern Federal Judges and Black Voters* (New York: Oxford University Press, 1973), 4–10.

30. Peltason, *Fifty-Eight Lonely Men*, 9.

31. Freyer, *Little Rock Crisis*, 118–26.

32. Ibid., 107–9.

33. James W. Ely Jr., *The Crisis of Conservative Virginia: The Byrd Organization and the Politics of Massive Resistance* (Knoxville: University of Tennessee Press, 1976).

34. Roy Reed, *Faubus: The Life and Times of an American Prodigal* (Fayetteville: University of Arkansas Press, 1997), 195.

35. Ashmore, *Civil Rights and Wrongs*, 126–28.

36. Reed, *Faubus*, 207–22; Ashmore, *Civil Rights and Wrongs*, 128–29; and Freyer, *Little Rock Crisis*, 86–109.

37. Reed, *Faubus*, 230–32.

38. *Arkansas Democrat-Gazette*, December 15, 1994, 1.

39. *Cooper v. Aaron*, 358 U.S. 1 (1958).

40. See Tony Freyer, "*Cooper v. Aaron*" in Hall, *The Oxford Companion to the Supreme Court of the United States*, 197–98.

41. 358 U.S. 18.

42. Ibid., 18–19.

43. Ellen Debenport, "Orval Faubus—Recall Crisis of '57," *United Press International*, June 7, 1981, 2.

44. "Orval Faubus Is Dead at 84, Governor Made History in '57," *Arkansas Democrat-Gazette*, December 15, 1994, 2.

45. See Ibid., 3. Faubus's actions and the constitutional issues they raised are analyzed in detail in Reed, *Faubus*, 348–62.

46. Debenport, "Orval Faubus," 3.

47. Ibid.

48. Ibid.

49. Ibid.

50. Ibid.

51. Arthur Bestor Jr., "State Sovereignty and Slavery: A Reinterpretation of Proslavery Constitutional Doctrine, 1846–1860," *Journal of the Illinois State Historical Society* 54 (1961): 170–80.

52. Ibid.

53. *New York Times*, November 4, 1997, 1.

54. Tushnet, *Making Civil Rights Law*, 98–101.

55. Freyer, *Little Rock Crisis*, 41–59.

56. The Court held that no state official had the authority to annul judgments of the federal courts, including but not limited to the Supreme Court itself. "No state legislative, executive, or judicial officer can war against the Constitution without violating his undertaking to support it." See *Cooper v. Aaron*, 358 U.S. 18.

57. Peltason, *Fifty-Eight Lonely Men*, 94–101.

58. Taylor Branch, *Parting the Waters* (New York: Simon and Shuster, 1988), 224–25.

59. Donald E. Lively and Stephen Plass, "Equal Protection: The Jurisprudence of Denial and Evasion," *American University Law Review* 40 (summer 1991): 1307–54.

60. Ashmore, *Civil Rights and Wrongs*, 125.

61. Rosenberg, *Hollow Hope*, 220–31.

62. Tushnet, "*Brown* and the Transformation of the Constitution," 23.

63. One of the most notable features of the CCRI has been the state-based attempts to mimic it. More than a dozen states have sought to limit affirmative action programs, although none of these efforts has achieved anything like the success of the California Civil Rights Initiative. See *New York Times*, November 4, 1997, 1.

64. Lively and Plass, "Equal Protection," 1312, 1316, 1317–20.

65. *Buck v. Bell*, 274 U.S. 208 (1927).

66. Tushnet, "*Brown* and the Transformation of the Constitution," 24.

67. Lively and Plass, "Equal Protection," 1317–29.

68. Peltason, *Fifty-Eight Lonely Men*, 33.

69. Ibid., 8–9.

70. Ibid., 32–35.

71. Harry Ashmore, "Orval E. Faubus," *Washington Times*, December 21, 1994, A21.

72. Freyer, *Little Rock Crisis*, 16–24.

73. Ibid.

74. Peltason, 244–54.

75. *Green v. County School Board*, 391 U.S. 430 (1968).

76. Tushnet, "*Brown* and the Transformation of the Constitution," 26.

The Past As Future: The Little Rock Crisis and the Constitution
TONY A. FREYER

1. The author wishes to thank Dean Kenneth C. Randall, the University of Alabama Law School Foundation, and the Edward Brett Randolph Fund for support; he also wishes to express his gratitude to J. L. Chestnut Jr. for assistance in a February 11, 1997, telephone interview. Except where noted, the following material is drawn from Tony Freyer, *The Little Rock Crisis: A Constitutional Interpretation* (Westport, Conn.: Greenwood Press, 1984); also, direct quotes from the text of this book and citation to reported law cases are in the notes. Joel E. Anderson et al., "Plain Talk: The Future of Little Rock's Public Schools," University Task Force Report on the Little Rock School District, University of Arkansas at Little Rock, 1997.

2. Freyer, *Little Rock Crisis*; Freyer, "The Constitution Resisted and School Desegregation" (Indiana University Foundation: Bloomington, Ind., 1985), 1–16.

3. Anderson, "Plain Talk," 53–65.

4. Ibid., 67–189.

5. Freyer, *Little Rock Crisis*; Freyer, "Constitution Resisted." See also Freyer, "The Little Rock Crisis Reconsidered," *Arkansas Historical Quarterly* 56, no. 3 (autumn 1997): 361–70.

6. Freyer, *Little Rock Crisis*, 70.

7. Ibid., 70.

8. Ibid., 160 n. 96. *Cooper v. Aaron*, 358 U.S. 1 (1958).

9. Freyer, *Little Rock Crisis*, 50. *Aaron v. Cooper*, 1 *Race Relations Law Reporter* 851 (U.S.D.C.E.C. Ark. 1956).

10. *Aaron v. Cooper*, 2 *Race Relations Law Reporter* 593 (U.S.C.A. 8th Cir. 1957).

11. Freyer, *Little Rock Crisis*, 58.

12. J. Clay Smith Jr., *Emancipation: The Making of the Black Lawyer, 1844–1944* (Philadelphia: University of Pennsylvania Press, 1993), 9, 321–29, 350–51, 573–74.

13. Quoted in Juan Williams, *Eyes on the Prize: America's Civil Rights Years, 1954–1965* (New York: Penguin Books, 1987), xiii–xiv.

14. Martin Luther King Jr., "Letter from Birmingham Jail," April 16, 1963, in Martin Luther King Jr., *Why We Can't Wait* (New York: Harper and Row, 1964).

15. Freyer, *Little Rock Crisis*, 97 n. 41.

16. Ibid., 133 n. 15.

17. Ibid., 96–97 n. 39.

18. Ibid., 105 n. 74.

19. *Tuscaloosa News*, Sunday, August 10, 1997.

CONTRIBUTORS

ANTHONY J. BADGER is the Paul Mellon Professor of American History at Cambridge University and fellow at Sidney Sussex College. He is the author of a forthcoming study about the response of southern liberals to the civil rights movement.

JAMES C. COBB is the B. Phinizy Spalding Distinguished Professor in the History of the American South at the University of Georgia. He is the author of, among others, *The Selling of the South: The Southern Crusade for Industrial Development, 1936–1980.*

MICHAEL J. DABRISHUS is curator of Special Collections at the University of Arkansas Libraries, Fayetteville.

TONY A. FREYER is University Research Professor of History and Law at the University of Alabama. He is the author of, among others, *The Little Rock Crisis: A Constitutional Interpretation.*

DAVID R. GOLDFIELD is the Robert Lee Bailey Professor of History at the University of North Carolina at Charlotte. He is the author of, among others, *Black, White and Southern: Race Relations and Southern Culture, 1940 to the Present.*

SHELDON HACKNEY is a professor of history at the University of Pennsylvania. He has served as chairman of the National Endowment for the Humanities, president of the University of Pennsylvania, and president of Tulane University. He is the author of, among others, *From Populism to Progressivism.*

KERMIT L. HALL is dean of the College of Humanities at Ohio State University. He is the editor-in-chief of the *Oxford Companion to the Supreme Court.*

ELIZABETH JACOWAY is a former history professor at the University of Arkansas at Little Rock. She is the co-editor of, among others, *Southern Businessmen and Desegregation.*

JOHN A. KIRK is a lecturer in American history at the University of Wales, Lampeter. He is the author of a forthcoming study of race relations in Little Rock before World War II.

ROY REED is the former chairman of the journalism department at the University of Arkansas. He is the author of, among others, *Faubus: The Life and Times of an American Prodigal*.

JOEL WILLIAMSON is Lineberger Professor in the Humanities at the University of North Carolina. He is the author of, among others, *The Crucible of Race: Black-White Relations in the American South Since Emancipation*.

GEORGE C. WRIGHT is provost and dean for academic affairs at the University of Texas at Arlington. He is the author of *Life Behind a Veil: Blacks in Louisville, Kentucky, 1865–1930*.

INDEX